S0-BRC-487

Bc

BX 5965 .L3 1961
**Lawrence, W. Appleton (William Appleton), 1889-1968.**
Parsons, vestries, and parishes: a manual

# PARSONS, VESTRIES, AND PARISHES

# PARSONS, VESTRIES, AND PARISHES A Manual

BY WILLIAM APPLETON LAWRENCE

THE Seabury Press

GREENWICH • CONNECTICUT • 1961

BX
5965
.L3
1961

© 1961 by The Seabury Press, Incorporated
Library of Congress Catalog Card Number: 61-12427
Design by Nancy H. Dale
358-861-C-3.5
Printed in the United States of America

LIBRARY
BERKELEY DIVINITY SCHOOL
NEW HAVEN 11, CONN.

TO ALL THOSE WHO BY THE EXAMPLE OF THEIR LIVES, THEIR LOVE, AND THEIR LABORS, HAVE HELPED TO WRITE THIS BOOK.

# FOREWORD

It is a privilege to write a foreword to this helpful book by Bishop Lawrence. He and I were classmates at the Episcopal Theological School, and we have been close friends for almost fifty years. In his Prologue he has told of his ministry, but what he could not emphasize is the fact that his service to the Church in every position he has held has been of remarkable quality. Appleton Lawrence was an indefatigable pastor of his people in Lynn. I went to his tenth anniversary as Rector there. His father was one of the speakers. He began, "My son can do one thing in the world better than any one else." I thought that this did not sound like the Bishop. Then he continued, "He can turn a new car into an old car quicker than anyone I know." The cars may have given out, but not Appleton Lawrence. Grace Church, Providence, was a parish of different character and outlook, but here the same effective ministry continued. As Bishop of Western Massachusetts his episcopate was marked by his love of clergy and people of all sorts and conditions.

I stress these facts because this book is not the product of an armchair theorist, but is written by a man of wide and long experience who knows whereof he writes.

The amount of general ignorance about the practical life and work of our Church is colossal! The canons of our Church, which are the supreme authority, are known by only a few;

yet they are guides to be followed and, incidentally, are a charter of freedom for both clergy and laity.

This book will be of especial value to church officials, rectors, wardens, and vestrymen. In these pages will be found many helpful admonitions and suggestions. A few will be familiar with much of the content; but there is no one, however great his experience, who will not find a great deal to consider carefully and prayerfully. For many this book will open vistas of opportunity and of service.

It is my hope that church people, without official positions in parish, diocese, or general Church, will read and ponder what Bishop Lawrence has written. In so doing they will find a new and deeper sense of the mission of the Church and of the privileges and the responsibilities of Christian discipleship.

Here are the words of a wise, compassionate, and deeply Christian man who has shown forth God's praise not only with his lips, but in the dedication of his whole life. Here may be found common sense and an inspiring call to the more effective service of Christ and his Church. I gladly commend this book to all people of our Church.

Henry Knox Sherrill

# CONTENTS

# PARSONS, VESTRIES, AND PARISHES

# PROLOGUE

The material in this book is so much a result of my experiences—and my reactions to them—during a varied ministry of nearly fifty years, that I feel it is important to begin with a short personal history.

Like many sons of clergymen, I rebelled at the idea of entering the ministry. To try to follow in the footsteps of my father, who was Bishop of Massachusetts, seemed to me an impossible task. I wanted to do something on my own and not be a pale shadow of his name and reputation. However, at the close of my freshman year in college, one of my best friends died—Otis Smith, a young man of unusual promise who was planning to enter the ministry. This was a great shock. It caused me to do serious thinking as to life's meaning and purpose, with the result that before I graduated I had come to the conclusion that the ministry was a "must" for me. My job was to try as best I could to fill the large gap he had left.

After a year in Union Theological Seminary, an experience for which I shall always be grateful, I transferred to the Episcopal Theological School in Cambridge. Upon graduation in 1914, I was called to be an assistant both by All Saints' Church, Providence, and Grace Church, Lawrence. Lawrence was a city which had been founded by my ancestors, and Grace Church was the only parish my father had ever served; and I was scared of this tradition. However, I went to both places to talk with the rectors. The advantages all seemed to be in favor of the Providence offer, and I wrote my letter of acceptance. I had been taught by my father never to make a big decision without sleeping on it. That night I wrestled with my conscience and came to the decision that although the advantages were all in favor of Providence, the needs were overwhelmingly on the side of Lawrence. So I tore up the letter and wrote another one accepting the position at Lawrence, to serve under Arthur W. Moulton (later Bishop of Utah); and I shall always be grateful for the rich experience and wonderful training I received there.

I had been there only a short time when my rector was called to St. Stephen's Church in Lynn. This was one of the largest parishes in the Diocese. He refused the offer; but in the course of his conversations with the Vestry, he mentioned that if he had felt called to leave Grace Church, he had confidence to believe that I would be elected Rector in his place. The result was that St. Stephen's called me to be their Rector. I had been in Lawrence only a short time; I was happy where I was; I felt I was altogether too young; and I didn't want a large parish. But I was persuaded to accept, because everyone I consulted said it was my duty. I spent ten happy years in Lynn. A man's first parish has a strange hold on him. It is his first love and he can never forget it. This one, I felt, was unique in that there were no other parishes combining all the opportunities St. Stephen's had to offer. And I still feel so.

The tenth year in Lynn had hardly been completed when I received a call which was both unexpected and upsetting. If the Vestry of Grace Church in Providence, who were looking for a rector, had sounded me out, I would have told them definitely that I could not possibly consider leaving Lynn. We had recently enlarged the parish house and it was not fully paid for. We had just purchased a new organ which was yet to be installed. The Vestry had also signed a contract for the building of entirely new quarters for a parochial mission which had for some years lived in rented quarters. But they did not sound me out, they called me. Because I had actually been called, I felt that simple courtesy demanded that I go to Providence to meet with the committee. I was excited by the opportunities presented; but I wanted to stay where I was supremely happy, where I had built up a fine staff, and where I knew the people and the place. I just didn't want to move.

However again, all the people I consulted were unanimous in saying that I ought to go and, because I recognized that sometimes others know you better than you know yourself, after several weeks of agonizing, I wrote the Vestry at Grace Church that I would accept if they wanted me enough to give me time to see the organ installed, the mission building constructed, and the money in sight to pay for them. To this they agreed, and I became Rector of Grace Church five months later. Again, I had ten very happy and busy years in this great parish situated at the very heart of downtown Providence. Grace Church was not only a parish church but, in a very real sense, a community and diocesan church as well. Its ministry was all-inclusive. Because of its position and tradition, it was everybody's parish. Protestants of all sorts, Jews, and Roman Catholics, all entered its doors and felt welcome.

But once again, after ten happy years, a call to wider service came from the Diocese of Western Massachusetts which elected me its Bishop. I hated to leave parochial life. It was for this that I went into the ministry. But my father told me that if a parish called a man, it was up to them to show why he should accept; but if the Church called him, it was up to him to show valid reason why he must refuse. This was definitely the call of the Church, and I could offer no valid reasons for refusing. This time, I had more than twenty happy years of service. During my episcopate, I learned that instead of having merely one parish, a bishop really has many. These "parishes" are made up of special groups such as the clergy and their families, postulants and candidates for the ministry, diocesan officers, leaders in the mission churches and institutions under his pastoral care, and all the people. Just as many pastoral opportunities and problems come to a bishop as any man can have as a parish priest, if he has the eyes to see them and takes the time to discharge them.

About this book, I want to say the following:

(1) It is definitely aimed to meet the needs of the smaller parishes and missions of the Episcopal Church.

(2) It is written from the point of view of the parish as the basic unit, but with the recognition that the old pattern of the neighborhood parish is fast being outmoded by our changing culture, and that the time has come for us to re-examine, re-evaluate, and radically rethink its nature, structure, and program.

(3) It is written chiefly for clergymen and vestries. But I hope it will be read by other laymen in order to try to help bridge the gap which too often exists between the thinking of clergy and laity.

(4) It will emphasize and underline the Church's Mission, in which the parish acts as a leavening influence in the community, nation, and world.

(5) It will inevitably reflect the culture and conditions in the Episcopal Church, but I hope it will be found helpful by those in other Christian communions, even as I am grateful for all I have learned from them.

(6) It is the product not only of my own experience, but has been evaluated and amplified by the contributions of others.

I am convinced that a guide book for the average parish is greatly needed, and I hope that I have written something that will save parsons, people, and parishes from some of the sad and often tragic experiences I have witnessed as Bishop in charge of thirty-three missions of which I was technically rector, and thirty-six parishes—all but six of which had fewer than five hundred communicants. There are a few helpful handbooks; but some of the best ones have been written by men of other communions, and those done by members of our own Church seem to apply chiefly to large parishes—in spite of the fact that sixty-one per cent of the parishes and missions of our Church have fewer than two hundred communicants, and eighty-five per cent have fewer than five hundred communicants.

No book on this subject can be completely original. I am indebted to known and unknown writers, and credit is given when I have been able to find the source; but there are undoubtedly many others from whom I have unwittingly borrowed phrases which have remained in my mind, and to whom I would be glad to give credit if I knew who they were. More than fifty persons—clergy and laymen, men and women—from different parts of the country and of different backgrounds and churchmanship, have had a part in the writing of this book. I am grateful to them all; but chief among them I would mention my father, the Right Reverend William Lawrence, who passed on to me much of his wisdom and experience. The clergymen and lay people who have been my co-workers, and all the clergy and laity who took time to assist in reading and criticizing the copy I presented to them—these have my special gratitude. I also express my indebtedness to Mary I. MacLeod, my secretary throughout my ministry, who typed most of the manuscript, checked numerous references and sources, and assisted in more ways than I can mention. Finally, I want to thank my chief critic, co-worker and helpmate—my wife, Hannah Cobb Lawrence.

This book will not provide the answers to all the problems, or give cures for all the sicknesses which overtake parishes. I hope, however, that because it represents the thinking of many who are deeply concerned and are trying to make parishes a more vital and relevant force, it may be helpful in stirring others to rethink their attitudes, practices and activities, and so give birth to new life and creative thinking in areas where they are so badly needed. If at times it seems that the Church as now organized has somehow lost its power and purpose, let us at the same time remember that only through the Church has the Gospel ever reached us, and that only through the Church can it reach the ages to come.

W. A. L.

# 1

## THE MINISTRY TODAY

### *The Ministry Defined*

> A minister is expected to have the wisdom of a scholar, the logic of a lawyer, the peripatetic energy of the family doctor, the wizardry of the financier, the rhythm of the poet, the imagination of an artist, the endurance of a horse, and the sanctity of a saint—all for the salary of an apartment-house janitor.

Whoever it was who first penned this description I do not know. But I should like to match it with one of my own. "The minister has an unequaled opportunity to make his life count for something supremely worth while. Every ability and capacity he has can be used to the full. He is brought in contact with all kinds of interesting people. His work is as varied as he cares to make it. Indeed, most of it can scarcely be called work, because he is doing what he loves most to do. By the very fact that he is a minister, hearts and doors and opportunities are open to him as to few others. He is his own boss in that he never has to punch a time-clock. He has the indescribable joy of discovering that as he gives himself in service to others, he receives back much more than he can ever give away. He has the high privilege of spending his life working with the forces of the Spirit, of being a humble servant of the Most High God, and of knowing that even though he may not be able to see all the results of his work in this world, in the long last, 'This is the victory that overcometh the world, even our faith.'"

The ministry is, or at least should be, the highest, happiest, holiest profession open to man; but no man should enter the ministry unless he is sure that it is God who has called him. God calls in many ways. Sometimes it is by a sudden, supernatural, or mystical experience. More often it is in the common experiences of life that we feel an incessant and constant call, or pressure, which gradually draws us into his service. Of this I am sure: there are many men outside the ministry who ought to be in it—and for some it is not yet too late—just as I know there are some men in the ministry who should never have been ordained. Some have the courage to ask for release; unfortunately others continue, and to the great detriment of the Church which should provide better means for their honorable retirement to some appropriate secular service.

## *Differing Images of the Ministry*

The confusion in regard to the call to the ministry is due partly to the different ideas that exist as to what the qualifications and duties of a minister actually are, what kind of a person he should be, what he is essentially called to do. The Church sets forth a very definite pattern in its Ordinal. The expectations and demands of the ordinary vestry looking for a rector to fill a vacancy are quite different. And the minister's own conception of his responsibilities and duties varies greatly from either of these. This disparity was quite vividly made plain to me by the answers received from a questionnaire I sent out to seven hundred fifty active clergymen in the Province of New England.

The clergy were asked to mark in order of importance the following aspects of the ministry: (1) administration (i.e. records, organizations, and correspondence); (2) community service and public relations; (3) pastoral (calling and counseling); (4) preaching; (5) priestly (administration of sacraments); (6) teaching (church school and adult classes); (7) worship (personal and corporate).

The vestry committees who were looking for a rector were

given a somewhat different list: (1) ability to preach acceptably; (2) organizing and administrative ability; (3) receptivity to new ideas; (4) a pleasing personality; (5) a helpful wife; (6) ability to work harmoniously with others; (7) definite convictions; (8) qualities of leadership which inspire action; (9) a genuine interest in people; revealed in being a good pastor; (10) concern for the Church beyond the limits of the parish; (11) a spiritual quality which clearly indicates that he is "a man of God"; (12) ability to accept criticism and to laugh at himself.

Almost unanimously the clergy placed "corporate and personal worship," "pastoral care," and "priestly responsibilities" as the three most important duties, in varying order. "Administration" and "community relations" came at the end; whereas with vestries, such matters as "pleasing personality" and "administrative ability" stood high in their estimation, and "a spiritual quality" and "definite convictions" were sometimes near the bottom of the list. I was glad to note, however, that pastoral interests and ability stood high in both groups. There was one vestryman who summed the matter up very well by marking the two items "spiritual quality found in a man of God" and "genuine interest in people," and adding, "Where these two are present, deficiencies in all other areas are bearable."

## *First Requirement of a Christian Minister*

It would seem self-evident that the first requirement of a clergyman is that he be a convinced and practicing Christian. Unfortunately, the obvious is sometimes forgotten or overlooked. Therefore, I would underline that for the Christian, the ultimate authority is Christ himself, who is "the author and finisher of our faith." He is also the source and final arbiter of what the ministry should be. We are called to "follow him." We are to be "light" and "salt" and "leaven" in the world. We are, by our influence and example, to bring God to men, and men to God. A Christian character is really the only irrefutable argument for Christianity. The special call of Christ to his chosen friends and apostles was that they were to carry on his work and spread his teachings; to be, as Paul puts it, "his body." The final commission of the risen Christ has fixed plainly and clearly the nature of the Christian ministry: go, teach, baptize. It is important that the Church, and we as individuals, clergy and laity, should ponder as to what this actually means today; for unfortunately, as someone has pointed out, the difference between actors and clergy is that actors make the imaginary seem real, and too many clergy make the real seem imaginary.

There may be varying interpretations of the meaning of many of our Lord's words, but the basic nature of this commission is clear. It is nothing less than the winning of the whole world for God. The goal is Christ-like lives and a Christian world. St. Matthew's version is perhaps best known, and reads as follows: "All power is given unto me in heaven and in earth. Go ye therefore, and teach all nations, baptizing them in the name of the Father, and of the Son, and of the Holy Ghost: teaching them to observe all things whatsoever I have commanded you: and, lo, I am with you alway, even unto the end of the world."[1] We cannot avoid taking note of its all-inclusiveness, and also of the intimate way in which our Lord identifies himself with the labors of those whom he sends into the world to do his work, and his promise to be with them even unto the end of the world. He reminds us more than once that the things which are impossible with men are possible with God. It is this which makes the Christian ministry so peculiarly sacred, challenging, and rewarding. We fight *with* and not against the ultimate forces of the universe.

I feel that this difference in concept of what the actual work of the ministry is on the part of clergy, laity, and the Church should be faced frankly and talked through to the advantage of both groups. Only when there is mutual understanding and shared goals can the work go forward successfully.

## *Calls for Sacrifice*

We need also to remember that when our Lord called men of his day to follow him, he told them quite frankly it would mean hardship, sacrifice, and suffering; that it was a difficult and dangerous adventure. It should be such—much more than it is today. Some years ago, there appeared in a London newspaper this advertisement: "Men wanted for hazardous journey. Small wages; bitter cold; long months of complete darkness; constant danger; safe return doubtful. Honor and recognition in case of success." Men answered that call of Ernest Shackleton. I believe that a similar call by the Church would have a similar response; and what the Church needs most today is just such men. About eighty per cent of the clergy vacancies today are in small places with meager means, in isolated communities, and in depressed areas. When a man of college and professional education marries a college-trained girl, they want their children to have their advantages, and these are not available in such deprived areas. Must the Church raise up an order of celibates to minister to these isolated places, or will the young men in the seminaries, and their wives, make this sacrifice? Or, should the older clergymen with grown children be called upon to meet this need?

## *The Church's Requirements*

If the Church is indeed the "Body of Christ," it is well that we should first consider seriously what she has to say on this subject of the ministry. Let us look at the services of ordination. Here we find a slightly different emphasis than is found in the conception of either the clergy or the laity. Indeed, the differences in certain respects are so great that it would seem that either the services should be revised to meet modern expectations and demands, or that we should do some very definite evaluation as to the rightness of our modern specifications and values.

In both ordination services,[2] we note the emphasis placed upon the call of a clergyman. The ministry is not something a man chooses as his vocation because he feels equipped to fulfill its requirements. Rather, it rests upon a compelling sense of being called by a power other than ourselves—not necessarily in terms of a vision or through a supernatural voice, but in the sense of inner compulsion and higher claims, or an unsatisfied hunger to serve God and man.

This is so important that the first two questions asked of an ordinand are centered on this question of "call." In the presence of the congregation, the bishop asks the ordinand: (1) "Do you trust that you are inwardly moved by the Holy Ghost?" and (2) "Do you think that you are truly called, according to the will of our Lord Jesus Christ?" This is not the first time the candidate has been asked these leading questions. His rector, his bishop, the vestry of his parish, the professors in his seminary, the examining chaplains, the standing committee of his diocese—all should have questioned and tested him in regard to this call in the process of his training. If a man enters the ministry with anything less than the conviction that that is where *God* wants him to serve, he is sure to run into trouble. The pressures to which he will be subjected, the discouragements and the indifference which he is bound to meet in the course of his ministry, demand that a man be undergirded and sustained and strengthened by powers greater than his own. Nor is this question of consecration one which can be answered at ordination for all time. A man may well reply with firm conviction and shining eyes that he sincerely believes that he has been so called; and yet, in the course of time, he may lose his vision and become tired "in the harness."

## A *Continuing Consecration through Refreshment*

It is generally recognized that professors in colleges, universities, and seminaries need sabbatical leave, but it is not so generally recognized that clergymen should have one. It is true that a minister gets a vacation of a month or more each year, but the professor usually gets three months. It is essential for a man who is constantly pouring himself out for others to have time for longer study and stimulation than a month affords. Laymen who work an eight-hour day, five days a week, should realize that clergymen are on call twenty-four hours a day, seven days a week. Even if they take one day off (as some try to do, often unsuccessfully), it still leaves a fifty-two day deficit as against the five-day week. From personal experience, I am sure that if the older clergy were polled, they would say almost unanimously that if they had a chance to live their ministries over again, they would want not only to devote more time each day to their devotions and study of the Holy Scripture, but would also make every effort to secure and use more time to refresh themselves intellectually and spiritually. Failure to take time off is sometimes not so much a matter of excess of conscience, but is due rather to a lack of orderliness and self-discipline. The Church and the seminaries have recently begun to awaken to their responsibility in this connection, recognizing how foolish it is to assume that they can pack into three years enough religion and biblical knowledge, or sufficient conviction and consecration, to last over a man's entire ministry. One of the chief characteristics of our day is that we want to do things, but the first necessity is to be Christ-like, to have time enough for reflection, "that he may dwell in us, and we in him." That will help to give a firsthand experience of God which is so essential to make a man's ministry effective. One means of doing this is through prayer and meditation (See Appendix). What I would press home here is that more important than what a minister does, is the kind of person he is; and that he should have that quality about him which the crowd recognized when, seeing the courage of ordinary men, and noting they were not scholars and yet possessed wide learning and deep convictions, "They took knowledge of them, that they had been with Jesus."[3] Therefore, it is of utmost importance that vestries should give their clergymen encouragement, and opportunity to revitalize themselves from time to time, as Jesus himself went off into the wilderness for spiritual refreshment.

## *Centrality of the Bible*

The next two questions asked the ordinand by the bishop have to do with the Bible. "Are you persuaded that the Holy Scriptures contain all Doctrine required as necessary for eternal salvation through faith in Jesus Christ?" and, "Will you diligently read the same unto the people . . . ?"

These questions put the Bible in its rightful place as the primary source of a man's teaching and ministry. In actual life, however, all too often the organizational activities and details of the parochial clergyman's work crowd out the Bible and the God who speaks through it. One learns much in the seminary about the Bible, and a good deal about what is in the Bible, but it takes a lifetime of regular, devotional reading of the Bible really to know it. And the responsibility to read the Holy Scriptures to people, with understanding and proper emphasis, takes a good deal more time than most clergymen accord it. I am constantly surprised at the hold that the Bible has over people. One busy doctor I know has read the Bible through twice from beginning to end; and laymen ask every clergyman questions from time to time, revealing a knowledge and interest which put most clergymen to shame.

There are few clergymen who know the Bible as they should. A recent survey of the habits of clergymen reveals that the average time devoted to scripture reading and personal devotion is tragically small. Many of us, in all honesty, would have to admit that the newspaper gets more time than personal devotions. I am glad to note that, in recent years, there have been signs which lead us to hope that the tide is turning. There has been a definite return to Bible-centered preaching. Clergymen are coming to appreciate increasingly the challenge and opportunity they have in exercising a teaching ministry. The many modern translations of the Bible, climaxed with the discovery of the Dead Sea Scrolls, and the publication of the Revised Standard Version, and now the New English Bible, have also led many to a deeper understanding as well as to a wider appreciation of Holy Scriptures. And it is encouraging to note the increased use of the Daily Offices by both clergy and laity.

## *The Catechism Is Still Important*

The deacon is then called to "instruct the youth in the Catechism." This may seem outdated in these days; but is it? There are many who still feel that it is important to have a solid foundation of well-learned facts on which to base one's faith. In later years, such a foundation is sure to be useful to help one describe the Christian faith to others simply and in official terms.

## *The Care and Cure of Souls*

The ordinand is also asked, as a deacon, if he will gladly and willingly "search for the sick, poor, and impotent people of the Parish." This opens wide the tremendous opportunity a man has to enter into the lives of his people. It is one of the most rewarding aspects of the ministry, and it calls for all the wisdom, tact, patience, understanding, courage, confident hope, and faith that any man can muster. Because he is their pastor and priest, people will open their hearts and their lives to him with a readiness rare in other relationships.

Doctors are called upon to perform delicate operations and to make life and death decisions; a clergyman is given the care and cure of souls which are eternal. The responsibility makes one humble, and throws a man back upon the resources only God can provide. No man, of himself, is wise enough, skilled enough, patient enough, loving enough to meet these situations in his own strength and ability. It is a rare privilege to be called to be one of the stewards of the mysteries of God—and the word "mysteries" is used here not in the modern sense of something vague and unintelligible, but in the Greek meaning of something hidden and then made known. Every clergyman should be glad and willing to render such service. The tragedy is that we miss opportunity after opportunity by not searching them out, remaining content to let them come to us. Actually, people usually postpone coming until things have become so critical that they are far harder to remedy or resolve. I know full well, by personal experience, how eager the laity are to secure a house-calling parson.

I realize that changes in our cultural habits have made parish calling more difficult: people are out of their homes far more than they used to be, and radios and television make serious

The King's Library



conversation difficult. But I am perfectly sure that setting office hours and advertising oneself as "always available and as near as the nearest telephone" is no adequate substitute. People hesitate to call, and even when they do, they miss the love and concern which has failed to send you out to them. There is no substitute for that. When your children grow up and leave home, you do not want them to wait until crises arise to get in touch with you. The parish is a family. Any real pastor will feel it is one of his choicest privileges to know that the latchstrings of his parishioners' doors are always out to him.

There is an important place for counseling in the office, and for prayer and confession in the church; but if they are to be of the greatest value, they need the background which friendly calling provides. Parish calling done only as duty and drudgery, a mechanical process of making the rounds of the parish, is not what I mean. "Will you do this gladly and willingly?" is the way the question is worded. There should be an eager expectation and personal interest behind such calls for, after all, one never knows just what he will find. To press a doorbell may open a door behind which there are almost endless and exciting possibilities, and serious problems. There are too many clergymen who lack the imagination to enjoy the privilege of spreading "Good News." Being a "troubadour for God" calls for a glad enthusiasm and a sense of anticipation in discovery which is sometimes sadly lacking in pastoral calls. To the real pastor calling is sheer joy—not duty.

## *The Clergyman's Family*

The next question asked the ordinand by the bishop has to do with the clergyman's family. It recognizes that the clergyman's family is of first importance in the success or failure of his ministry, both through the happy home that they should provide for him as well as the example that they set in the parish. In the secular world, the family example may be a minor matter in a man's work. With a clergyman's family there must be no difference between his preaching and practice. There is always the temptation to avoid family responsibilities by overemphasizing parochial responsibilities. Both must be of one piece: not only on the minister alone, but on all the family, lies the difficult, demanding, and continuing responsibility to be "wholesome examples of the flock of Christ." This question quite naturally calls forth the reply, "I will so do, the Lord being my helper." Without his help, without his being the silent partner, a man's ministry is handicapped from the very start.

## *Order and Obedience*

The last question is one in which the candidate promises reverently to obey his bishop and other chief ministers who have charge over him, and to follow "with a glad mind and will their godly admonitions." This is much more important than is generally recognized in these days of lawlessness. We are well aware of the "out" so often used by clergymen when told unpleasant facts—that such admonitions are not "godly." It may be true that the bishop and others in authority are not all-wise; but because they have been given responsibility and authority, their decisions should not be casually set aside as "not godly" because they are unpleasant. Clergymen, by the very nature of their office, are constantly admonishing others, and should, therefore, be sensitive and quick in their willingness, as men under authority, to obey. The Constitution and Canons of the Church are important and should be observed. We are men under authority. At ordination, we solemnly promise "to conform to the Doctrine, Discipline, and Worship" of our Church. It is well that we should remember that fact.

## *A Bishop Acts for the Whole Church*

When a bishop lays his hands upon an ordinand and says reverently, "Take thou Authority to execute the Office of a Deacon (or Priest) in the Church of God," he does so in his representative capacity and is, in a certain sense, the symbol of the combined hands not only of the people in the congregation, and of

Christians down through the ages, but even the hands of Christ himself. Through the bishop, we receive the strengthening power of the Holy Spirit, and come into the inheritance of the saints and martyrs through the centuries. We believe in the "Apostolic Succession," and would "continue stedfastly in the Apostles' teaching and fellowship."[4] This act is a most impressive one, if one sees it with this background. We must accept the discipline of the Church if we want to best serve the Church.

When, again, the bishop gives the deacon the New Testament and says, "Take thou Authority to read the Gospel in the Church of God, and to preach the same, if thou be thereto licensed by the Bishop himself," the authority is not simply that of the Church, but of the Gospel itself. We recall that when our Lord spoke, people noted that he spoke not as the scribes and Pharisees, but with an authority of his own. The Gospel needs not to be supported by argument or quotation from other authorities. It is itself the truth which was written into the very act of creation. Christ is indeed "the way, the truth, and the life," and our life rings truest when we are true to him.

The Ordering of Priests[5] follows very much the same pattern, and once again, not only does the service presuppose all that has gone before, in the way of training and testing, but it again gives any individual in the congregation the opportunity to speak if he knows of "any Impediment, or notable Crime . . . for the which he ought not to be received into this holy Ministry." This is to emphasize the democracy of the Church. The right of protest and the responsibility of protest rests with every individual in our Church in this most important area.

## *The Exhortation—A Different Picture*

The long Exhortation which the bishop uses in this service gives a picture of the priesthood which in many points seems out of focus with the expectations of most people and with the activities of the ordinary parish priest. It points out that priests are "to be Messengers, Watchmen, and Stewards of the Lord; to teach, and to premonish, to feed and provide for the Lord's family; to seek for Christ's sheep that are dispersed abroad, and for his children who are in the midst of this naughty world, that they may be saved through Christ for ever." The ordinary round of a rector's life, with all the administrative responsibilities and the petty secular demands being made upon him, is often a far cry from the picture of what is expected of him in this statement of the bishop.

With the trend towards mass production and mass movements, too many of us are impatient with the possibility of ever attaining such perfection, and become too easily content with half measures and "getting by." This is often due to a fault which is pointed out in the next paragraph, which stresses both the high dignity of the office, and our natural inability to accomplish our goals on our own initiative. We indeed have "to pray earnestly for his Holy Spirit," and, seeing that we "cannot by any other means compass the doing of so weighty a work" . . . consider how studious we ought to be "in reading and learning the Scriptures, and in framing the manners" both of ourselves, and of them that specially pertain unto us . . . and how we "ought to forsake and set aside," as much as we may, "all worldly cares and studies."

Thus the prayer book provides a picture of a man whom today we would call a holy man—a man of God. It is certainly the most important requirement of the priesthood—but how many clergymen come anywhere near qualifying? And are not the expectations and demands of most congregations more nearly approximated in the description of "a man's man?"

So the Exhortation goes on to hope that we "have well weighed these things" with ourselves long before the time of ordination, and that we have clearly determined, by God's grace, to give ourselves "wholly to this Office," whereunto it hath pleased God to call us, and that we will "continually pray to God, by the mediation of our only Saviour Jesus Christ, for the heavenly assistance of the Holy Ghost; that, by daily reading and weighing the Scriptures," we may wax riper and stronger in our ministry; and that we may so endeavor ourselves, from time to time, to sanctify the lives of ourselves and our family, "and to fashion them after the Rule and Doctrine of Christ," that we may "be wholesome and godly examples and patterns for the people to follow."

You have heard the definition of a minister as one "who is invisible six days a week, and incomprehensible the seventh." Anyone who knows the facts realizes how grossly overdrawn it is. It may be that the clergymen of today are altogether too visible, are over-active, are over-busy and immersed in too many things. There is such a thing as yielding too much to the demands and expectations of the laity. The recollection of these promises should bring judgment and repentance into the hearts of many of us who made them.

## *Our Ministry—Reconciliation*

There is one additional and most important question which the bishop asks of the priest-to-be: "Will you maintain and set forwards, as much as lieth in you, quietness, peace, and love, among all Christian people, and especially among them that are or shall be committed to your charge?" The ministry of reconciliation is a great and most important ministry. How far we fall short is evidenced by the pettinesses, jealousies, and squabbles, which sometimes take place in parishes. To be known as one who can keep his temper, and bring such differences as exist to a new level of consideration—as seen in the sight of God—is a goal toward which every priest should strive.

If we put the picture of the parish priest, as drawn by the questions asked and answered in the ordination service, beside the picture of the priest as he is exercising his parochial ministry today, there is a striking contrast. Nothing is said about administrative duties, financial drives, the care of the fabric, ceremony and ritual, parish-house activities, community interests, diocesan responsibilities, or of national and international affairs. I recognize that each and every age must have its variations of the basic pattern, but I would point out that sometimes the basic demands seem to get smothered and forgotten in a mass of the less consequential.

What I am trying to emphasize here is that I believe it would be a stimulating and profitable experience if both clergy and laity would spend more time in thinking through, seriously and prayerfully, what the life and work of a parish clergyman ideally should be in today's world, that there may be a better understanding between them on this matter. Only by working towards a jointly acceptable goal can a man's ministry rightly accomplish its basic purpose of spreading the love of God and the love of one's neighbor in the local community and throughout the world, as charged by Christ.

To do this intelligently, it is necessary that we should also have some common idea of what a parish is or should be in this day and age. We shall consider this in our next chapter.

---

REFERENCES

1. Matthew 28:18-19
2. Prayer Book, page 530
3. Acts 4:13
4. Prayer Book, page 291
5. Prayer Book, page 536

2

# THE PARISH—AN EXPANDING FELLOWSHIP

What is the purpose of a parish? Why do some parishes seem to be alive and vital, while others are dull and ineffective? Why do we have parishes? It is well to stop from time to time and ask such basic questions, to discover whether we are merely perpetuating an ancient and outdated institution, or are participating in a vital, organic experience essential to the perpetuation of the Christian faith.

Here are two pictures of a parish: one by a layman describing what he actually sees in the average modern parish; the other by a clergyman, about what he wanted his parish to be on the Lower East Side of New York. The layman writes:

A fellowship of middle-class people who enjoy being affiliated with an organization of good standing in the community to which they can belong with comfort and without heavy expense; who believe in brotherhood within well-defined limits and in social progress, if it is not carried too far; most of whom cast a conservative vote, and who find real satisfaction in listening to good sermons and tolerable church music and in being associated with respectable people of their own class.[1]

The clergyman describes what he would like his parish to be:

A body of people under the divine directive which is to reach out in love to those whose lives are torn and mangled by personal and social sin. It seeks to draw into its fellowship those who do not belong to anything or anyone. It is the center of acceptance. It consists of people who are in relation to each other on the levels of love and forgiveness. It therefore does not, can not, exist for itself. The object of the parish in the history of the community which it encompasses is peace, salvation, wholeness, unity and health. This objective is God's, who chooses to embody himself in the person, the place, and the thinking, in order that men may be saved from sin and death.[2]

Where does your parish fit in between these two? What is it really like? What do you want it to be?

## *Parishes Are Essential to the Church's Life*

I believe that parishes are essential to the life of the Church; but that each age must have its own adaptation of the vital fellowship which is its very essence. We know that there are all sorts of parishes, and that every parish is different from every other one. It is very important for every parish to think through the fundamental principles and procedures which make the difference between a vital, contagious, living fellowship of concerned Christians, and one which has outlived its usefulness and is being perpetuated through sentiment or endowments and a natural unwillingness to die.

We sometimes hear it said that "the only thing that can save this world is the Gospel," or, "Christianity is the hope of the world." I believe this to be true. But we can hardly blame the outsider from raising his eyebrows when he looks at the local parish, wondering at what he sees and how it can possibly be considered necessary to the saving of the community, much less the world. Certainly, unless the average parish can become a more effective agent in producing more convinced Christians, such statements about the Gospel and the faith are empty boasts.

Someone has said that a thing only becomes real when it becomes local. The local parish church is therefore the means by which man must be reached where he is. If so, it is of vital importance that every single parish and mission be a shining witness of Christian life and a focus of Christian concern. Archbishop William Temple has given us our cue when he says, "Within the Christian fellowship, each is to be linked to each by a love like that of Christ for each . . . If a church really were like that, if every communicant had for every other a love like that of Christ for him, the power of its witness would be irresistible." You will undoubtedly agree with this statement, but will immediately inquire, "How can we make it so?" It is my hope that what is written in this book will reveal ways in which we may recover some of the conviction, courage, and contagion of the early Christians who, in spite of their small numbers and their lack of position and prestige, were accused of turning the world upside down.

## *Four Steps to Recovery*

Every religion has its origin in man's sense of inadequacy. Man reaches out for something beyond himself which will give unity, purpose, and meaning to his life. In his heart he realizes that he is not what he should be. The Gospel is not just pleasant information. Rather, it tells of a dynamic Person and Power which transforms life, and makes it free and full and joyous. To us who are Christians, Christ came, as he himself says, to give us abundant life. The Christian Gospel begins with the conviction that man cannot solve all his problems by himself. If he could, there would be no need for the Gospel. But, tragically, there seem to be many people and many parishes who are so self-satisfied that they apparently feel no such desperate need.

The very first step in this recovery is to face the fact that the local parish is not all that it ought to be—that it falls far short of the description which Archbishop Temple gives—and that we should be deeply concerned about this fact. We need to be disturbed by a divine discontent with things as they are, and unwilling to be satisfied by anything less than a new breaking through of God's Holy Spirit.

If the first step is a recognition of need, the second step is that we must be ready and willing to do something about it. The case is not hopeless. One may look with regret and even alarm at the lack of influence of the Christian Church as a relevant factor in the community, nation, and world; but Christ is still "the way, the truth, and the life." As Paul told Timothy, "God hath not given us the spirit of fear; but of power, and of love, and of a sound mind." We must therefore face facts with faith.

It is not enough just to try harder. When our Lord finally withdrew his presence from the sight of men, he left behind him not a formulated creed but an exemplary life, not an accumulation of "Sayings" in which his philosophy of life was expounded, but a group of ordinary men and women who were so convinced that he was "Lord of Life" that nothing could stop them as they proclaimed the Good News of Jesus Christ, crucified, dead, buried, and risen again. The New Testament term *Koinonia* suggests not only a contagious, dynamic fellowship, but a community solidarity such as should be perpetuated in our present parishes. Is it? If not, the second step is to repent, and to rethink our goals and program.

This brings us to our third step: the realization that although there is an important place in the parish for the clergyman, he is not the whole Church. There is within the Church a diversity of gifts. Again we quote Paul, "God hath set some in the church, first apostles, secondarily prophets, thirdly teachers, after that miracles, then gifts of healings, helps, governments" [3]—and he might have added, "some mothers, some lawyers, some engineers, some nurses, some cleaners, some clerks . . ." Christianity is not something added to life: it must permeate and penetrate all life, all our doings, all our thoughts. The local parish preaches the Gospel not only through the mouth of its priest on a Sunday, but more definitely through the activities and spirit of all its members throughout the week. The Good News is that God cares for us, and cares so much that "he gave his only-begotten Son, that whosoever believeth in him should not perish, but have everlasting life." [4]

In the fourth place, there must be a new understanding of worship. It is not something apart from life—for Sunday—but rather, a way of life throughout the entire week. We cannot pull ourselves up by our own bootstraps, nor is it sufficient to have an individual relationship with God. We need to be brought together into the presence of God regularly and formally. We need to renew our spirit and be strengthened by the fellowship of others. We need to confess not merely those sins of omission and commission for which we ourselves are personally responsible, but those great social sins for which all of us are partially responsible but none of us fully responsible—sins of war, juvenile delinquency, pressures on minority groups, slums, waste . . .

The average parish today has tremendous unrealized potential, much of which can be uncovered and developed. This can be accomplished, if together we stop long enough for some self-criticism—humbly, searchingly, hopefully recognizing the tremendous responsibility that rests upon each parish and mission to be a living witness to Jesus Christ, a voice spreading the Good News.

From what I have said, you can see that I believe a parish exists to nurture and deepen the spiritual life of its members who, through their lives and influence, will reach out and bring others to our Lord. In brief, it is to increase among men the love of God and the love of their neighbor.

## *The Two Families*

The way of doing this, I believe, is found in God's pattern of family life. We are born into a family, and in this matrix of love and concern we learn the lessons of unselfishness, the importance of discipline, the warmth of forgiveness, and the joy of helpfulness. "God setteth the solitary in families." [5] This is God's way of providing for the physical welfare and the spiritual growth of the individual; it is, therefore, a beneficial climate for the development of Christian character and personality.

Through baptism we are spiritually born into Christ's family, the Church. We receive an indelible mark that we can never lose, any more than we can escape the physical inheritance of our fathers and mothers. As the child's human family is the means by which he grows in wisdom and in stature, so the parish is the unit of Christ's family in which children grow spiritually in favor with God and man. It provides a natural nursery with a friendly climate in which children and others can have wider relationships and more varied experiences than the family offers. Unfortunately, there are still many parishes where there is strife and contention, often over trivial matters. Until there is harmony within the parish, its usefulness is negated and its witness as "a family of God" contradicted.

## *The Parish Family: Organism, Not Organization*

It is one of the hopeful signs in our Church today that there is a definite trend which indicates that we are leaving behind the pattern of the highly organized, institutional parish with its elaborate structure, its emphasis upon activities within the parish house, and its breakdown into age groups. We are returning to the idea of the parish as a family. We are restoring the family pew to its rightful place. We are changing the emphasis in the church school from instruction in facts to group experience, with a leader rather than a teacher. We are emphasizing couples' clubs rather than separate groups of young men and women. We are having parish gatherings with pot-luck suppers for all. We are arranging for Parish Eucharists rather than Corporate Communions. Indeed, in some places, Holy Communion is being taken right into the homes, and emphasis is laid upon the "house Church." A simple family Eucharist celebrated around the breakfast table must be similar to that which was held in the very early days when there were no churches.

To the generation who have known the parish in its organizational pattern, it may come as a bit of a surprise to realize that it is less than a hundred years ago that the first parish house was built by St. George's Church, New York City, under the leadership of Dr. Rainsford, to meet a particular situation in a rapidly changing area. It served its purpose so well that it was copied widely throughout the Church, so that in recent years parish-house activities have often overshadowed the worship of the Church. The parish house has done much to strengthen the spiritual life of individuals and to widen the influence of the Church during these years of cultural change. But gradually we are recognizing that it has often been overdone: men's clubs have duplicated service clubs with secular programs; women's groups have often considered themselves quite independent of the work of the Church, sometimes becoming exclusive clubs. They have raised money which they have given and spent as they pleased. Youth groups, although meeting on church property and opening their meetings with prayer, have often become competitors with similar groups in the community.

## *The Family Unit under Pressures*

The family unit is being put to a severe test in the changing culture of our secular society. The automobile, the emphasis upon pleasures away from the home, the pattern of mass production and labor-saving devices, and the large increase in substitutes for home and homemade activity—trade schools and extra-curricular programs provided by the school system, packaged foods which make cooking largely a matter of opening and heating containers—have all helped to make a home merely a place in which to sleep, dress, and eat. The greatest contribution that the Church can make to our present culture is to emphasize that the home is God's way of training children, and to stress the fact that there can be no adequate substitutes for the love, concern, intimate fellowship, and training that a Christian home ought to provide. We have condemned the efforts of the Communists and Nazis to substitute community nurseries and dormitory living under State control for the raising of children in their own homes. Yet too many parents, under the pressures of modern demands, are defaulting their responsibility by accepting the cultural pattern around them, failing to hold firm to the conviction that the family is God's way of training children, and that the Christian family is the basic unit of the parish which itself is part of the larger family of Christ.

The parish can do far more to instill courage and provide fellowship for parents who are striving to uphold moral standards and to maintain Christian principles and practices in home and community. Clergymen are assuming larger responsibility for counseling parents and young people. Sermons are no longer moral exhortations, but are becoming Bible-centered, and are directed to answering basic theological questions inevitably arising out of the circumstances and culture in which we live. Why shouldn't we eat, drink, and be merry, if we can afford it? Why should we keep our word, if others don't keep theirs? Why shouldn't we seek a divorce, if our marriage does not seem to be working out? Why should we go to church when others we admire rarely, if ever, do? Why shouldn't we spend our money as we please? Our people want and need definite, practical, and helpful answers to such questions.

## *New Patterns of Relationship Must Be Found*

We must continue to search for new forms of parish life which not only will maintain and strengthen the lives of our Church members, but more especially will meet the needs of the majority who are still outside and to whom the Church is largely irrelevant. Without realizing it, we have drifted from a civilization built by Christian men and women of strong convictions, to one which, under the impact of two world wars, has been shaken from its earlier spiritual foundations and is now largely secular and materialistic.

Underneath, however, there is a deep yearning for what God, as revealed in Jesus Christ, can supply. We no longer face a pastoral situation in which it is enough to take good care of our own members: we face a missionary situation right in our own community and among our own friends. We are now a minority group. Our job is to reawaken the Church out of its concern for the whole of man, important as that is, to challenge the whole of life, to call in question the very structure of the society in which we live. For after all, the God that we have worshipped is not only concerned with birth and marriage and death, but also with politics, wages, industry, housing, war, and good manners. Dr. George MacLeod says, "The Church must be turned around so that it faces the market-place." He asks for the establishment of the Church as the center of the life of the community. This is a large order and what parish is there today actually meeting this challenge? But it is a goal which we must pursue, and we must remain dissatisfied until it is realized. There must not be the complacency which too often reveals our parishes as oases of refreshment for the few, while the neglected multitudes pass by outside. Too often a parish is largely irrelevant—a harmless and pleasant place where one can enjoy the niceties of life, while the world outside, as of old, boils in a caldron of "adultery, fornication, uncleanness, lasciviousness, idolatry, witchcraft, hatred, variance, emulations, wrath, strife, seditions, heresies, envyings, murders, drunkenness, revellings, and such like." [6]

We cannot continue in old patterns and expect the Church to minister to modern society. The identification of the ministry with the clerical profession is, I believe, on its way out. It is becoming increasingly evident that if we are going to have an indigenous Church, expanding within an industrial society, it will have to have indigenous leaders. It is even becoming evident in some areas that the priesthood, as a separate and somewhat isolated class is evangelistically ineffective and economically unsupportable. The coming pattern of the Church's ministry may include priests who will also work in secular jobs. We must, if the Church is to meet the needs of the present day, raise and train a leadership which is quite different from what we are training today.

## *A Fresh Baptism of the Spirit*

The parish pattern, in the sense of a family of Christ, must continue; but there is no assurance—indeed, no necessity—that it should be formed on a geographical basis. It may very possibly be a fellowship based on common occupations and interests. What the future holds, no one of us knows, but of this I am convinced: that the old pastoral pattern with the simile of the shepherd watching over his sheep, is no longer real or pertinent in our industrial, mechanized, materialistic society. If the Church is really to leaven society, as I believe it is called to do, every priest and parish must take a completely fresh view of the present situation and, cutting loose from outworn patterns, persistently seek a new baptism of the Spirit, that their parish may indeed be a family of Christ, and a factor in making the kingdoms of this world in truth the kingdom of our Lord and Saviour.

---

REFERENCES

1. Wilbur La Roe: *The Church We Love* (Abingdon)
2. C. K. Myers: *Light the Dark Streets* (Seabury)
3. I Cor. 12:28
4. John 3:16
5. Psalms, 68:6
6. Galatians 5:19,20,21

3

# THE LAITY

Webster defines "laity" as "the people, as distinguished from the clergy."

They are the ones who, for better or worse, keep the machinery of society running. One may be a governor, another a garbage collector. Lofty or lowly in the scale, they are the men and women, the boys and girls, white, black, yellow, and brown, to whom the Church is supposed to minister through her priests. How are they all getting along together? How are they fulfilling their responsibilities as witnesses to the Christian faith in the particular positions they hold? Are they concerned about one another? Are they working harmoniously together to fulfill the command of their Lord and Master: "Go ye therefore, and teach all nations . . . to observe all things whatsoever I have commanded you." There is much that can be done to improve the relationship that at present exists between clergy and laity. I believe that both clergy and laity have equal responsibility in bearing witness: both are equally necessary in the Body of Christ.

It is true that over the years the apostles, and later the bishops and the clergy, being set apart and trained for full-time service, have had special functions and responsibilities. But the laity, on their part, have definite responsibilities which are also important and vital to the life of the Church. Indeed, the laity make up ninety-nine percent of the Church and, as the second World Assembly at Amsterdam stated, "Only by the witness of a spiritually intelligent and active laity can the Church *meet* the modern world in its actual perplexities and life situations." It has been well said that the remedy for clericalism is not anti-clericalism, but a frank recognition of the place of the laity as well as the clergy in the life of the Church.

St. Jerome has described Confirmation as the "ordination of the laity," and down through the centuries the Church has made use of the laity in varying degrees. The Reformation re-established rights which gradually had been taken away from the laity. The nineteenth century was outstanding in the spiritual achievements of the laity in political and social reforms. The twentieth century, however, has seen a growing emphasis upon the position and power of the priesthood, and we have often failed to give the layman his rightful place in the life and work of the Church. However, recently there has been a re-awakening of interest in this matter. I believe that this has been due not only to an effort to supplement the overburdened and understaffed clergy, but springs, rather, from the rediscovery of the essential nature of the Church which combines both clergy and laity. The word "laity" should, therefore, not be understood negatively, as meaning those Church members who are not ordained. Indeed, the Greek word "laos," from which "laity" comes, signified the whole people of God, all of whom had a necessary share in Christ's ministry.

## *The Laity—The Church at Work*

The laity are not only people who come together for worship and fellowship, to receive the Sacrament, and to hear the word of God from the clergy: it is they especially who are called to bridge the gulf between the Church and the world. They, indeed, are the Church wherever they are. They are called to this great and significant ministry whether they recognize it or not. Without the laity, the Church is as incomplete as if it had no clergy. Every baptized lay person is, by implication and obligation, a twenty-four-hour-a-day representative of the Christian Church—whoever he is, wherever he is, and whatever he is doing. It is true that sometimes he is a very poor sample, but it is also true that sometimes he is a shining light and bears witness in a way not possible for any clergyman. It is tragic indeed if a man's lifework is only a job by which he earns his living, but claims neither his interest nor his enthusiasm.

## *The Clergy—Teachers and Leaders*

The clergyman is, or should be, the teacher and leader of the laity. Too often he succumbs to the pressure and temptation of trying to do the work of evangelism that is really the task of the laity. He does not have the patience to learn how to teach the laymen who, in most cases, can do it far more effectively. I know of a dramatic instance of how one clergyman challenged a layman to a task which he did better than the clergyman himself. The clergyman was called by a member of his parish who was frantic because his partner had suddenly gone berserk, climbed out of the window of a high office building, threatening to jump if anyone followed him. He wanted his rector to come immediately and talk him out of it. I am sure my first reaction would have been to get there without stopping for anything. But this clergyman was wiser than I. He reassured his parishioner that he would get there as soon as he could, but stopped long enough to call the man's golfing partner, who had an office in the same building, asking him to go and persuade his friend to return to safety. The layman went and soon had accomplished his object—long before the clergyman could possibly have reached the place. This pattern of expecting the clergyman to do all the spiritual work has unfortunately often been encouraged by the laity. Sometimes they seem to think it is sufficient if they employ him to do the witnessing and the evangelizing, while they attend church services, pay their pledges, and go about their secular business.

We find the same tendency in sports today. Too many Americans are content to sit in the stands and watch others play. This is not a healthy situation. The present thought-pattern reveals the clergy as the active participants, and the laity as the spectators or, at best, workers under the direction of the clergyman who assigns them "church work" in certain routine responsibilities within parish life. This, I believe, is bad, both theologically and practically. It results in misunderstanding and a feeling of tension and frustration on the part of both clergy and laity; the clergy, because the laymen are not always too ready to accept the limited and often fruitless trivialities assigned them; and the laity, because they do not feel that their full abilities are being used.

## *The Problem of Authority*

Another contributing factor to the friction that sometimes exists is that, unfortunately, there are too many clergymen who, as seminary graduates, feel that they have all the answers, and proceed to proclaim them to men and women on a take-it-or-leave-it basis. This tends to arouse resentment in the minds of mature people who have learned by hard experience that life's problems are not so simply solved, and that morality cannot be divided so clearly between right and wrong. It takes time, patience, and tact to apply profound formulas to local conditions and changing circumstances. The result of such an authoritative approach is liable to decrease church attendance and exhaust the patience of the remaining loyal ones.

On the other hand, there are members of the laity who expect the clergy to speak with authority, not only upon matters of Theology, Church History, and the cultivation of the personal religious life, but upon a wide variety of moral and ethical problems when, if he is to grow spiritually, the individual must learn to make his own judgments and his own decisions. The clergy should always be ready to act as coaches and counselors, to help by listening to lay people talk their way through problems and difficulties, and to reveal new insights; but they should not be asked, nor should they try, to make the final decision. As a priest, he can tell of God's forgiveness and of his all-powerful love; but it is God's forgiveness he pronounces in the Absolution—not his own—and it can only be received when the necessary conditions of true repentance and amendment of life are present.

Our Church is both Catholic and Protestant: Catholic, in its firm belief in the use and value of the Sacraments and in the nature of the ministry; Protestant, in that it does not provide neat answers, but demands that each person be responsible in his own right before the Throne of God. I believe it would be well if both clergy and laity could come to a better understanding, by free and friendly discussion, of just what place authority has in the life and work of the Church.

## *Christian Work in the Community*

Clergy should be encouraged to discover and make use of the particular abilities and interests of their lay men and women, and to find the patience to work out with them the varied ways in which their special gifts and abilities can be put to use. This is fairly common when it comes to doctors, lawyers, teachers, nurses, and social workers, who can be called upon in definite cases of need. There are many parishes where men and women have these skills and are most helpful. They serve in particular instances which the rector may call to their attention, and they bring to their professions the special insights and values which the Christian faith provides. The famous surgeon, William Osler, is said to have replied to someone who asked him about his religion, "If you want to understand my religion, come and watch me operate."

This latter aspect, of influencing their fellow-workers, is probably even more valuable than the particular service they may render within the parish, and is actually the best way in which laymen or laywomen can make their lives count most for Christ. The businessmen who, without ostentation or pious profession, are so deeply concerned about the highest welfare of those with whom they work that they give vivid and practical evidence of their Christian concern and conviction, cannot escape general recognition. This Christian witness is definitely open to almost everyone, whatever job he may perform. If we remember that

Brother Lawrence washed dishes "to the glory of the Lord," we see that it only requires a sanctified imagination to figure out ways in which laymen can do the same in their particular activity. Many of us know invalids and handicapped people who show us how adversity can be transformed into an opportunity as they bear witness to a patience, courage, and spirit which even the ordinary person will recognize as essentially Christian.

Another difference which separates clergy and laity grows out of the fact that clergy are, for the most part, taught to think in terms of the abstract and to deal with ideas and attitudes. The layman may recognize the truth of what the clergyman says and want to grasp it, but he is as often lacking in the capacity to apply it as the clergyman seems to be in relating it to everyday living. This leads many laymen to think that their clergyman seems to live in another world, protected, and to a certain extent insulated from life as they know it. The result is that people adjust their conversation to his presence, and shape their conduct temporarily to what they feel he expects of them.

## *The Clergyman's Predicament*

It is tragic that so many lay people tend to regard their clergyman as a different genus, made such by the title he holds, the clerical collar he wears, and the spiritual service he is expected to render—failing to recognize that clergy are human beings, with the weaknesses, desires, drives, and emotions of everyone else. To offset such an attitude, many a clergyman is tempted to become a "man among men" and to seek a common familiarity, a casual easy-going manner, an intimacy of relationship, that cheapens his profession and is more likely to repel than to win. For instance, I believe that the average layman who is accustomed to his cocktail and who believes it is quite all right for him to drink with moderation, does not like to see his priest drinking in public. In these days when alcoholism is so common, I believe that the clergyman does well to set the example and so strengthen his weaker brothers, rather than to conform to the common social pattern. There should be, I believe, a greater sensitivity on the part of the clergyman to the fact that the position which he holds calls for a dignity and conduct which befits his office as a representative of Christ's Church and "an ambassador for Christ." The tragedy so often is that the clergyman thinks that the office makes the man, whereas we all know it is the man who makes the office.

This does not mean that he needs to be so pious as to irritate, or that he should assume the holier-than-thou attitude which repels.

## *Worship and Work*

There is today, in the minds of many, a great gulf between church worship and workaday life. This should not be. The real battles of faith today are being fought in factories and stores, in business offices, in politics, in the press and on the air. There are still some who do not believe that the Church should enter such areas. The truth is, that the Church is already there, in its laity; and the important thing is that it should have something definite to contribute. Too often, the official Church has failed to give its laity the proper support and leadership which could make them more intelligent and effective in this area. There was a time when the clergyman was "the parson," or "person," of the community. As one of the few educated men, he gave leadership in community affairs. With the growing complexity of life and public education, such a position can probably never be recaptured; but the Church certainly should have a more significant role than it is now playing, in lifting community standards and in guiding its thinking in national and international affairs.

One of the difficulties is that in the minds of many of us there seems to be a lack of any clear-cut distinction between the behavior of a genuine Christian and the conventionally accepted behavior of ordinary secular society. Modern Churchmen are often as blind to the shortcomings and evils of present-day society as our forebears were to the evils of slavery or witch-burning—both of which were accepted by some of the most religious and respected people of their day. One of the great needs today is for clergymen who can supply such basic biblical and theological convictions as will give the laity the sensitivity and understanding needed to make clear this difference. The failure to produce a sufficient number of such clergymen is one of the weakest aspects of the work of the Church. It is all too often a case of "the blind leading the blind."

## *"With one accord . . . with the women."*

In all I have written so far, I have been speaking generally in terms of the lay*man*. This is not because I have not appreciated the fact that in today's world lay*women* are more numerous and are equally important; but because they seem to be more sensitive to the understanding and application of the Christian faith, as well as being far better informed and organized for its application. I hope that nothing I have said would seem to exclude them. I considered starting this chapter with an explanation of the fact that the term "laymen" should automatically be understood to include laywomen and not require any explanation or definition. I refrained because I wanted to conclude the chapter by emphasizing the fact that, just as we must get away from the idea that the clergy are specially called to deal in spiritual matters and with holy things, and in the minds of some are considered the only first-class citizens—the laity being relegated to a position of second-class citizen—so we can no longer continue to allow women to be classified as third-class citizens in the organizational and legislative aspects of the work of the Church. Women hold leading positions as legislators, ambassadors, scientists, physicians, and heads of large industries. Why not within the Church? There is no logic in the present situation, where women are allowed to serve on vestries and in diocesan conventions, but are excluded from serving as deputies to General Convention. This may be delayed, but die-hard conservatism cannot stop this rising tide any more than could King Canute stop the ocean tide which faced him. The wholeness of the Church can only be achieved when every part of its membership is enabled to contribute fully to its life. It is inherent in our faith that men *and* women are both called to do God's will and to witness for him. The Holy Spirit was given to women as well as to men. This emphasis implies that neither men nor women can be considered separate or isolated from each other. Each sex has its own special abilities and responsibilities, but neither is superior to the other. It is a difference of function, not of fact.

If we face our present practices frankly and fearlessly, we must, I think, acknowledge that there is still, especially in economic fields, and within the Church itself, injustice in compensation, and inequality in the lack of recognition of the abilities and special insights of women. Deaconesses, social workers, and parish secretaries, are cases in point. It is not only in less civilized countries, but also here in the United States, that the Church, instead of being the leader, has been the laggard in providing equal opportunities for women. There is still a carryover of the ancient idea of the subordination of women to men. Of course, as with the clergy, there is and should be a difference of function. There are naturally some things for which men are better fitted than women, and vice versa. Nevertheless, we should never lose sight of the fact that for the fullness of the Church, it is necessary that there be no inequality, as in the sight of God, between men and women. Clergymen, laymen, and laywomen, are all equally important, and all are essential for the wholeness of the Church. The Lambeth Conference of 1958 said, "The world-wide task of evangelism is not an 'optional extra.' It is the high calling of every disciple . . . There is a growing recognition today that too sharp a distinction has been made between clergy and laity. All baptized persons have the priestly vocation of offering life as a living sacrifice, acceptable to God through Jesus Christ. There is a ministry for every member of Christ; every man and woman who is confirmed is commissioned in this ministry—in the Church, the home, the community, the world of business and social life."

4

# THE IMAGE OF A BISHOP

If the Church wants her bishops to be what they are called to be—chief shepherds of the flock of Christ—something must be done to review and rethink what is currently required of them. In doing so, I am afraid that we shall discover that the Church, instead of converting the world, has fallen victim to a good many of its ways and methods. Actually, I believe that much of the present organization has slowly become top-heavy, so that a bishop spends more time in keeping the machinery in order than in "the care and cure of souls." We cannot, of course, return to the simple pastoral ways of ancient days; but I believe that, as clergymen and laymen, we can do much to see that the bishop is relieved of some of the responsibilities which can be far better handled by concerned laymen of training and ability. Already, some large dioceses employ such lay assistants, but even in the smaller dioceses there is need for exploration and study.

There are some aspects of organization which extend a bishop's pastoral relationships, serving to lengthen his arms, widen his concerns, enlarge his influence, and increase his effectiveness. There are other areas which have to do with contracts, legal matters, insurance, construction, statistical reports, and financial procedures—these often consume too much of a bishop's ordinary life. In recent years these have multiplied greatly; and if a bishop is to fulfill his responsibility as chief pastor, he should be freed from many of them.

## *The Image of the Bishop*

In the Offices of Instruction found in the Book of Common Prayer, we are told that the office of a bishop is "to be a chief pastor in the Church; to confer Holy Orders; and to administer Confirmation." As a matter of fact, we discover that over the years, especially during the past half-century, a bishop seems to have acquired a great many other responsibilities and duties, many of them administrative and secular. It is a good thing to have our attention called to the service of consecration where there is no mention of these other responsibilities, so that we may try to recapture some of the historic understanding and purposes of the episcopate as set forth in this service.

In the service, as well as in the Office of Institution, it is emphasized that he is to be a "chief pastor." This pastoral picture may seem remote and outdated in this mechanized age. This very fact, however, makes it all the more important for the bishop to fulfill the image as set forth in the prayer book. This relationship as chief shepherd to his clergy is not a one-way affair in which all the responsibility for initiative is placed upon the bishop. The clergy should feel that the bishop is concerned about their general welfare, and should make a point of sharing with him, more often than they usually do, their problems and their joys.

Unfortunately, there is a feeling among some clergymen that a barrier is raised when a man is consecrated bishop. They tend to think of him officially, and allow the exalted level of his office to blind them to the fact that he is also a brother priest and, even more important, that he is still a human being. A bishop needs the confidence, friendship, and prayers of his clergy as much as they need his. He wants to be regarded as a friend and not just as an official, when he comes to a meal. He wants to feel included in clergy gatherings as one of the group. Here he is priest as well as bishop. It is true that he sometimes has to act in an official capacity and speak with the authority of his office; but, actually, these occasions are surprisingly few.

## His Authority

A bishop's authority must inevitably be used very sparingly, and this authority does not extend very far beyond what should naturally be given a man whom they have chosen to be their leader by virtue of his ability, integrity, and Christian character. This limit of his authority is evident, in that if a bishop is deliberately disobeyed, there are no penalties which he can impose except those that are so drastic and difficult to invoke that they are very rarely, if ever, exercised. What a bishop cannot secure through the power of his position, persuasion, and personality, is rarely worth the cost of what inevitably follows the official, canonical, disciplinary action.

## His Responsibility

There is, I know, a general feeling among clergymen that a bishop should always support his clergy. It is certainly true that he should be ready to back them up every way he can in maintaining their rights and defending and upholding their interests in the face of unjust criticism. On the other hand, I have become increasingly impressed over the years with the long-suffering patience of the laity in the face of laziness, arrogance, stupidity, and even immorality. Most bishops could easily quote "chapter and verse" on all these counts. There should be, I feel, a recognition on the part of the clergy that although stores may consider it good business to sell on the principle that "the customer is always right," a bishop cannot condone or vindicate a priest under circumstances which call for condemnation. A bishop has the extremely difficult task of acting in three capacities—as friend, as judge, as critic. Sometimes he must sit in judgment and tell a man plain and unpleasant facts about the weakness of his ministry. Even though such criticism is born of deep concern for his best welfare, the priest may nevertheless resent it and be very angry. Very often, as time goes on, he will come to recognize the truth of what the bishop has said, and at a later date return to thank him for it. The best kind of friendship, and the most helpful pastoral relationships, are not those nurtured by a sentimental love that avoids all that is unpleasant, but those bred of honesty in accepting criticism as well as giving it. A bishop should never allow the laity to condemn a priest with vague generalizations. He will defend to the limit the clergyman's right to preach the Christian faith as he understands it, even though it may run counter to public opinion.

### His Relationships

A bishop should constantly assure his clergy, over and over again, that they are his first concern, and should prove it by being always ready to see any who seek his counsel. He should visit them, as often as he can, as he travels about his diocese. His telephone should be at his bedside as well as in his office, and he should remind his clergy that they must not hesitate to use it. Younger clergymen especially, because they sometimes are more timid about approaching their bishop, should realize that the bishop is eager to have them come to see him and consult with him. In this way he can often save them and also himself many a "headache."

The families of the clergy are also a bishop's special responsibility. I believe that clergy wives should feel that they have as easy access to the bishop as their husbands. If the bishop has a wife, she can do much to provide the fellowship so important to a parson's wife, especially if she is living in surroundings which lack many of the cultural opportunities to which she has been accustomed.

Both bishop and clergy have often failed adequately to realize the importance of taking the initiative in strengthening and deepening the relationship which is so important in building up the morale of the diocese. I realize that in the dioceses where the number of clergy runs over a hundred, this becomes much more difficult. However, less than one-third of the dioceses have more than a hundred clergymen, and almost all of these have more than one bishop. A lack of such a loving relationship is therefore a difficulty more imagined than real. I have known many bishops of large dioceses who have managed to be effective pastors to their clergy.

### The Bishop and His "Men"

A bishop's relationship to his postulants and candidates is a responsibility which is carefully spelled out for him by Canon 28. This gives him superintendence of all candidates in his diocese, both as to their daily life and their theological studies. Most bishops take this responsibility very seriously, for there is nothing more important than the careful selection, competent training, and wise guidance of the future leadership of the Church. Every hour a bishop spends with his candidates, trying to fulfill his responsibility as their chief shepherd, is important and fruitful because the favorable results are multiplied many times through the lives of those who themselves are called to be shepherds.

The canon provides that postulants and candidates write their bishop a letter each Ember season. This can be a mere formality, or it can be a significant opportunity. The letters need not be long, and sometimes should be only a brief report. At other times, however, they should be used by the candidate to bring his doubts and difficulties to his bishop, his "father in God." Even when such a letter is only a formality, it has its value in enabling the bishop early to discover whether a man fulfills even simple duties on time. Too many clergymen greatly handicap their ministry by failing to answer letters promptly. Candidates are very appreciative when bishops visit them in seminary. They are also grateful when they are included in the annual clergy conference or retreat. This is not only good for them but brings new life into the group, thus benefiting the older clergymen as well.

When a man graduates from the seminary, the canon provides that he shall continue to be under the direction of his bishop until he is ordered priest. This seems to carry out the idea that a man's diaconate is still definitely part of his training. At the present time the need for clergy is so great that the diaconate all too often becomes merely an irritating waiting period of six months until a man can be advanced to the priesthood. I believe very strongly that something of a canonical nature should be done to remedy this situation; that this period should serve as an internship in which a man's understanding of human nature and his relationship to individuals is tested under skilled guidance. Until something is done to make it a useful office, it is a wise bishop who makes a special point of seeing to it that a man's first appointment is not made merely on the basis of his filling a vacancy, but takes seriously into account the practical training and preparation it provides for his lifelong ministry. Rectors who secure assistants just out of seminary should remember, more than many of them do, their responsibility to train the new deacon by giving him a well-rounded experience, than merely using him as a glorified errand boy.

The need for more priests to take care of a rapidly-increasing population is pressing. One does not need to quote statistics. But in the face of this need, the bishop must be even more sensitive to the necessity of selecting only the men best fitted to serve. The Church suffers greatly today through its failure to go out, as industry goes out, into the colleges in search of top-flight men. It is interesting to note that the New Testament tells us that Jesus "chose" twelve men. There were no volunteers. He even turned away a rich young man who wanted to serve him, but could not free himself from the comforts and security of wealth.

We have faith to believe that many more of our very finest men would respond to the call of the Church if we could make more clear to them that the real ministry of the Church is not a matter of "serving tables," of ministering to women and children, or of preaching a mild doctrine of comfort which will help people to adjust to the status quo. Unfortunately, that is too often what they see it to be, and for that reason some of the best men are not interested. We have even reached the point where too many clergymen rationalize themselves into accepting only calls to places where they want to go, rather than to places where the Lord most needs them. The Church as a whole has, I feel, become so entangled with the deceitfulness of riches, and the ways and values of the world, that if our Lord should return to earth, he would have difficulty in recognizing his own. To remedy this situation is certainly one of a bishop's first concerns.

When Churchill called England to "blood, sweat, and tears," people rallied to his call. When the Church calls young men to the ministry in the heroic and revolutionary terms which the Gospel sets forth; when it confronts them face to face with the challenge to give their lives to Christ, to find the fullness of living in the service of mankind and in spreading the knowledge and love of God; when it refuses to shackle them with ecclesiastical conventions; then I believe that the very best men will answer that call. This is not solely a bishop's responsibility. The clergy and laity have a responsibility to seek out the finest men they know and to challenge them to give their lives to the salvation of mankind.

### Refreshment and Placement

Every bishop should make the effort to see that his clergy are given opportunity for study and refreshment. No man can long continue to "spend and be spent," as clergy are called to be, without regularly replenishing the source and continuing to add to his knowledge and skills, by seeking stimulation outside his parish. Our Church should be doing far more to provide opportunities for such study. There are altogether too many clergymen who, through pressure of work, inadequate resources, or simple inertia, slowly but surely exhaust themselves, losing their enthusiasm, and gradually drifting into a rut of routine which is completely devoid of the contagious spirit of the bearer of the Good News of Jesus Christ. A clergyman, above all others, should be at his prime in his fifties and sixties, when he has had wide experience and opportunity for deeper knowledge—but this is far too seldom true.

Bishops shall, so far as they are able, see that a young man's enthusiasm and strength are not prematurely used up by being called to a responsibility beyond his years and experience. Vestries should remember, when calling a man to a parish, that they should not only consider their own needs, but also have in mind the total ministry of the clergyman being considered. Their bishop's suggestions should be given first consideration, for he is better informed from all points of view, and is most concerned to strengthen the manpower and build the morale and leadership of the diocese.

### The Bishop as Mediator

From time to time, circumstances in a parish may cause tension between the clergymen, vestry, and people. The difficulty may be only a simple misunderstanding, sometimes a mannerism, or sheer tactlessness on the rector's part, or stubbornness or petty bickering of the people. This must not be allowed to run on indefinitely because soon it undercuts a man's ministry and hampers his effectiveness; and people stay away because they don't want to get involved. The result is that the parish slowly diminishes to a handful of "the faithful," with a vestry made up, for the most part, of the rector's few remaining friends. Unless, however, the bishop is called in by either the minister or the vestry, he has no canonical right to enter such a situation. I believe that conditions such as this should be more frankly faced. Very often the minister is as unhappy as the parish. Sometimes he realizes he has chosen the wrong profession and wishes he could enter some other work; but he has a family to support, and no training that would bring him an equivalent income elsewhere. Sometimes a clergyman, through inexperience, has happened to get off to a bad start, has learned his lesson, and could make good in another parish. Sometimes the parish is split by questions of churchmanship which the Archangel Gabriel would find difficult to solve. Sometimes the parish fails to pay its priest a living salary, so that worry about debts seriously affects his work. Whatever it may be, I feel sure the bishop would be willing to try to fulfill his consecration promise —to set forward as much as shall lie in him, "quietness, love, and peace among all men; and diligently exercise such discipline as by the authority of God's Word, and by the order of this Church," is committed to him—if his counsel were sought more often by both clergy and laity, and he were given the chance to help resolve their problems before they reach the breaking point.

### Confirmation

The bishop's third responsibility, as set forth in the Offices of Instruction, is his special authority to confirm. Confirmation, as has been said, is the ordination of the laity, and with its reverberations in eternity, it should be a high moment in a person's life. Yet we often fail to be sufficiently sensitive to its great significance.

Certain it is that the bishop should make clear to his clergy that no person should be presented to him for The Laying on of Hands merely to swell the number on the parish list; that all should be properly instructed and prepared, and brought to a full recognition of the nature of the promise they are making to "follow Christ, to worship God every Sunday in his Church; and to work and pray and give for the spread of his Kingdom." [1] The bishop should make perfectly plain to every parish priest that Confirmation is not intended to be a converting experience, but is the seal and symbol, the public affirmation of a conviction already held that Jesus Christ is their Lord and Saviour, and that God's gift of the Holy Spirit is given them in Confirmation. It should be a witness to the fact that they recognize the need of the strength of God's Holy Spirit, and of the fellowship and sacraments of the Church, to carry out this responsibility.

The bishop should take the lead in calling the clergy to study the meaning of Confirmation, pointing out the importance of a careful follow-up of those who are confirmed, which I believe to be fully as important as the preparation. As part of the follow-up, I used to send them a card before the first Sunday of the month for a year following Confirmation, asking them to place it on the alms basin when they came to Holy Communion. This helped them to establish a regular habit, as well as to notify me that they were present. The bishop, with the help of the clergy, should establish a set of minimum diocesan standards which would include not only a certain knowledge of the Bible, Book of Common Prayer, and church history, but also a habit of church attendance and a Christian practice and attitude in one's daily life. The tragic falling away over the years of so many presented for Confirmation is evidence that our present procedures are far from being effective. If you do not believe me, check carefully what has happened in your parish to those presented during the past ten years. Then try to visualize the tremendous gain to the Church, in terms of their Christian influence, multiplied over the years, if they all had remained active and faithful communicants.

### Special Duties and Responsibilities

The bishop is called not only to be the chief shepherd of his clergy, postulants, and candidates, and to watch especially over those he has confirmed, but he has very real responsibility towards other special groups.

First, there are those who come to him for decisions in regard to their remarriage following a divorce. This is a very great responsibility which has recently been placed on his shoulders and, if it is taken seriously, takes a large amount of his time. He will, of course, ask the help of his clergy in screening the applicants and recommending only those whom they feel fall within the scope of the canon. He will also wish to have the counsel of lawyers and other responsible persons in making his decisions. In the last analysis, the final decision is his. Knowing how deeply his decision is going to affect the lives of the persons concerned, the bishop recognizes that this is no simple task. He needs your prayers and your support to help him carry this new and heavy responsibility. After five years as a bishop, I made a study of the marriages which resulted from the permissions I had granted for remarriage. I was happy to discover that out of approximately fifty, only two had failed to be a Christian marriage. This represents a much better average than most of us have with first marriages.

The canons also provide that, "Every Bishop shall visit the Congregations within his Diocese or Missionary District at least once in three years, for the purposes of examining their condition, inspecting the behavior of the Clergy, administering Confirmation, preaching the Word, and at his discretion celebrating the Sacrament of the Lord's Supper. At every visitation it shall be the duty of the Bishop to examine the records required by Canon 45, Section 3."[2] Most bishops try to make such a visitation every year, and prepare their list in May or June for the year beginning in September. These services are usually arranged on the basis of tradition and convenience. If, therefore, a rector wishes to change the date or season usually assigned, he should write his request to the bishop early in this period, giving the approximate date desired. The bishop certainly will try to meet his request. However, it is both unreasonable and annoying for a man to make a request for a change after the list has been made up, or to cancel a visitation a few weeks before it is to take place because the candidates are not sufficiently prepared (which is usually due to his delay in getting them together). Actually, it is not necessary, or in some cases even desirable, to present a class every year. Many clergymen make a practice of having a continuing "Inquirers' Class" throughout the working year—an idea which has much to commend it.

What is wanted as preparation for his visitation depends entirely upon the individual bishop. When he sends the notification, such information may well be included, as the canon provides. Some bishops have a regular diocesan usage with definite procedures and practices for the service and in regard to their entertainment, groups they would like to meet, the canonical inspection of records, etc. Other bishops try to fit themselves into the tradition and plans of the local rector and parish. In any case, the parish should realize that when he comes, the bishop is the guest of the rector and parish and should be treated with the consideration that we would accord any honored guest. One courtesy which would save the bishop time and worry, especially in visiting large parishes, is to notify him that a parking place will be reserved for him.

The duties of being chief shepherd, ordaining clergy, and confirming laity, are unique to the office of a bishop; but there are three questions in The Consecrating of Bishops, that I would like to stress.

The first has to do with his responsibility to use "All faithful diligence to banish and drive away from the Church all erroneous and strange doctrine contrary to God's Word; and both privately and openly to call upon and encourage others to the same." [3] In other words, the bishop is called upon especially to be a defender of the Faith. What does this mean to us today? The fact that we no longer seem to have heresy trials should not relieve a bishop of the responsibility of defending the Faith, but should make him all the more sensitive to discharging the responsibility in a more positive way—by trying to see that both clergy and laity are given stimulation and opportunity to study the Bible and the Faith. In recent years there has been a resurgence of interest in the Scriptures, sparked partly by the discovery of new and important manuscripts. Parallel to this is a new interest in theology brought about by the growing recognition that behind the cold war there is the more important battle for men's minds. People are no longer content to listen to moral exhortations. They want the answer to really basic questions in regard to existence: Why are we here? is God really a Person? if Christ arose from the dead, what difference does it make in my life? if God is our Father, why is there so much sin and suffering? why do we call the Church "the Body of Christ?" what is its function? what is meant by "The Incarnation," and "Atonement?" what actually happens in Holy Communion? There are no easy or simple answers to these questions. But if, as Christians, we believe Jesus is "the way, the truth, and the life," we must bear witness to these truths in our human relationships.

Bishops of today, with some few exceptions, are not theologians. They need to be given more time to study, to think, to pray, and to write. They ought to be deeply concerned about relating life to God and God to life, not simply within the Church but in the world. Their position presents them with a definite responsibility and opportunity to speak openly and boldly on the application of Christian convictions to public affairs. It is not enough today merely to try to define the Faith in outworn phrases. Bishops are called to lead the way in proclaiming the Faith in terms that are relevant to the present day. By the expectations and demands made upon bishops, clergy and laity are both responsible for the fact that the diocesan office has displaced the bishop's study. The multiplication of meetings has been allowed to crowd out the more important obligation of proclaiming the Faith and Gospel of Jesus Christ as Lord and Saviour of the world. This must be changed.

Another question asked the bishop is, "Will you maintain and set forward, as much as shall lie in you, quietness, love, and peace among all men?" The world of today is full of conflict, not only in the international sphere but right down through every level of society to the family. Even the individual finds within himself a constant conflict between the ideal and the actual, and, like Paul, finds that the good that he would do, he does not, and that which he would not do, he does. Quietness, love, and peace, are more evident by their absence than by their presence. It is the bishop's responsibility to have such a sense of the eternal, and of God's power, that he will create by his very presence a sense of serenity and quietness in place of the clash and clatter of secular life. He is called to incarnate the prayer of St. Francis to serve as an "instrument" of peace. Where there is hatred, he is to sow love; "where there is doubt, faith; where there is despair, hope; where there is darkness, light; where there is sadness, joy." But how many bishops would you describe in these terms? The blame is not all theirs. The demands and expectations of the clergy and laity have deprived them of their true role.

And the last question. How remote and almost absurd it sounds in the light of modern practice and actual fact! "Will you show yourself gentle, and be merciful for Christ's sake to poor and needy people, and to all strangers destitute of help?" One of the things which a bishop misses most in his work is the intimate contacts which as a parish priest he had with the poor, the needy, and the sick. The office of bishop seems to build a barrier. When he visits jails, or state institutions, or slum areas, he goes as an official—a bishop—and it is very difficult for him to divest himself of that sense of awe and aloofness which is associated with the office. Bishops might do well, however, to remind themselves from time to time of this solemn promise, and in doing so, might at least be more sensitive to the needs of those whom they rarely see without making a real effort to do so.

There is another way, too, in which the bishop can fulfill his responsibility towards the poor and needy. He can speak strong words publicly in behalf of the underprivileged, the dispossessed, and disinherited. He is in a peculiarly strategic position to do this because he is not under economic or political pressures to remain silent. He can, and should, speak on controversial public questions as did the prophets of old. The world badly needs men who will speak out boldly and fearlessly. Thought-control is not something which is practiced only in other countries; it is already at work here in the United States of America. But he must be careful to speak not to some particular solution, but on the basic moral and spiritual issues which lie beneath. I can well remember being called to account by my senior warden at the time the Child Labor Amendment was being nationally considered, and I spoke in its favor. He was right in calling me to account. He was against the use of child labor as much as I was, but he felt that each state should make its own decision. He taught me a lesson I have never forgotten.

### A Shepherd to the Flock of Christ

The charge given to the bishop at the time he receives the Bible from his consecrator reads:

"Give heed unto reading, exhortation, and doctrine. Think upon the things contained in this Book. Be diligent in them, that the increase coming thereby may be manifest unto all men; for by so doing thou shalt both save thyself and them that hear thee. Be to the flock of Christ a shepherd, not a wolf; feed them, devour them not. Hold up the weak, heal the sick, bind up the broken, bring again the outcasts, seek the lost. Be so merciful, that you be not too remiss; so minister discipline, that you forget not mercy; that when the Chief Shepherd shall appear, you may receive the never-fading crown of glory, through Jesus Christ our Lord."[4]

The Church has the wisdom and experience of years in setting forth her picture of a bishop. Customs and culture change, and bring to the front additional duties and characteristics, but the primary responsibility unique to the office of a bishop is still as chief shepherd, with the power to ordain and to confirm. In our day and age, especially, he should remember those promises made at the time of his consecration—to be a defender and proclaimer of the Faith; to set forward quietness, peace and love in a world full of clatter and conflict and hate; and to be gentle and merciful, for Christ's sake, to poor and needy people and to all strangers destitute of help.

In this chapter I have tried to show the difference between the picture of the work of a bishop, as given in the official formularies of the Church, and the actual expectations and demands made upon the bishop today; and to make clear to both clergy and laity that any misunderstanding and difficulties, if they are to be resolved, require their cooperation and help.

The initiative for establishing a closer relationship between clergy and bishop is not only the bishop's responsibility. It is often in the hands of the clergy. When a clergyman receives a call from any parish, let him come and ask the bishop's counsel, even if he is happy where he is and his first reaction is to politely turn down the call. If he thinks some decision or action of the bishop is all wrong, let him come to the bishop and tell him so, rather than criticize him before others. The bishop may have good reasons for his action. Or, just possibly the bishop may be wrong, and will be grateful for such concern and help, and for the friendship it shows. Laymen would be amazed and chagrined, I am sure, to find out how often the bishop has to spend his time and energy on details and jobs which no executive in secular work would ever be expected to do, because he has a totally inadequate staff. And usually, especially in the smaller diocese, he has insufficient and secondhand equipment to work with. Bishops of Missionary Districts have shamefully low salaries, and yet they often are expected to pay out of their own pocket some office and other expenses which would certainly be included as business expenses in any secular work. We need more lay men and women concerned about the superhuman task which a modern bishop is called to undertake, and this is just as true of the bishop in the small diocese as of those in larger ones. A time-study and job-analysis of the work of most bishops would plainly reveal how overloaded and understaffed he is.

## *Pray for Your Bishop*

So, in closing this chapter, I ask you—clergy and laity—not only to read but to pray the prayer which comes at the very close of the Consecrating of Bishops, because bishops need your prayers as well as your help, much more than you imagine or think. Your prayers are asked at his consecration. They are needed throughout his ministry. Every time you participate in the service of Holy Communion, Morning or Evening Prayer, you pray for the bishops of the Church. As you do so, pray in secret for your bishop by name. Pray earnestly, sincerely, devoutly, that he may receive the blessing, guidance, and strength of the Almighty. His is a hard task, with great demands, yet with great possibilities. It is heartening and important for a bishop to know that his people are praying for him; that what he does, he does not in his own right nor in his own power, but in your name, and through the grace of God.

> Most merciful Father, send down, we beseech thee, upon this thy servant (N) thy heavenly blessing; and so endue him with thy Holy Spirit, that he, preaching thy Word, may not only be earnest to reprove, beseech, and rebuke, with all patience and doctrine; but also may be, to such as believe, a wholesome example in word, in conversation, in love, in faith, in chastity, and in purity; that, faithfully fulfilling his course, at the latter day he may receive the crown of righteousness, laid up by the Lord Jesus, the righteous Judge, who liveth and reigneth with thee and the same Holy Spirit, one God, world without end. Amen.

REFERENCES

1. 2d Office of Instruction, Prayer Book 291
2. Canon 43, Section 2 (a)
3. Prayer Book, page 555
4. Prayer Book, page 558

5

# THE RECTOR'S DUTIES AND RESPONSIBILITY

The canons of the Church are very explicit in stating that "The control of the worship and the spiritual jurisdiction of the Parish, are vested in the Rector, subject to the Rubrics of The Book of Common Prayer, the Canons of the Church, and the godly counsel of the Bishop. All other Ministers of the Parish, by whatever name they be designated, are to be regarded as under the authority of the Rector." [1]

## *Broad Powers of a Rector*

As this book is written chiefly for parishes and missions with fewer than five hundred communicants, it is not likely that the staff will consist of more than one minister. However, most parishes with more than two hundred fifty communicants ought surely to supply the rector with additional lay assistance of some sort. It is good economy and it makes his work much more effective by freeing him from routine tasks to do the special work for which he has been trained. I have a deep conviction about the size of a parish: I feel strongly that when a parish begins to grow beyond four hundred communicants, serious consideration should be given to the question of founding a mission, instead of enlarging facilities. Of this I am certain: that as a parish rises above five hundred communicants, it is subject to the law of diminishing returns. No matter how large the staff may be, there is bound to be duplication of effort, and no rector can keep the personal touch and relationship which are so important in good pastoral care. The parish becomes an organization, rather than a living organism.

The canons also set forth that "For the purposes of his office and for the full and free discharge of all functions and duties pertaining thereto, the Rector shall, at all times, be entitled to the use and control of the Church and Parish buildings with the appurtenances and furniture thereof." [2] The vestry should know this. In many cases they do not; and it might be well, before some question becomes an issue, to review with the vestry the relevant canons of the Church and of the diocese, perhaps each year at the first meeting after the election of new vestrymen. Even good church members often are poorly informed. After all, why should we expect them to know, unless the rector recognizes his responsibility to explain to them how they can work together to the best interests of all?

The fact that this canon gives the rector such broad powers does not mean that he should use them. A wise rector will consult his vestry about matters in which there may well be a difference of interpretation. For example, offering the use of the parish house to certain community agencies might be considered within the range of the rector's office—but then again, it might not be. This may well become a touchy subject, if it is an organization of a political or left-wing character. The lending of tables, chairs, or dishes to individual members of the parish might be another debatable matter. I know that many such requests come up unexpectedly, and an answer should not have to wait for a regular vestry meeting. To cover such matters, policies should be drawn up by the rector and vestry and put into writing for general information. These will serve as helpful protection to the rector, who in disputed cases can point out that these are parish policies and not merely his personal decision. (See Appendix)

## *The Vestry Should Know the Canons*

The vestry should also be adequately informed about some of the duties which are laid upon the rector by the canons of the Church. For example, many rectors quite rightly believe that young people are the future Church and are therefore of supreme importance; that time spent with young people may yield higher returns for the kingdom than a similar amount of time spent with adults. Some vestries, in such a situation, might think that the rector was spending too much time on the children while they, the adults, paid the bills. I can remember distinctly one occasion when I was taken to task for this; and it takes patience and tact to help the vestry understand that in engaging a rector, they are not engaging a private chaplain to serve them as they desire but, rather, a man who is to serve the young as well as the old, the indifferent as well as the active communicants and supporters, the community as well as the parish, as he deems it to be in the best interests of the Church.

Another possible bone of contention is the reluctance of some vestrymen to allow money to go outside the parish for missionary work elsewhere, when they see at hand so many needs unmet and, perhaps, an unpledged budget. The rector has a responsibility to see that they are informed about the missionary work of the Church; and here again the canons are of help to him: he can call attention to the responsibility laid upon him to instruct all persons in the parish "concerning all the missionary work of the Church at home and abroad, and give suitable opportunities for offerings to maintain that work."[3] It is hoped, however, that the rector will not think that he has discharged this duty by giving one or more missionary sermons a year, or by asking a missionary to preach from time to time. He should recognize that practically every sermon should, if it be the Gospel, have an evangelistic note in it; and also that definite plans should be formulated and carried out to see that the church school, the young people, and the members of other organizations, should all be brought to a realization of their responsibility of bringing the knowledge and love of the Lord to others outside their group—in the community, the nation, and the world.

## *Confirmation and the Episcopal Visitation*

There is another responsibility which is laid upon the shoulders of the rector, and its great importance is not always recognized. The canon says, "It shall be the duty of Ministers to prepare young persons and others for Confirmation; and on notice being received from the Bishop of his intention to visit any Church . . . the Minister shall announce the fact to the Congregation on the first Sunday after the receipt of such notice; and he shall be ready to present for Confirmation such persons as he shall judge to be qualified, and shall deliver to the Bishop a list of the names of those to be confirmed."[4] I have found that these explicit instructions are not always followed, that a congregation is not always informed of the bishop's coming when notification is received, and that in some cases clergymen hand over to others the training of the children. Lay people may give such instruction as well as, and sometimes better than, the clergyman, but it is tremendously important that the rector should have some personal and intimate contact with those he is to present to the bishop for the Laying on of Hands. There are few things more important than the training of new communicants, and it is precisely because of inadequate and poor training that the Church loses so many of those who are confirmed. With the wisdom that comes from experience over the centuries, the Church deliberately spells out these provisions.

The canons also provide that the vestry is jointly responsible with the rector, "to exhibit to the Bishop the Parish Register and to give information to him of the state of the Congregation, spiritual and temporal, under such heads as shall have been previously signified to them, in writing, by the Bishop."[5] I believe it is unfortunate that some bishops seem to be so pushed these days that they do not take time to fulfill this canon, and sometimes even neglect to sign the parish register. It is therefore a desirable practice for the rector and wardens to be ready to exhibit the parish register to the bishop and, perhaps, to have some prepared statement giving him a general picture of the parish activities and its plans for the future. He would, I think, appreciate it; and it might be a gentle reminder to him of the provision of the canon.

## *Discretionary Fund*

Still another section of the canon provides that "The Alms and Contributions, not otherwise specifically designated, at the Administration of the Holy Communion on one Sunday in each calendar month, and other offerings for the poor, shall be deposited with the Minister of the Parish . . . to be applied by the Minister . . . to such pious and charitable uses as shall by him be thought fit." [6] I have sometimes discovered that this canonical source of income for the rector's discretionary fund is not known and, when it is, that the vestry feel that the rector should give an accounting as to how it is used. Usually, the amount received in this way is altogether insufficient, and should be supplemented from the parish budget. The rector is definitely not called upon to give an accounting of the money he often uses confidentially. But it is a wise rector who, even though the amount is small, requests that it be paid to him by check rather than in cash, and disburses it through a special checking account—perhaps making a voluntary report at the annual parish meeting in order to show that the monies are carefully handled.

## *Records*

One of the most important responsibilities that the canons charge the rector to perform is "to record in the Parish Register all Baptisms, Confirmations, Marriages, Burials, and the names of all Communicants within his Cure." [7] Failure to keep such an accurate record may result not only in serious inconvenience to some persons, but even may be the cause of great distress to individuals who need such a record in order to establish certain legal rights. In order to be sure that it is complete and correct, it is good practice to publish such vital statistics monthly in the parish leaflet, to post the record on the bulletin-board for all to see, or have it mimeographed yearly for distribution at the annual parish meeting.

The matter of recording and removing communicants in the parish register is a touchy one. General Convention many times has refused to define what is meant by a "communicant," and unfortunately many communicants are lax in securing a Letter of Transfer when they move, while many rectors are equally easy-going in recording persons as communicants who have never been formally transferred. Of course, there should be a clear differentiation between the permanent Parish Record Book (which should be carefully preserved in a fireproof safe) and the active card file of the parish. Communicants should only be recorded in the permanent register when they have actually been confirmed within the parish, or "received" formally into the Church, or have presented a Letter of Transfer from the former parish. Communicants should not be removed from the permanent register unless the Letter of Transfer given them has been accepted by some other parish of our Church, or, they are known to have died. This will mean that inevitably there will be a difference between the number of registered communicants and the number of active communicants. (For statistical purposes, an active communicant is sometimes considered to be one who is known to have received Communion within the parish at least once during the calendar year.)

One of the commonest complaints I used to receive as a bishop was from rectors who, beginning work in a new cure, reported that the parish lists were incomplete, out of date, and sometimes even partially missing. This latter is most reprehensible, as the canons are very definite in saying that such records are the property of the parish and may not be removed by the retiring rector. The burden of responsibility for keeping them in good order lies ultimately with the rector, even though he may have assistance. The bookkeeping of parish souls should certainly be as carefully done as the bookkeeping of finances. Carelessness in this area is a serious matter. Bishops, rectors, and vestries should all work to see that it is done very conscientiously, with the records completely filled in. The term "vital statistics" means exactly what it says. These records are both vital and necessary to the Church, as well as to the individuals concerned. It is said that there are only three persons who really know a man: his wife, his secretary, and his successor. If this is so, it should make us want to leave the records of a parish in the same kind of condition that we would like to find them.

## *Leaving a Tale Behind Him*

Inasmuch as we have referred to retiring rectors who leave poor records behind them, or even carry them off with the best intentions of returning them when they have had time to bring them up to date, I want to mention another uncanonical discourtesy which is all too common—namely, of returning to one's former parish for the wedding, or funeral, of some special friend. The canons are explicit in stating clearly, "No Minister of this Church shall officiate . . . by performing any . . . priestly or ministerial function, in the Parish, or within the Cure, of another Minister, without the consent of the Minister of that Parish or Cure." [8] It may be that the parties concerned have secured that consent from the present rector. Even so, it is a wise man who will still refuse—because he is taking time from the parish he now serves for what is purely a personal matter; and also, because most rectors, when put on the spot in such a case, will grant the necessary permission. But often with a reluctance which has real justification: because each such "invasion" postpones his fulfilling the responsibilities which are by right his. Before a man leaves a parish, he should make it clear to the people that their new rector should have their full loyalty and support, and that he is no longer to be called upon for any official act in that parish. Only in the interim before a new rector arrives, is there any justification for his returning.

There is one exception to this rule, and this applies to a clergyman who is invited to preach or to officiate in "any Church, Chapel or Oratory, which is part of the premises of an incorporated institution (such as a school or college) . . . provided that such place of worship is designed and set apart for the convenience and uses of such institution, and not as a place for public or parochial worship." [9]

## *Three Important Points*

There are some very important points which need to be made, although they are not spelled out in the canon.

The first is that the spiritual level of the parish rarely rises higher than its leader. An ordained man is privileged to use "The Reverend" before his name. This should not be an empty title. It should mean that there is a quality in his life which calls for reverence. This does not necessarily mean an otherworldliness which lifts him above the level of ordinary duties, but rather that these duties are fulfilled in a way which shows that he does them as in the service of God. As Archbishop Temple has somewhere put it, "The proper relation between prayer and conduct is not that conduct is supremely important and prayer may help it, but that prayer is supremely important and conduct tests it." Another wise bishop, when he heard I was writing this manual, said, "Be sure to emphasize the importance of a clergyman keeping his shoes shined, his nails clean, and his clothes free from the spots that show what he had for breakfast." Such details may seem absurd; but many a man's ministry has been ruined just because he has not realized that when we are in the service of the King of Kings, it behooves us to reveal that fact by our manners and behavior. George Elliot has a caustic word about some parsons "whose celestial intimacies do not improve their domestic manners." Clergymen are not called to act as spiritual thermometers, merely reflecting the spiritual temperature of those about them. They are called to be thermostats, serving to raise that level. A Christ-like character is the best and only irrefutable argument for Christianity.

The second point I would make is that such a life must be a disciplined life. The words "disciple" and "discipline" come from the same root. Dietrich Bonhoeffer, who was executed a few days before his concentration camp was liberated, said, "When Christ calls a man, he bids him come and die." Bishop Bell of Chichester, in commenting on Bonhoeffer's life, says, "There are different kinds of dying, it is true. It may not be suddenly or dramatically, as it was in Bonhoeffer's case, but the essence of discipleship is contained in these words of St. Paul when he calls us 'to die daily unto sin, that we may live unto righteousness.'" Here, again, I would bring high-sounding phrases down to very practical matters. Take such simple matters as getting up in the morning or going to bed at night. Too many clergymen are undisciplined in these respects, especially the latter. It is so easy to stay up reading or talking, or tending to unfinished business. In the long run, such lack of discipline leaves its mark. A wise dean of a seminary said, "Beware of the momentum of youth." He had seen so many young men leave the seminary full of promise—enthusiastic, abounding in vigor and on fire with the desire to serve the Lord—then he had watched those same young men come back in their forties, tired and discouraged and with barely enough energy to keep going, with their vision dimmed, their spirits wasted away. The enthusiasm of youth passes, and both clergy and vestry should realize this. If one runs in a mile race, one doesn't sprint all the way. He disciplines himself so that he will have sufficient energy for the last lap.

Finally, I would say a word of warning in regard to professionalism or clericalism. Because clergy meet so many people, they are prone to get careless in their recognition of each and every person as a soul, a child of God, who likes to be recognized as an individual and not simply as one of a group. It is important to know and to call children by their name. It gives them a status which they need as they struggle towards their own individuality. Even adults like to be called by their name. As a bishop, I used to ask the clergy to introduce the people to me by name as I shook hands with them when they left the church. Of course, in a large parish this is impossible; but even in the small parishes there were only one or two clergymen who could do this. I knew that these clergymen cared for their sheep because they "knew them by name." Sometimes, with the best of good will, we fail because of the lack of this personal concern. I recall that one clergyman told a story of how his parish had adopted a refugee family. They were most grateful for all that had been done for them. As they left for another city, the mother came to express her thanks. She thanked him profusely, but then added her regrets that she had not come to know him better, and said, "You know, I always seemed to be a cause, and I so wanted to be a person." This "clericalism" is very common in connection with the clergyman's voice. Many clergy have an entirely different and unnatural voice when they conduct a service or preach. It is extraordinary how easily this mannerism is acquired. I know how important it is for a parson to have a frank critic. One time when I was speaking over the radio, my wife asked one of our children if he recognized who it was. He replied, "No, but I think it must be a minister." Judgment had come home! How useful it is to have children to stick pins into one's inflated ego.

All three of these points—the importance of the Christian quality of a clergyman's life being reflected in his manner and behavior, the necessity of a disciplined life, and the danger of professionalism—all these require persistent effort. The value of our work is really measured, as someone has said, "not merely on the basis of one-third inspiration but of two-thirds perspiration." We must be continually on the watch, constantly working to improve ourselves. These are things that don't just happen. The insurance agent knows that if he makes a certain number of calls, although he may be turned down again and again, over the weeks there will be a percentage of sales. The parson, too, should take heed to the words of the exhortation read to him when he was ordered priest: "Wherefore consider with yourselves the end of the Ministry towards the children of God . . . see that ye never cease your labour, your care and diligence, until ye have done all that lieth in you, according to your bounden duty, to bring all such as are or shall be committed to your charge, unto that agreement in the faith and knowledge of God, and to that ripeness and perfectness of age in Christ, that there be no place left among you, either for error in religion, or for viciousness in life." [10]

## *Lay Readers*

There is one more responsibility which I must mention, and which is taken all too lightly by many clergy. I refer to the proper training of lay readers. The parish priest, for the sake of his congregation's worship and edification, has the duty to train the reading habits of these men, particularly if they are used to take any of the portions of Morning and Evening Prayer. They should be well instructed in the rationale and order of the service as well as in oral reading. The clergyman should also see that these men are duly licensed by the bishop. A corps of well-informed and efficiently performing lay readers is a great asset in many aspects of the life of the parish.

REFERENCES

1. Canon 45, Section 1 (a)
2. Canon 45, Section 1 (b)
3. Canon 45, Section 2 (a)
4. Canon 45, Section 2 (c)
5. Canon 45, Section 2 (d)
6. Canon 45, Section 2 (e)
7. Canon 45, Section 3 (a)
8. Canon 45, Section 4 (a)
9. Canon 45, Section 4 (a)
10. Prayer Book, page 538

# 6

# THE CLERGYMAN'S WIFE

"Don't ever let the parish get the impression that they hired you when they called your husband." These are the words of a wise bishop to a young girl about to be married to a clergyman, and will serve as the theme for what follows.

When a clergyman is ordained deacon, and again when he is advanced to the priesthood, he promises to be diligent to frame and fashion his life and the life of his family according to the Doctrine of Christ, and to make both himself and them, as much as in him lies, wholesome examples of the flock of Christ.[1] But there is nothing in this promise about his wife being his private secretary, or the laundress for his surplices, or the head of any parish organization; nor is there demanded any of the other hundred-and-one things that some parishioners assume are a natural part of her role as wife of the rector. It doesn't even require her to be prim or staid. Indeed, it seems to say she is to be a good Christian, a faithful wife and, if it please God, a mother of a fine family.

Her primary obligation and privilege is to make her home a happy one, full of Christian love and devotion. It will be very much like that of many other Christian homes in the parish. Inevitably there will be circumstances which will vary because of the simple fact that she is the rector's wife. The telephone may ring more often than in many homes, her husband will be home for most of his meals, and he will work on Sunday.

But these differences are true of many other homes. Her husband will be given confidences which he will not be able to share with her, some of them by women; but this is also true of the doctor or lawyer. There may be some inconvenience in living in a rectory provided by the parish; on the other hand, there are very often conveniences and advantages which might be beyond their means if they had to rent their own house.

The advantages of being a clergyman's wife far outweigh the disadvantages. The overwhelming testimony of those who have had this privilege is that their lives were greatly enriched and broadened by the interests and opportunities which came to them through their husband's profession. A clergyman's wife has the rare privilege of being able to share in almost all of his interests in a way that is not true of many wives of husbands on the road, or wives of commuting husbands who rarely are at home except when they are worn out by a long day at the office, or on weekends.

When the clergyman moves to a new community, the people of the parish are as eager to welcome the new rector's wife as they are the rector. This is a very different situation from that of a man moving for business reasons. His business will offer some contacts, and his church will give him additional ones, according to his interest in it. But the rector and his wife are immediately known and accepted in quite a different way. They are known, recognized, and welcomed not only for themselves, but for the position he holds. They enter into a rich legacy of good-will and good wishes. Instead of a feeling of loneliness and strangeness, they often find the flood of engagements and new friends almost embarrassing.

Because her husband has promised to devote his life to the Church and to be an example in Christian living to others, he is expected to live a life of moral rectitude and integrity, of self sacrifice rather than of self indulgence; and, by these expectations, is helped to live on a higher moral level. A clergyman's wife, therefore, not only has the privilege of sharing in his work and welcome in a unique way, she should be grateful that she is also protected from many of the worries which come to the wives of men who have no such firmly set standards and goals.

She can be of invaluable help in giving counsel and advice to her husband, especially when asked about the many matters in which women's intuition is more sensitive. She must remember, always, that there are some things which a clergyman must keep to himself—from the confessional—and also other information which comes to him about which she must have the grace to refrain from being over-inquisitive, or to be resentful at being left out.

## *The Rectory Family*

To offset the disadvantage of having to live in a house which is provided, there are certain definite advantages. I believe that clergymen and their wives—for the very reason that they do not have to rent or maintain their property, and are often provided with utilities—do not always fully appreciate how much these items actually cost. In addition, Pension Fund premiums are paid by the parish to the amount of fifteen per cent of the clergyman's cash salary, plus one-sixth more. This provides family protection which otherwise might be beyond their financial ability. Too often, a clergyman compares his lot with others in terms of his cash salary, and fails to realize how much he benefits by these advantages. And there are other advantages: the generous action of some doctors, and others who are glad to help with free or partially-billed services, and clergy discounts. I wish that clergymen might be paid sufficiently so that they would not be dependent upon these benefits which I feel tend to put the parson and his wife in an embarrassing position and sometimes to detract from the dignity of his office. There are disadvantages, in that in some small communities the clergyman and his family are expected to trade at stores and automobile agencies owned by parishioners, and to call the parish doctor—all of which is an undesirable situation and makes the clergyman's family different from others. A clergyman's wife prefers to be allowed to be like other women, independent of such special privileges and discounts, so that she can shop where she wishes and buy what she needs.

It is hard enough to raise a family these days, but even more difficult when the children are treated differently than others. Often, a clergyman's children get labelled at school as "preacher's kids," and sometimes get excluded from groups when a shady story is being told or some mischief planned. This may be considered a happy circumstance by some grown-ups; but in the eyes of the youngster it has its tragic aspect; and this sometimes makes him pretend a recklessness in behavior that is not natural to him. So far as possible, the rector's family should be treated like other families. No more should be expected of the rector's wife than is expected of the wives of other members of the parish. If she wants to be a teacher in the church school, or to sing in the choir, she should be permitted to do so; but to expect such service of her is both unjustified and unfair. Children, as they grow older, often are a man's most helpful critics, in their honest and casual side remarks which come out with such complete frankness and candor. A clergyman may indeed be grateful if he has teen-age children to tell him off from time to time, and to keep him in touch with what is going on in life as they live it.

Like everyone else, the clergyman should try to take some time off each week, although this is often difficult to do with any regularity. He has, however, the great advantage of being able to choose his own time for doing things with his family. A clergyman is fortunate, too, in being allowed to take a month's holiday, which should be a family affair. He is lucky not to have to crowd all he wants to do into two short weeks.

Because of the low salaries of many clergy, lack of sufficient support often becomes a major issue and irritant; and sometimes, because of unexpected illnesses or accidents, borrowing becomes a necessity. In such a situation, the husband should not be ashamed to share his situation with his senior warden or some other vestryman in whose business ability he has confidence. However, it is important that the ordinary budgeted expenses be somehow cut to the income. Even with salary of

$10,000 per year it is easy to incur debts unless one watches expenditures carefully. With an income of $5,000 and expenses amounting to $6,000, the result is misery; but with an income of $4500 and expenses of $4,000 there can be happiness. A clergyman who is constantly in debt contradicts the life he professes, and needs the help and cooperation of an understanding wife.

## *A Goldfish Bowl*

To be a rector's wife is not an easy task because inevitably she lives to a large extent in a goldfish bowl, and every word she says and everything she does, and the very clothes she wears, are subject to scrutiny and judgment by many. She may well say to herself, "It is none of their business"; but I believe that in the vast majority of cases the interest shown is not merely idle curiosity and inquisitiveness, rather it is a real, although perhaps unrecognized, admiration and affection. A rector's wife may wish that she were not so much of a public figure, but she is, just as are the wives of men who hold public office. She must not be hyper-sensitive about it. The fact is that the parish and community are genuinely interested. This has its disadvantages by the invasion of what one may consider "private affairs," but it also has its advantages in making a parson's wife an influence for good in the community, far beyond her imagination, if she will go about her business of being a wife and mother in a perfectly natural way.

It is wrong to expect her to do all the things her predecessor did. She may not want to sit in the same pew, or to have the same friends, or trade at the same stores. She must be free to be herself. If she doesn't come to the early celebration, as her predecessor did, this is no cause for criticism. How many other parish women are regular in attendance at this service?

It is very important that a clergyman's wife should be genuinely loyal to the truths of the Christian faith, and of the great importance of the work her husband is doing. She will often have to give priority to it; therefore, she needs deeply to believe in it. She may not do any more than other women are called to do, but she must be deeply interested in the parish and attend its services as regularly as she can.

A clergyman's wife will hear gossip from time to time, but she will treat it for what it is and try to forget it. She will occasionally be annoyed by long and boring telephone conversations. She will listen patiently for a time; then, kindly but firmly explain that she is called to other duties. She will never spread hearsay, but will find a tactful way to change the subject. She will try to understand the background of other women's lives in order to be more sympathetic to their problems. She will often be silent in discussions, or try to lead the conversation from small talk to matters of real consequence. In smaller communities, some parishioners may resent a clergyman's wife having any special friends, and a feeling of jealousy may arise which must be met with understanding and kindness. There is no need for a clergyman's wife to be petty because some parishioners are small-minded; and it is important that the parish recognize that she has as much right to have special friends and interests outside the parish as within it.

Kindly parishioners may bring gifts to the rectory, and such should be gratefully received, even though they may not be wanted. In some cases the donors can ill afford to give them. The clergyman's wife will remember that they are gifts of love, and should be accepted in the spirit in which they are given.

## *The Critic—A Thankless Job*

Because so many kindly people tell a clergyman so many times how much they enjoyed his sermon, or what a beautiful service it was, or how much he had helped some friend, he is constantly led to think he is doing a pretty good job—and to be oblivious to the fact that he may be failing miserably—by pleasing the conventional Christians with pleasantries and platitudes. Clergy have special temptations to self-delusion, and it is the business of a clergyman's wife to nip this in the bud.

Clergy wives who married before their husbands entered the ministry may have a very special and difficult adjustment to make. When the wife gives her consent to the new venture, perhaps even encouraging him to take the step, she may realize in theory that adjustments will be necessary. When she is brought to face them and has to live with them, it is a different matter. It is important, therefore, for the husband to be very sure that he and his wife have talked through these problems before the definite break is made; and that the bishop be taken into their confidence, especially as to their financial needs. The husband must be particularly anxious to see that his wife is not called upon to make any more sacrifices than he does.

The clergy wife has many important privileges and responsibilities which can make or break her husband's future. Uniquely hers is the job of being coach and critic. She knows him best and loves him most, so he will accept from her what he might not accept from others. She is closest to him, and has opportunity to see and hear him more often and to know something of the background for what he says and does—and this makes a world of difference.

She will have to entertain people she does not like; so do other wives. She may have to go places when she would rather stay at home; so do we all. There should be no room for self pity in her emotions. There are disadvantages and discomforts—there are also joys and satisfactions and happiness beyond measure.

The bishop I quoted at the beginning of this chapter added this advice: "You are to be your husband's critic—a thankless job, perhaps, but an essential one." I suppose this is true in almost any marriage, but it is especially important for a clergyman's wife. She is also the best one to praise and give encouragement to her husband; and at times he will need this desperately.

## *Not in Their Own Strength*

I think it is significant that when the clergyman promises at ordination that he will be diligent at making his family wholesome examples and patterns to the flock of Christ, his reply is, "I will so do, the Lord being my helper." I believe that, on the whole, clergy families do a remarkably fine job in this respect; and this, we are confident, is due in no small measure to the fact that they realize they cannot do this in their own strength, but need to seek the constant and continuing help of God. Private prayer, grace at meals, family prayers, regular church attendance, happy association with other faithful Christians, opportunity as well as responsibility to be helpful to others—all are a natural and almost inevitable experience which does much to bring courage, strength, faith, and loyalty into their lives. They are richly blessed by the regular duties they are called upon to fulfill. They are being constantly held up to their best by the demands that are made upon them, and the high expectations of the people they serve. It may be a very busy life, and that very fact helps to make it a happy one. It may be a public life; that helps to make it a worthy one. It may call for the sacrifice of some of the things that others have; but it is rich in its opportunity and its gifts in human relationships. No other profession has the advantages for a married couple that the ministry offers: the wife and husband working as partners in the service of the Lord. I have often called attention to the fact that one of the most important decisions a clergyman makes is in the choice of his wife. By and large, clergy wives are effective Christian women, and deserve far greater credit than most of them get for the very large contribution each makes to the success and usefulness of her husband.

So I would close this chapter with very real thanksgiving and high praise for the wives of our clergy. They include many of the finest women I have been privileged to know. God has blessed them, and, in calling them to this special ministry, has richly blessed us, too.

---

REFERENCE

1. Prayer Book, page 533

# 7

# THE RECTOR, WARDENS, AND VESTRY

The canons of the Church regulating the duties of the wardens and vestry of a parish are simple and meager. This is advantageous in that latitude is given to meet varied circumstances and conditions; and disadvantageous in that there are practically no instructions to give guidance and authority. The canon does state that, "Except as provided by the law of the state or of the diocese, the vestry shall be agents and legal representatives of the parish in all matters concerning its corporate property and relations of the parish to its Clergy."[1] Another section provides, "Unless it conflict with the law as aforesaid, the rector, when present, shall preside in all the meetings of the vestry."[2] And a third section says, "The wardens and vestrymen elected . . . shall hold office until their successors are elected and have qualified."[3] However, the number of members, the mode of election, the qualifications in regard to voting, and the times of meeting, all are left open unless state law provides them.

With so few limitations, it is all the more important that the parish by-laws should be carefully and properly drawn up. It is very likely that the diocese may provide a set of model by-laws. If so, it would seem sensible to follow them wherever possible. For instance, the number of vestrymen would naturally vary according to the size of a parish, with perhaps a minimum of six or eight, and a maximum of twelve or fifteen.

The question of a rotating vestry is another matter which may well be debated. It has certain advantages where the parish is rich in potential leadership or seems to be running in a rut. It has certain disadvantages in its lack of stability and the loss of experience gained over the years. Very few vestrymen can come to know the ways and working of a parish in a term of three years. With vestry meetings only once a month, even regular attendance provides too little opportunity for finding out what one needs to know. It is certainly important that the wardens, clerk, and treasurer be elected on a yearly basis, with the assumption that they will be continued in office as long as their service is satisfactory and they are willing to serve. Membership on a parish vestry is an important and responsible office, and to introduce rotation in order to interest more persons is a dangerous procedure.

## *The Wardens*

The wardens are usually designated as senior and junior, although sometimes they are called the "rector's warden" and the "parish warden"; and the rector may be given the privilege, in the parish by-laws, of appointing his warden. At any rate, the duties usually are assigned on the theory that the ultimate responsibility is with the senior warden, who is closest to the rector. The junior warden is often given the special responsibility of the care of the property, and is expected to represent the interests of the people of the parish. The position of warden should never be allowed to become an honorary office; it is too important for that. If a man has served long and faithfully, he may be elected an honorary warden, with a seat on the vestry. Because embarrassing situations sometimes arise by a man aging in office, it may be well to make provision in the by-laws for a retirement age of seventy-two. If there should be a case of a poor choice, or of a man losing interest and holding the office but failing to function, the nominating committee ought to have sufficient courage to approach him tactfully and present him with a graceful way out. One of the handicaps of church work is that it is voluntary, and there is always the inference that a church should act in a kindly manner. This means that we too often allow the perpetuation of conditions which would not be tolerated in business. We recall the old adage, "When is a business man not a business man?" and the reply, "When he is a vestryman." It is extraordinary that capable business men will act in the most unbusinesslike way when they serve on a vestry.

To be a member of the nominating committee of a vestry is to hold a very responsible position. In most parishes this group determines the calibre and character of the vestry over the years. By taking pains to secure the very best persons available, they can make the vestry a board on which it is a signal honor to serve.

## *Vestry Women*

In the last sentence I used the word "persons" rather than "men," because there is a growing number of vestries on which women serve with distinction. We know the familiar objection to such a practice: if the women serve, the best men won't; that men don't like women around when they smoke and talk; that, after all, many women are not business-like, and the vestry is a business body; and finally, that there is an innate conservatism and prejudice against such a practice. It can safely be said, however, that where it has been tried, it has worked out so well that they wonder why they did not do it long ago. Women can make a unique contribution. Some of the most able persons in a community are women, and it is too bad that the parish should be deprived of their services by excluding them from vestries. The fear that men lose interest when women serve has proved contrary to fact. When opposition is ingrained, the by-laws can provide that the number of women should be limited, if this will help to include them in the membership. Or, as an alternate, the heads of the women's work and the altar guild can be included *ex officio*.

## *The Organization of the Vestry. The Parish Council*

Actually, the vestry should not be—although, unfortunately, it too often is—merely a business body. Their primary responsibility is fabric and finances, but these are intimately related to the worship and activities of the parish. The vestry should, in fact, be the rector's council of advice in all matters. In some parishes, the vestry is not broken down only into the ordinary standing committees of finance, property, music, and nominating; sometimes it is set up to serve as the central board which is responsible for the activities of the parish. This is a service often rendered by a separate body termed the parish council, composed of the heads of the various parish organizations, and others. This works very satisfactorily in some places. However, there is sometimes a division of authority and a lack of communication which can be overcome by widening the work and interest of the vestry, so that every vestryman will have a knowledge and measure of responsibility for some part of what is going on day by day. This has many advantages over the parish council, in that it brings the parish into a unity which is not possible when only one group is interested in and responsible for finances and fabric, and other groups responsible for the activities of Christian education, organizational work, and the human and community relationships of the parish. The difficulty comes in educating the vestry to a recognition of its true and all-inclusive function. Tradition and inertia are hard to overcome; and this education, with patience and tact, must fit each parish situation. It is not a paper program or an easy solution to the problems and frictions which are common to every parish. The parish council idea is in itself a long step forward from the disorganized situation often found, with each organization sufficient unto itself, performing its function with varying degrees of usefulness and efficiency, and with no particular interest in the work of the other organizations. Sometimes organizations are so tenuously connected to the real purpose and life of the parish that they tend to be social cliques. Others often provide such a purely secular program that they are more of a detriment than an asset to the parish.

In order to emphasize and dramatize the spiritual aspects of the vestry's work, it is helpful to have an installation at the regular morning service following the annual meeting. Such a service dignifies the office and brings home to the congregation, as well as to the vestrymen, the responsibilities which are laid upon the wardens, vestry, treasurer, and clerk. The rector may well take the occasion, either before the sermon, or as a part of it, to speak of the work and future plans of the parish, and also to express to the vestry the gratitude of the parish for their willing service, which, especially in the case of the treasurer, involves many hours of painstaking work which too often goes unrecognized and inadequately appreciated.

## *Moribund Organizations*

What can we do with organizations which have outlived their usefulness? Sometimes one has to have the patience to let them die slowly. Sometimes they have to be endured. And sometimes, with patience and tact, they can be revived and made to understand what the real purpose of the parish is, and be stirred to make their contribution to it. It is only very occasionally that the rector has to ask them to disband. Their roots are usually sufficiently deep that drastic action of this sort is liable to cause more disruption and division in the parish than it is worth. Gossip, hearsay, distortion of facts, are impossible to control and are quite the opposite of the peace and harmony that the rector, in his ordination vows, promised to cultivate and preserve.

## *Candidates for the Ministry—A Vestry Responsibility*

One of the most important and far-reaching functions of a vestry is its responsibility in the enlistment and screening of candidates for the ministry. The idea that they have any responsibility at all in this area will probably come as a completely new idea. But has a vestry the right to expect to have a clergyman available whenever the rector leaves, if the parish never produces a candidate for the ministry? I have known some century-old parishes that have never produced one candidate. There are other parishes (and some of them comparatively small) where there has been a constant procession of candidates over the years. The rector's interest in this matter is, of course, important; but a parish tradition should be built up which will continue from rector to rector. There should be a sense of expectation and responsibility in the vestry to guarantee that the parish produces its share of men for the ministry. It must not, like a parasite, live on the harvest of other parishes.

When a suitable candidate is found, the vestry should take a personal interest in his training, and the parish should help to finance his education in college, if necessary, but certainly during his seminary years. Canonically, he does not need the official endorsement of the vestry until he has been one year in the seminary; but actually, the rector will be wise if he asks him to meet with the vestry when he has been accepted by the bishop as a postulant. It is no small responsibility to encourage, or even allow, a young man to spend a year in seminary if there is any chance that he will not be endorsed by the vestry at the end of that year. After meeting the candidate, the vestry must have time to find out more about him before they meet again to discuss his qualifications (or lack of them), remembering that *they ought not approve any man whom they would not be willing to have as their own rector.* All too often, the signing of a candidate's papers is a pro forma matter. The rector presents a man, tells something about his background, extols his virtues, and then asks the vestry to sign the proper papers. No man would engage a responsible employee in such a casual way; and yet here is a situation where a man is to be trained to be "an ambassador for God," a priest of the Church; and a misfit can do irreparable damage. There are more of these in the ministry than there should be, and they are there partially because of the laxity of some vestries. This can be changed if vestrymen will take their responsibility seriously.

## *The Vestry—A Legal Entity*

The powers and duties of the wardens and vestry, as generally defined by diocesan canon or state statute, usually include the right, as trustees, to hold legal title to all property belonging to the parish. Before a parish purchases, receives, or sells any property, the bishop's counsel and advice should be sought. The diocese often has resources which will be found very helpful; and in any case, the parish, as a part of the diocese, should feel a relationship to it that should make consultation a natural procedure. Costly mistakes are thus often avoided; and the wisdom of those who have had wide experience in this field will save time and trouble. In the case of fiscal property, this procedure will provide for greater security and wiser management than might be available at the local level where personal considerations of individual vestrymen might be of influence.

## *The Vestry's Relation to Rector and Parish*

No vestryman should ever trade on his parish position for personal advantage. Such practice is ruled out in politics; it is far more reprehensible in the Church. Service on the vestry is service to the Church; and a vestryman should be scrupulous in all his conduct, his integrity should be above question, his character beyond reproach. Indeed, his example in loyalty to the Church, and his witness as a Christian in the community, are probably his most important responsibilities. Regular attendance at church on Sunday, and at vestry meetings, should be as much a part of his office as his daily faithfulness at work is assumed to be part of his job.

The rector has a right to expect of his wardens and vestry a willingness to consider seriously his plans for strengthening the life and work of the parish. The fact that some proposal he may make has been tried at some time in the past, and failed, is no adequate reason for thinking that it will fail again. New leadership, proper training, avoidance of past pitfalls, and perhaps new conditions, may well prove the difference between past failure and present success. On the other hand, the rector should recognize that what worked most successfully in his previous parish may be inappropriate and unworkable under different local conditions. And he must realize that in the vestry the Church has provided a check upon the impractical and unsound ventures of rectors.

In proposing anything new, it is always well for a rector to test it out on one or two of the officers of the parish and certain key vestrymen. If they are generally skeptical or opposed, a wise rector will bide his time, postpone the presentation, and re-examine his position. If, on the other hand, they are favorable, he will at least have an informed and enthusiastic minority to support him when he presents the matter to the vestry as a whole. These individuals might even be willing to advance the proposal themselves, which is much to be preferred. The work in most parishes would go forward more effectively if rector and people were not so concerned about who gets the credit.

## *Vestry Meetings*

The rector is by canon chairman of the vestry, and no meeting of the vestry can legally be held without his knowledge and, as a matter of courtesy, should not be conducted without his presence unless he is away from the parish for an extended period of time. It is very important that there should be a regular time for vestry meetings, and that for these meetings the rector should have his agenda (which might well be included with the notice of the meeting) prepared in advance. The clerk will have the minutes of the preceding meeting recorded, and the treasurer will present a written report of the financial condition according to the instructions given him. Date and time of meeting should not be suddenly changed, nor should the meeting start late, or without the proper information available. As the presiding officer, the rector is primarily responsible; but every member of the vestry, especially the officers, should be on time and ready to report on the business for which they are accountable. *They should be reminded from time to time that the business to be considered is not merely that of another organization, but is God's business; that mundane as it sometimes is, it has to do with the extension of Christ's kingdom and fulfillment of his word.*

Every vestry meeting should begin with a prayer. This need not—indeed, preferably should not—be offered by the rector. The rector may close the meeting with a blessing. Some vestries make a practice of having the rector spend half an hour, either at the start or close of the meeting, in the presentation of some aspect of the work or worship of the Church—at which time they discuss together the general purpose of the parish. Or a guest may be asked to speak on some aspect of the work of the Church outside the parish. If the proper committees are set up, do their work well and make their reports concise, the vestry will come to have confidence in their sub-committee recommendations. The time thus saved—now often spent in useless discussion—can be used to acquire a greater knowledge of the work of the Church and a better understanding of what she expects of her officers and leaders.

## *Rector and Vestry—A Team Ministry*

Members of the vestry should be fully aware that they are part of a diocese, and that what they do, or fail to do, affects the life and work of the diocese, and is lifting or lowering the morale and effectiveness of the work of the general Church. Many parishes are heavily colored by "congregationalism" which is contrary to our polity in the Episcopal Church. The rector and vestry must work together as a team, and a spirit of mutual recognition and appreciation should be far more visible and articulate than it often is. It is amazing how, year after year, vestrymen meet, transact business, and scarcely give a thought of recognition of the good work of the rector, who, as well as his people, needs and deserves evidences of appreciation. I have known some parishes to continue a man's salary at the same figure for five, ten, or even fifteen years, without the slightest recognition that some tangible evidence of their appreciation for his increasing ability and growing expenses is deserved and long overdue. Even though the recognition may be only a small amount, the fact that a raise has been given will be appreciated by the rector as an evidence of interest in him and his needs as his family and obligations increase. If the rector is called away, and the vestry has to secure a new man, almost inevitably it will have to pay him considerably more than the former rector—although, in engaging a new man, there is no assurance that he will ever be as fine a pastor or as good a leader as the one just lost. Every vestry should make a practice of reviewing the salary of the rector and other staff members every year. On the other hand, the rector should make a practice of recognizing the faithful and devoted service of many members of the vestry. It is astounding how much time and thought many wardens, treasurers, and clerks gladly give to the church; and this should be given public recognition.

Occasionally it is a pleasant custom for the rector and his wife to invite the vestrymen and their wives (or husbands) to a meal, perhaps before a vestry meeting. Such an informal occasion helps to break down the formal relationship and to build good will and understanding. Having them come into the rectory may even bring about a recognition of the fact that improvements and redecoration are needed from time to time. It also helps the parish officers to come to know the rector's family.

---

REFERENCES

1. Canon 13, Section 2
2. Canon 13, Section 3
3. Canon 13, Section 1

# 8

# THE CALL

## *On Calling a Rector—for Vestries*

When the rector of a parish resigns, and his resignation has been accepted by the vestry, the parish faces a critical situation. Decisions must be made which inevitably will affect every member of that parish for years to come, and the reverberations of which will reach out into the community and the diocese. This is as true of a small parish as of a large one. Canon 47 provides that as soon as such a vacancy occurs, "the Churchwardens or other proper officers" shall notify the bishop of the diocese. This is a wise as well as a necessary provision because the bishop has had more experience in this area than anyone else. It underlines, too, the fact that we are members of an episcopal Church and not simply of a congregation. In addition, it recognizes the fact that the diocese has a very vital interest in the choice made by the parish.

### First Steps

The Bible tells us that "a prophet is not without honour, save in his own country, and in his own house."[1] The truth of this observation is often revealed in the way committees turn away from men within the diocese and give preference to a man in another. This is often due to the fact that nearby clergymen have weaknesses which are known; and distance lends enchantment. Here, I would like to interject the observation that most bishops, and others who deal with personnel procurement, soon discover that most letters of recommendation have to be read in terms not of what they say, but of what they leave out. It also makes a great deal of difference who writes them. Sifting evidence is an important part of the work of any nominating committee.

Because the bishop is the more experienced, often has access to confidential information not available to a committee, and also because he is the bishop, it is well first to ask him for suggestions. He will probably make one or more suggestions of clergymen within the diocese. He will do this not merely because he usually knows them better than men outside the diocese, but because a diocese partakes of the nature of a team, and it is important to have team-play. A high morale can only be maintained when men feel that good work is being recognized and faithfulness rewarded. Every man likes to feel approved and wanted, even though he is not eventually called; and to know that the bishop has recommended him bolsters his spirit. In officially notifying the bishop of the vacancy, it is therefore well to ask for an appointment to talk the matter over with him. Most bishops regard the choice of men as one of their most important responsibilities, in that over a period of years the quality of their leadership can make or break the work and life of the diocese as well as of the parish.

The by-laws of the parish should state what body has the power to call the rector. Sometimes a parish meeting is necessary. More often, and better, the responsibility is in the hands of the vestry. Whichever it is, the best procedure is to set up a nominating committee to report to this body. Preliminary thought should be given by the rector and wardens as to what persons should serve on such a committee, because it calls for the wisest and most discerning people the parish can provide. In making the choice, it is well to remember that the committee should be representative of the parish, and yet sufficiently small to be effective. The members should not all be from the vestry. At least one should be a woman, and one or more should be representatives of the young element of the parish. This committee is to receive and secure names of prospects, screen them, and eventually nominate one or more to the vestry or parish. It should be given a general outline of the conditions of the call in terms of salary, living facilities, utilities, automobile allowance, and so forth. It is well to leave such matters as age and other qualifications entirely in their hands. Too many preconceived limitations are unwise. The thing to do is to choose the committee carefully, and then trust them to bring in the nominations. The proper authorities will have their chance to judge the wisdom of their choice, and the reasons for it, when the time comes to elect.

In addition, it may be well to appoint another committee to consider what the parish has to offer to challenge the clergyman in terms of parish equipment, human and financial resources, schooling facilities for his children, community and cultural advantages, growth statistics for the community, and other data which might be helpful in securing the right man. Nearby colleges, possibilities for parish growth, lay leadership resources, opportunity to work with young people, missionary interest, diocesan relationships, all these are things a man will want to know when he is called. He will be favorably impressed if such facts are in the hands of the vestry or nominating committee when he begins to ask questions about them. The conference with the bishop will be helpful in giving a committee both suggestions of men to be considered and a procedure to follow.

### Some Basic Considerations

After meeting with or hearing from the bishop, the committee should meet immediately to consider some of the basic questions as to procedure and needs. I would offer the following comments.

(1) No one man has everything, and in seeking a successor it is usually wise to try to get a man who has interests and abilities somewhat different than his predecessor. If he has been a good organizer, it may be well to look for a good preacher; or, if he has been young, enthusiastic, and successful in work

with young people, it may be well to get an older man to solidify these gains and deepen the life of the parish. One mistake many nominating committees make is to think that success is to be found in youthful enthusiasm, and that they must have a man in his thirties or forties. Actually, if one thinks about it, he will realize that a clergyman, because of the nature of his work, ought to be at his prime in his fifties and early sixties; and that a younger man, if he is really good, will probably not remain in the parish long enough to know the people as they can only be known through years of working together in the parish family. If the committee makes an error and chooses a young man who has zeal but lacks experience, a tragic mistake may be made which may continue over many years because of the right of permanent tenure which a rector has. This will cause many a heartache and lost opportunity.

(2) The ability to preach a good sermon is important, of course, but it is absurd to imagine that one, two, or even half a dozen sermons, are adequate criteria on which to base so important a decision; and it is unrealistic to think that a man can preach naturally and freely when he knows he is on trial. *A clergyman should never be asked to preach in the parish considering him as a candidate.* Indeed, the word "candidate" is obnoxious. The idea behind the Christian ministry is quite different from the assumptions of business. In business a man wants to better himself, and from time to time he may seek a new position which will offer greater opportunity for growth, a bigger salary, and better educational resources for his family. In the ministry, we believe that a man is "called," not employed or hired by the parish. He is called of God to serve, and wants to go to the parish or community where he feels he can serve most fully. If he is married, he must consider the happiness and welfare of his wife and children; but essentially, he is called on a full time basis to provide the skill and the leadership needed in every parish or community. Each parish and community is different, and he naturally wants to serve where he feels he can be most effective with the gifts God has given him. The man for a particular parish should be hand-picked for par-

ticular needs and a special situation. He will want to feel that he fits, and that the parish wants him because it feels that he has "what it takes." This does not mean that, as an employed person, he should be called upon to do all the work; nor should he regard his vestry or members of his parish as his unpaid laborers. This is a family affair. Responsibilities are to be shared. It is a cooperative effort in which all are called upon to join, both for their own good and that of the parish and the community. Right relationships are essential. The titles he holds are indicative of his special responsibilities: rector, father, priest, pastor, preacher. In the last analysis, however, it is his total personality which is of the essence. In brief, is he the sort of man whom, in the best sense of the word, you can love and who will love you?

(3) Although the committee may be limited in numbers, it ought to have the right to call on others for help, those who have had experience in this field, both in the parish and outside. It might be well—the members of the committee having met with the bishop and organized under a chairman (preferably appointed by the vestry) and a secretary—that they call an open meeting for all the parish, to receive further nominations from members of the parish and ideas of special needs or qualifications. If names are presented, the person suggesting the name should be asked to secure all possible information about the man. However, *the clergyman suggested should not be written to, nor asked if he would allow his name to be considered or presented.* This is a very unfair and unsatisfactory practice—somewhat similar to a man sounding out a girl by asking her if she would accept him if he proposed. No man can say that he is interested, or would accept, if he were called. He cannot know all the facts he would want to have before giving an answer; nor can he know how much he is wanted or needed until a call has been extended. No nominating committee should ever send out a sheaf of letters to the men whose names have been given them, saying in brief, "Will you allow your name to be considered, or are you interested, or would you accept if we should extend you a call?" Every resource should be used to find

out about a man, by letter and by telephone, from people in his community, from those who know him, his bishop, the dean of his seminary, nearby clergymen, and businessmen. I would here add that people will tell you in conversation what they will not put in writing; and I would repeat that all letters of recommendation must be carefully evaluated.

### The Search

When the list has been reduced to a half-dozen or less, these few should be visited by teams of people who are not all members of the committee. It is wise to include one or two members of the committee in each car. Teams of husbands and wives are useful. When investigating a prospect, care should be taken to be on time for the service and to ascertain whether the prospect is preaching. If there are two or three carloads, the groups should not arrive together, and should park their cars a short distance away, walking to the church in pairs or alone, remaining incognito so far as possible. If questioned, they may introduce themselves as strangers in town for the day.

Reports on these visits should be made to the whole committee. When a month or more has passed, a report of progress should be made to the parish at a morning service. This should be continued from time to time, either by verbal reports or information in the parish leaflet, in order to keep people aware that the committee is working faithfully. It should be stressed again and again that it is far more important to get the right man, and to spend the necessary time in doing this, than to get a man immediately and be sorry later. A temporary vacancy is definitely of secondary importance. Indeed, an interim of a month or more between rectors is a good thing to have as a settling-down period—to prevent odious comparisons, to redecorate and prepare the rectory, to build up a keen desire to welcome a new man, as well as to develop lay responsibility which will be a real asset to the new rector when he comes.

Some of the things a committee might do well to look for and consider are listed in the Appendix, and have been compiled by those who have had wide experience in their field. Many of these may seem foolish, but they have proved of help to others. For instance, one suggestion is to find out everything possible, tactfully, about a clergyman's wife—perhaps seeing her and talking with her. This may be regarded as desirable but not important, and it may seem unfair to judge a man's qualifications by his wife; yet those who have had experience in such matters regard this as of very great importance in a parish ministry, as you will discover, if you do not already know.

If one of the men being seriously considered has a parish too far away to visit, effort should be made to discover some nearby clergyman who knows him well enough to invite him to preach in his parish. It may be necessary to tell him why such an invitation is extended, although it is better not to do so. The parish inviting him should be told that his expenses and an honorarium will be paid. As many committee members as possible, and other parishioners, should hear him; but his visit should not be publicly announced. Those attending the service may meet at a predetermined point after the service; and if the reactions seem sufficiently favorable, some members of the committee may be authorized to talk with him, either by inviting him for lunch, or meeting with him in the afternoon and urging him to visit their parish and to meet with the vestry. The procedure will depend upon how far he has come and how much he has been told ahead of time. The important thing to remember is that he should not be asked to commit himself, and that the committee not commit the parish; other men may still be under consideration. It is only a friendly meeting in which he is asked to match his time and interest against your provision of expenses and hospitality. After all, most men that you may want are happy where they are, and unless they have been there ten years or more, will have to be persuaded that your parish presents a greater opportunity for service. Even those who have been in a parish for ten years may need persuading. Many clergymen will refuse to preach under such conditions, or even meet with a committee until they have been called. If this is so, it should not be charged against them. Indeed, it may well be credited in their favor.

## The Decision

The time will come when the commitee feels that it has all the information it needs, and that it is ready to make its choice of a man to nominate. A time should be set sufficiently far ahead so that all the members of the committee can be present, and when they can meet in a leisurely fashion. The name of each man still being considered should be brought up in alphabetical order, and should be freely and fully discussed, with everyone given a chance to ask questions. The best procedure then is to cast a secret straw ballot. If there is serious division, more time should be taken to gather more information; or perhaps even some new names might be followed up, because the nominating committee should, if possible, make a unanimous recommendation. This is far more important than a delay of a few weeks. Remember, this decision involves a choice which should be effective, over many years, and concerns very personal and extremely important relationships. Therefore, minority opinion should not be pressured into agreement, or democratically overridden. This is a time when it pays to be patient.

During this whole period the committee should be in constant touch with the bishop, making reports of progress and seeking his counsel. When the clergyman to be nominated has been chosen, and his name is ready for presentation to the vestry for definite action, the bishop should be notified officially of this fact; and the canons provide that he has thirty days "in which to communicate with the Vestry."[2] Some bishops interpret this to mean that in so communicating, the bishop has a right to veto the nomination (if he considers the man undesirable for reasons he regards as adequate) without stating what his reason is, or preferring charges. Another bishop may think such a communication is only for the purpose of telling the vestry what he knows about the clergyman, both favorable and unfavorable; and if he feels the unfavorable points are sufficiently strong, he may want to meet with the vestry. He may add that if the call is issued, he will want to see the man before he accepts. If the committee has been in continuous touch with the bishop, matters should never reach this stage, as the bishop would also have been investigating the men most seriously considered, relaying his findings to the committee. And if these findings were distinctly unfavorable, both out of respect for the bishop's judgment as well as his office as bishop, the man's name would have been dropped in the process of screening. Although the vestry may meet to consider the nomination before they hear from the bishop, they cannot proceed to the actual election until they have received his communication.

Again, it is important that when the committee reports to the vestry, there should be no serious division in the vestry. It is as important here, as in the committee, to have general agreement, and to take sufficient time to arrive at a unanimous decision. And again, I would press home the fact that it should be genuinely unanimous, and not merely the generous gesture of the minority who, seeing that they are outvoted, move to have the vote made unanimous. Again, time is of secondary importance. If only one person is unconvinced that the man nominated is the right man, his convictions should be heard and respected. If it is still maintained, it is only fair that the man who is called should be informed of this fact.

### Immediate Procedures Following the Call

At the time of the election, the preliminary details of salary, housing, and utilities given to the committee should be reviewed and made reasonably firm and explicit. Some things must inevitably wait for a conference. For instance, if the rectory is to be redecorated, the new rector and his wife should be given liberty in the choice of wallpapers, paints, and equipment, with a top total cost mutually agreed upon. If moving expenses are to be paid, it is well for both parties to have an estimate made in advance, and the vestry should see that a certified check is available upon arrival of the goods. If utilities are included, it is well to specify what they are (See Appendix.).

When a clergyman has received a written "call," it is only natural that he will want to meet formally with the vestry, and see some of the people who are active in the parish. This will be true even if he has previously made an informal visit; because at that time, when the matter was entirely tentative and exploratory, he could not be expected to ask personal and practical questions. For instance, although he may have seen the rectory, he could hardly expect to inspect it carefully, and could scarcely ask questions about its renovation and redecoration until he had been asked to occupy it. He may want to probe more deeply into the finances of the parish, and will want to know the attitude of the vestry with regard to certain matters which he considers important, and to sound them out on proposals he may want to present for the future. He will probably want to visit the bishop at the same time, both as a matter of courtesy and to see what the bishop has to say in regard to the parish and the work in the diocese. Previously, the bishop will have given consent to the "call," it is true; but a chance to talk personally with him is important and begins his relationship with the bishop properly.

Of course, his wife is invited to come with him on this visit, thus providing her with an opportunity to meet with some of the women of the parish. She may want to go over the rectory with them more thoroughly, and to discuss such questions as schools, medical and other resources.

He should not be expected to give an answer immediately. Just as it has taken time for the parish to come to a decision so it will take time for him in that his decision inevitably will affect his whole future ministry. He will want to consult with his own bishop, with his vestry, and with friends in whom he has confidence. No matter how sure he may be, when a man has received a definite call, he should not rely on his own judgment alone. His bishop may have plans in the making for him which would make a difference in his decision; and it is hardly courteous to his vestry to come before them with a *fait accompli.* His vestry must accept his resignation before he can accept another call. They will probably do this as a formality, realizing the foolishness of trying to hold a man if he is determined to go.

There will naturally be a feeling of regret; but if, after working with them over the years, he does not now take them into his confidence, there may also be unnecessary resentment.

### The Announcement

When a parish has issued a formal call to a man, and he has received it, both the parish and he have a right to make it public. It is an official action. At the same time, the parish is not eager to have the unfavorable publicity if the call is declined; and the clergyman may wish to have it kept quiet so that he may make his decision free from the pressures of the people of his parish. Therefore, the question of the announcement should be decided at the time the call is presented. It would be undesirable if it were to become public in one place and not in the other. If it is to be kept confidential for a time, it is very important that all those who know it officially should be impressed with the importance of keeping the confidence. In passing, let me say that it is a very poor practice for a man to use a call as a lever on his vestry to accomplish something which he has not been able to accomplish otherwise, or to cause them to raise his salary to match the one offered him in the new call.

When a man receives a call to another parish, he is in for a very uncomfortable period as he seeks to balance the pros and the cons and genuinely tries to fulfill God's will. His decision should not be unduly prolonged: a week to ten days should be sufficient.

## *On Being Called—for Clergy*

We commonly speak of the ministry as a "calling," and of a clergyman as being "called" to a parish. This not merely pious vocabulary. It has behind it the thought that God is still actively at work in the world through his Holy Spirit and through people; that one does not choose the ministry as a vocation, but that in a very definite way a man feels called by a power outside of himself which seems to lay this challenge, opportunity, and obligation before him. Here I want to make it clear that when a man is called to a certain parish, this is not like the offer of a new position, as a business firm might approach a prospect. A clergyman definitely is not hired or fired. His calling is on quite a different level, in which God's Holy Spirit is invoked both by the parish and by the clergyman who is called.

This is particularly evident when it comes to being called to a diocesan or national church office, when it is the voice of the Church speaking, rather than that of a single parish. When a parish calls a clergyman, it may be said that the burden is on the parish to persuade the man that he can be of greater service, and is more badly needed, than in his present position. But when a clergyman is faced with the larger call of the Church, the burden is upon the man to show adequate cause why he should not accept the call; and these reasons must not be based on personal opinion as to fitness or preference, but in terms of some basic inability. The Church is often called "the Army of Christ." Even so, its clergy sometimes seem to forget that there is of necessity a chain of command, and that they are men under authority. When there is a definite call from a parish, it must be assumed that this represents the carefully and prayerfully considered decision of a duly authorized group, like the people of Macedonia who called to Paul, "Come over and help us."

### First Steps to Take

He will then notify his bishop, for certainly his advice should be obtained. I believe that before any call is definitely refused, a man should take a few of his most intimate friends on his vestry into his confidence. They, too, may have helpful advice to give. It is sometimes possible that some may feel that a change of rectorships might be as good for the parish as for the incumbent, even when a man is doing good work. If he has been there for some time, and has ten or more years before retirement, this fact should be carefully weighed. If he is in his forties, this may be the last call he will receive.

### Conference with the Vestry

When a parish calls a man, he should plan to have a frank and informal conference with the vestry of the parish calling him, to discuss all sorts of matters which can much better be discussed before accepting their call. In making arrangements for this conference, if he is married and the distance is not too great, it is well for him to suggest that he bring his wife with him. I believe that this is of sufficient importance so that considerable effort should be made to accomplish this. The wives of most clergymen have excellent judgment, especially about matters concerning the rectory, and they have a woman's intuition about many other things as well.

In planning the trip, he should allow plenty of time. Being late for the first appointment may get him off to a poor start; and if he is early, he can "case" the neighborhood and get a quick idea of the general character of the community. Whether his wife will wish to sit in on the vestry meeting or not, is a matter of mutual personal preference.

In his conference with the vestry, he will want to find out, first of all, what their plans and hopes are for the future of the parish. He will have looked up the statistical report, and inquired about the parish from friends. He will want to know about the attendance at Sunday services and at church school. There is often a vast difference between figures reported in the diocesan journal and the actual facts. Also, at this time he should make sure that the vestry has the right to call him, as some parish by-laws call for election by parish meeting. He will share with them some of his hopes and plans should he accept the call, and discuss frankly with them matters of churchmanship and stewardship. He will enquire how they stand in regard to their share of the missionary program of the Church, and the place they have in the life of the community; and will tell them how he feels in regard to these matters.

He will want to see the fabric, and will note how well it has been kept up. Little details—the condition of the prayer books and hymnals, the comfort or discomfort of the kneeling benches, the condition of the sacristy and the kitchen—can tell him much about the parish.

He and his wife will want to see the rectory. He will be sure to look at the cellar and note its condition, inquiring if water ever seeps in, or if there is dry rot in the beams. He may find that the rectory is somewhat run-down, especially if the previous family was of long tenure. He should not be astonished at this, but should make a note of what he would like to see changed; and when he talks with them, should state frankly his hope that some member of the vestry will be appointed to be responsible for its repair and continual upkeep. The vestry will probably be cooperative, and will do most, if not all, of what he requests. They may even be willing to buy a new rectory, if he points out that the neighborhood has changed and that his children should be in a good school district. His decision must not hang on the question of the rectory alone; comfort should not be a first consideration in our ministry.

At the time of his visit to the vestry, the newly-called man should plan for an appointment with the bishop of the diocese. The bishop will know the situation objectively, and be able, if necessary, to talk with the vestry about more adequate housing better than the man involved. Only the bishop can give him much valuable information about the parish as a whole. Of course, he has given his consent to his call; but even so, a man's position will be greatly strengthened if he can be assured that he is gladly received canonically into the diocese. If a man is called as a deacon to be an assistant, or as vicar of a mission, many bishops make a practice of delaying canonical acceptance for a period of time.

Upon his return, he should again seek the judgment of his bishop and some of his closest friends. Discussion with these, and with officers of the vestry, must be confidential because there are certain canonical procedures to be fulfilled before a man is free to accept a call. Then there is the whole matter of public relations.

## Setting the Date

Before making the final decision, he should determine, if he plans to accept the call, not only the date of his departure, but also the date of his arrival to take up his new work. This will depend upon many circumstances, too many to enumerate here; but actually, he will discover that his usefulness in his present parish will definitely diminish when they know he is going elsewhere; and that about all he can accomplish is to tie up certain things, making sure that various duties are definitely assigned to responsible persons. Naturally, he cannot make any plans for the future of the parish he is leaving. How long it will take to prepare the new rectory is another matter; the usual time is about a month.

When, finally, he and his wife have come to a decision, he should telephone or write to the vestry of the parish to which he has been called, informing them of his decision. If he decides to remain where he is, he should make every effort to word his refusal as kindly as he can, because this will be a sad disappointment. If he decides to accept their offer, he should tell them he intends to do so, but also that he wishes to discuss in detail such matters as have not been definitely cleared; adding that, by canonical courtesy, there are certain definite formalities to be fulfilled before he can give them his official acceptance. He will then call a special meeting of his own vestry as soon as possible, as the canons definitely provide that, "A Rector may not resign his Parish without the consent of the said Parish."[3] Few vestries will refuse to accept such a resignation; but it is a matter of courtesy to give them adequate opportunity. Acceptance of his resignation being voted, he can read them his acceptance of his new call, if he wishes to do so; and he should immediately notify the bishops of both dioceses, and send his official acceptance to the vestry of the parish which has called him—forwarding with his official acceptance the basic facts they will need for publication, together with two glossy prints of himself, one for the newspaper and one for the parish.

It has been found desirable to arrange for the public announcement of acceptance to be made simultaneously in both churches at a Sunday morning service. It seems reasonable that the people who come to church should be the first to know of his decision; they are the most deeply concerned. Practically, Monday morning is usually an easy time to get good space in a newspaper, particularly if the information is sent ahead of time with a definite release date clearly noted. It is important, in order to keep the good-will of the newspapers, that this be done in both communities at the same time.

## *Leaving, and Beginning Anew—Primarily for Clergy*

Once a man has accepted a call to a new position, his mind inevitably turns to a consideration of his new work, and he begins to make plans for the future. It is for this reason that it is best to move as soon as it is possible and fair to do so. Too many men remain too long, thinking they are doing the parish a service. They are not, because most vestries will not really begin seriously to look for a successor until the rector has left. It is good, anyway, for the parish to have a short period between rectors so they can develop lay leadership. Also, it is a good thing to have the parish reach a point where they are tired of supply clergy and long to have a man of their own.

### Advance Planning

The best way for a man to make plans for the new work is probably not to sit down and think, trying to write out some theoretical plans, but rather to make notes as situations arise and problems confront him. Later they can all be evaluated together, and general plans formulated. It will not be possible to draw up complete blueprints for some time; and whatever is drawn up should be subject to continual review and revision. He can, however, put down certain goals and certain emphases for the deepening of the fellowship and the lifting of the vision of his people. It is interesting and worth while to put these in such a shape that he can look them over after six months, or perhaps even a year, and then make revisions as a result of his more intimate knowledge.

It is well for a clergyman to have a little break between responsibilities—resigning in the middle of the month, and taking up his new duties the first of the month following, or, perhaps, working it out in connection with a Church season. Most parishes will want to pay the full salary of a broken month, in appreciation of the service given over the years; and he will probably have some vacation due him, as well, on a pro rata basis.

### Interim Vacation

The matter of vacation should have been settled at the time of the call. The usual and fair procedure is to have one month —although in a few cases it is six weeks or two months—with the expenses of clergy supply provided. He should certainly be allowed time-off in between, in proportion to the number of months he has served since his last vacation. If a man leaves in the spring and takes the vacation due him between positions, most vestries will realize that the summer is usually a slack time and will recognize the wisdom of having the rector begin the fall season refreshed and with new perspectives. They will be willing to grant him a reasonable, additional summer vacation even though he may have been with the parish only a short time.

### Tying Loose Ends

If a man has been in a parish a number of years, it is well for him to get a running start in his preparations for leaving: first, by bringing all the canonically required parish records and address lists completely up to date. In addition to this, it is helpful to leave a detail of the general parish practices and procedures, and something in the way of a skeleton program in terms of special events. In addition to this, the rector should provide a complete list of names and addresses of the people to whom has been entrusted responsibility for various parish activities. In a rural parish, particularly, it is extremely helpful if a man leaves a map marked with the location of the various families, as usually there are no numbers on the houses or names on the streets. *All basic records belong to the parish, and in no case should they be removed, even with the best intentions of making them more complete.* This is a primary responsibility. There should be no exceptions. Throw away all the "dead" and personal material which has accumulated. This will take more time than anyone anticipates. Everything helpful to the incoming rector should be left definitely in someone's care, and the wardens should be informed who is responsible for the various areas of work assigned. To sum it all up, a man should plan to leave behind him all that he would like to find in his new parish, and thus earn the admiration and gratitude of his successor.

## *Beginning Work Together*

One of the first things a new man will want to do on his arrival is to report personally to his senior warden. He should obtain from him a list of the very sick persons in the parish, in order to call on them as soon as possible. He may want to see the choir director and church school superintendent before Sunday.

He has thought over his first sermon, and it is desirable to have it well in hand before he arrives. A "dry run" from the new pulpit, with wife to listen, helps greatly in discovering and solving special acoustical problems before the first service.

One rector I know, upon arriving at his new parish, worked out a visitation schedule with the members of the vestry, and they drove him around, introducing him to the parishioners. Beginning at ten o'clock in the morning, and often continuing until nine in the evening, they covered the whole parish within a month's time. The vestrymen seemed to enjoy it, and the members of the parish were most enthusiastic at this evidence of their rector's concern and friendliness. During the first week, it is helpful for him to meet with the teachers of the church school and the leaders of the various parish organizations, as well as the other members of the vestry. He should attend the first choir rehearsal after his arrival. As soon as he can work it in, he should introduce himself to the civic and welfare agency leaders, both as a courtesy, and in order to have personal relationships with them before any acute problems arise in which he may need their help.

The shut-ins would naturally take priority over ordinary parish calling, but it is tremendously important to begin making regular parish calls as soon as possible. This is a dramatic and effective way of indicating his concern for his people, and his interest in them. It is remarkable how quickly the "grapevine" passes the word along that he has already called and he will be astonished how appreciative people are. During the first weeks, he will have fewer administrative details and interruptions; therefore it is important to start at once making calls through the parish every afternoon (especially Saturday), and as many evenings as possible, in order to find the men at home.

## First Vestry Meeting

In preparation for his first vestry meeting, it would be well to ask for a copy of the constitution and by-laws of the parish, and as opportunity offers, request the same from the various organizations of the parish. It is extraordinary how easy it is for them to become lost, or so far forgotten that many of the purposes and practices which have been wisely provided are being ignored. Every parish should have carefully considered policies in regard to such matters as the use of church equipment, approval of bills and pledge statements, counting of the offering, competitive bids on purchases over a certain figure, and the audit of books (See Appendix.).

If there is a regular vestry meeting soon, it is not necessary to call a special one; but it is important to have the first meeting run on a high level. What happens at this meeting will be a pattern for subsequent meetings. The new rector should, therefore, ascertain from the clerk what the business in hand is likely to be, make sure that the treasurer has a monthly report and, with the help of the senior warden, prepare a definite agenda which should be read at the beginning of the meeting. He will want to start with prayer, and perhaps explain to them how he feels a vestry meeting should be different from an ordinary, secular meeting. He should use committees just as much as he can, and expect them to report at each meeting. The usual committees are: buildings and grounds, church school, finance, sometimes one on memorials, every member canvass, and a nominating committee. This latter is most important of all because, over the years, it will help determine the caliber of the vestry and parish leadership. He will probably want soon to hold meetings of the heads of parish organizations, and of teachers and staff of the church school, especially to find out what they are doing, and what their plans are for the future.

It may be desirable to send a general letter to the members of the parish, expressing his happiness at being with them, and his desire to serve them in every way. This can be done through the weekly leaflet. If his original letter of acceptance has already been sent out, this procedure may not be necessary.

His first annual parish meeting will give a wonderful opportunity to review and to plan, to make goals clear, and to raise the sights of vestry and people.

## *The Service of Institution*

I suggest that the vestry arrange a service of institution with the bishop. This can be a very significant event, and a dramatic presentation of a man's new relationship as their rector, pastor, and priest.

A clergyman locating in a new parish should see that the bishop is sent the canonical letter containing the vote of election (and, if he has not already done so, should present to the bishop his *Letter Dimissory*, because he has no canonical standing until he has been officially accepted into the diocese). The vote of election is provided for in the opening statement of the service of institution. If the bishop does not arrange to bring the Certificate of Institution (he usually does), one should be prepared, sufficiently large to be impressive. The clergyman should go through the service carefully with his wardens, to be sure they know precisely what to do. A key should be prepared and must be sufficiently large to make visible the symbolic act of the rector receiving it. And of course, the Bible, The Book of Common Prayer, and the books containing the General Convention Canons and the Canons of the Diocese, should be readily available.

The service of institution is of sufficient importance for a carefully prepared special service leaflet. This should give instructions to the congregation, and might contain a short historical introduction telling about the background of the service, and the meaning of the various symbolic acts performed by bishop and wardens. Attention should be called to the fact that the final blessing is given by the newly-installed rector—the only service in which a priest takes the final blessing when a bishop is participating. It dramatizes and emphasizes the new relationship which is embodied in this service. It is also interesting to note that, as his first act, the new rector kneels before the altar humbly to present supplications for himself, and then stands as he prays the prayer for the Church. The bishop decides who shall preach the sermon; he often does so himself. It offers an excellent opportunity for him to make some plain and helpful statements about the canonical and personal relationships which should exist between rector and people, and to clear up some of the misconceptions, which some church people still have, about the clergyman being employed by them, and their strange expectation that he should be a glorified errand boy to do all the things they fail to do. In most places it is courteous and worth while to invite clergy of other communions, and perhaps dignitaries of the community, to march in the procession, and make this service a significant community event.

If it is an evening service with a reception following, as seems desirable for many reasons, it is best to omit an offering as the faithful will have already given their pledge envelopes, thus making this a collection from outsiders rather than an offering. It is appropriate, too, to point out that the priest is offering himself anew, and to call the congregation to make an offering of themselves, their souls and bodies, unto the Lord.

## *Make Haste Slowly*

The beginning of a new ministry is extremely important, and careful thought should be taken for the details involved. It is well to continue for a time, as far as he can, the practices, procedures, and program of the preceding rector, and to make as few changes as possible. Indeed, it is desirable to make none at all for the first few weeks, unless the new man feels that his predecessor has not been completely following the canons or rubrics of the Church. In this case it is desirable to explain why he is making the changes. As a matter of fact, this is good procedure in effecting change. There are few things more irritating to people than to have a new rector immediately make changes; but it is remarkable how loyal people can be, after they have gained confidence in him, in following the suggestions he makes. It is always important, in making any change—whether large or small—to talk the matter over with the vestry. No group likes to have anything sprung upon them, with immediate action requested; and it is much more important to have them strongly behind a man, than it is to accomplish some special personal desire he may have, or some plan which he may have conceived. In the last analysis, this is their parish more than it is his; but first and foremost, it is the Lord's parish, where there should be peace and harmony.

---

REFERENCES

1. Matthew 13:57
2. Canon 47, Section 2
3. Canon 46, Section 1

# 9

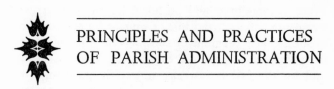

# PRINCIPLES AND PRACTICES OF PARISH ADMINISTRATION

## *The Rector as Leader and Administrator*

There is much truth in the old adage, "Never do anything yourself which you can get somebody else to do"; but if you are a rector, there are some things which you alone must do. A leader should always be out in front, setting goals and giving direction to the enterprise. It is the rector's responsibility to lead; although he will be wise to seek counsel from others who have been longer in the parish than he. It is the rector's job, also, to see that the work is evaluated regularly, and redirected according to the experience gained.

There is a happy medium in this matter of administration. A parish cannot be run effectively without it, but if it gets out of hand it is difficult to live with it. It is said that there will be no partings in heaven, but one can understand the feeling of the rector who also hopes there will be no meetings there, either.

The head of any organization has a special responsibility to plan for the months and years ahead. Yet rectors find themselves so pressed by the many immediate tasks that they fail in this most important obligation. Time must be set apart solely for this purpose. A few clergymen regularly go on a yearly retreat, alone or with their parish leaders. Time spent in finding and developing lay leaders is most productive. It yields rich, long-range returns. However it is done, planning ahead is a "must" item in every rector's schedule. The time and place for such planning should be set far in advance, and should be adhered to against any temptation to cancel it. If this is not done, some adequate substitute must be provided for the clergyman to get away for a time from all parish activities, in order to look at himself and the work objectively. This matter of planning ahead is far more important than is generally recognized. If the rector and parish leaders do not know what the parish is trying to accomplish, or in what direction it wants to move, how can it be expected to get anywhere? Attendance at services may be good, activities many and varied, and numbers steadily growing, because the parish happens to be in a fast-growing community. But a yearly appraisal is essential, even in smaller places. A quarterly meeting of rector and leaders is helpful, if it is not allowed to become merely a clearing-house for dates or cluttered with minutiae.

The second important ingredient of any good administrator is the ability to get along with people. This calls for a recognition of what others may have to contribute, even though one may disagree with them, and a willingness to support other than one's own special schemes for the good of the whole. One of the best ways of meeting individual opposition is to put the objector on the committee. It is far better to give opportunity for expression inside the group than to have its work undercut by criticism on the outside. Team-play is essential to any organization, and spirit and morale is very largely measured by the ability of the leader to weld individuals into a group, to keep the discussion on the subject, and to be as free as possible from dealing with personalities. A leader has the responsibility of injecting enthusiasm into the whole group—and when we use the word "enthusiasm," we are thinking of it in terms of its derivation, "God in." In other words, he should relate the work being done—even though it may seem insignificant at its local level—with the great purposes of God in spreading The Good News and building his kingdom.

## At a Meeting

Meetings should be called to order on time, even though all may not be present. When sufficient time has been allowed to secure attention and a sense of expectancy, a prayer of special intention for the business ahead should be offered. This must not be allowed to become a mere formality. God, having once been called upon, is often completely forgotten. How far away he sometimes is becomes painfully apparent, if the leader calls for a pause and suggests that it might be well for all to stop for a moment, to lift the whole level of discussion beyond argument to a new point of view, asking God for light and leading. So far will the conversation have wandered that this idea will often come as a shock. Why is this so? If two forces meet head on, there is sure to be disaster, but if you can merge them at a tangent, there is much less destruction.

## Delegation of Authority

Too often, leaders are so fearful that important plans will fall through, or that assigned duties will not be done that they take them over themselves. Such action upsets the person concerned by revealing the leader's lack of confidence. If one is sure that the person knows what his responsibility is, and is equipped to discharge it, it is often more important to allow failure to take place. One of the handicaps of any voluntary service is that, because it is voluntary, some are inclined to feel it need not be performed with the same faithfulness as the paid job. This must be changed, and we should have courage enough to do so by a frank talk with the parishioner concerned. If this is not effective, a tactful request for his resignation is in order. Before a person is replaced, it is always courteous and fair to notify him of the fact that this is planned unless the responsibility laid upon him has been discharged within a certain period of time.

It is important to add here that one of the reasons for failure is that the person assigned responsibility is not sufficiently instructed in what is expected of him. For instance, how many clergymen are guilty of enlisting a teacher for the church school by outlining a few important ideas, providing the textbook, and then assuming that the vacancy is filled and the work will be done. A little imagination will make clear that most people will have many questions to ask, and that continuing guidance and encouragement will be needed throughout the year. One needs only to imagine how inadequate a clergyman would feel, if asked to fill in as a foreman in a machineshop, or behind a sales counter, with as little guidance and instruction as are sometimes given to a new church school teacher or other appointees.

Another very important principle of good administration, is that new leaders must be continually sought out and trained. Organizations rise and fall very largely on the basis of the leadership provided. For example, it is poor practice to put a frantic appeal for church school teachers in a parish leaflet, or to make a general appeal from the pulpit for more men for the Every Member Canvass. Those who volunteer under such circumstances either have a sensitive conscience or offer their services reluctantly because they are already carrying more than their share of the burden. Or else, as is far more likely, they will not be adequately qualified. To open positions of responsibility and opportunity to volunteers is a dangerous practice, and sometimes tragic in its consequences both to the individual and to the parishioners assigned to them. It is far harder to get rid of the wrong persons than to secure the right one.

Time and care taken to choose, persuade, and train the right person for a position of responsibility is time well invested. Few things demean the work of the Church more than the casual way in which we choose our leadership. Proper choice can be greatly aided by parish calling. Only so can we discover the available skills and human resources. If the work of the Church is important at all, it is of first importance; and the only reason it sometimes seems of small value is because we have sometimes allowed its leadership to slip into the hands of small people whose capacity and vision are limited.

It is a good practice for every organization to have a vice-chairman, but the office should never be given as a "consolation prize"; someone who has potential for future leadership should be appointed. It is good practice for the leader to allow the vice-chairman to take over from time to time, both to instill confidence and to develop ability.

It is very important not to jump over the heads of people who have a right to recognition. It is so easy to go directly to the people at the top, especially when they happen to be personal friends. The sexton isn't around when he is expected to be; so someone tells the rector who proceeds to instruct the sexton on his duties, completely overlooking the fact that there is a building committee responsible for this work. He should not be surprised if the chairman should say, "If the rector wants to run things, let him, I'm through!" The result will be that the rector may find more and more responsibility falling on his shoulders. Some rectors like this; but it is not good administration, nor is it good for the people or for the work.

### Healthy and Unhealthy Criticism

Almost all of us occasionally fall victim to the fault of criticizing someone in the presence of others, only to find later that we were too hasty, and that there were extenuating circumstances which, had we known them, would have greatly modified our judgments. Our annoyance over some mistake or neglect may be so keen that we allow sarcasm to creep into our rebukes; or, perhaps even worse, make a joke at the expense of the person in a way which cuts deeply. The damage done can never be fully undone. It is much better to wait until temper cools. Then, with facts in hand, a friendly talk is in order. Instead of creating ill-will, you may discover that you have won good-will for yourself and perhaps even be thanked for your interest, help, and tact.

The reverse is equally, if not even more, important. When good work is done, it should be recognized. There are those who feel that Christians should be expected to be willing and hard-working, and that they should not expect praise—indeed, do not deserve it—for they are merely fulfilling a duty and privilege in serving the Lord. This may be true, but we need to remember that all of us fall short of being perfect Christians. (Actually, it is amazing how much is accomplished, considering how imperfect we are.) When I say that good work should be recognized, I do not mean to imply that a person should be thanked every time he sings in the choir! Nevertheless, many congregations assume too casually the presence of choir, organist, and clergy, and yet themselves are careless and irregular in joining in worship. In the eyes of God, they have just as much responsibility to be present as has a member of the choir. A church full of people can create a spirit of contagious joy and praise which even a good choir is unable to produce, or a bad one to ruin.

Occasions arise when the rector is sorely tempted to "sound off" to the parish as a whole. Such explosions are to be stoutly resisted, and they rarely produce the desired results. Certainly the weekly leaflet should never be used to lower one's blood pressure. Rebuke, if it be occasionally necessary, should be on a limited basis. Nothing is more discouraging to a congregation than to have a rector complain about poor attendance at services, when the people who should be told are not there. Never publish in a parish bulletin what could not be said face to face to anyone, and never try to be clever. It will always be misinterpreted by some.

At least once a year, at an appropriate time and not as a routine matter, it is good practice to say words of appreciation for the faithfulness and helpfulness of the different groups without whose labor the work of the church would greatly suffer. It is dangerous to use names unless you are sure no one is forgotten. Such an expression of gratitude is even more important for the parish to express, than for the people to receive.

## Not unto Us, O Lord

We often hear it said that "The rector has built a new parish house," or "has raised a mission to parish status." This was not a single-handed achievement by a long shot! It was the result of the devotion, sacrifice, and concern of many parishioners, some of whom inevitably may be even more deserving of the praise than the rector himself. It is quite common for clergymen to refer to their cures as "my parish." In a certain sense, this expresses a real truth, in that it reveals his love and concern for the people. But in another sense, it has a very undesirable overtone and contains an ugly truth: it may indicate an authoritarianism by which he regards the parish as his achievement. Most parishes were carrying on the work of the Church long before the rector appeared, and they will continue for many years after his departure. Most emphatically, therefore, it is *not* "The Rector's Parish"; much more is it the people's parish, because they are the continuing body. The rector should, therefore, be careful to carry on the fine traditions, rejoice in the fabric that has been given him to use, and the prestige which the parish has won over the years. These are his inheritance. But even before it is the people's parish, it is the Lord's parish. It is Christ's work that is being carried on.

I have been told that in the parish where President Roosevelt was a vestryman, there was a sign on the lawn, "This is President Roosevelt's Parish." On this some wag had chalked the words, "Formerly the Lord's." It may be fiction but it drives home a truth which should be remembered by every rector and member of the vestry.

### So Many Different Things to Do

Laymen may often wonder how a parson spends all his time between Sundays. I have often wished that critical parishioners could follow him around for a week's time. I am sure they would be astonished by the many and varied responsibilities a clergyman has, and the hours he puts into discharging them, and how exhausting some of these tasks are. They are rarely routine or mechanical. A clergyman can never close his office and walk off free of mind, certain of leisure hours until the next day's work begins. He is always on emergency duty as long as he is in town; and even when out of town, he should take care to see that someone knows where he can be reached in case of personal need.

With so many different things to do, it is of first importance that there should be a time schedule, and a set of priorities, set up for each day. Almost inevitably it will be upset, and it will be a rare day when a parson completes what he has set out to do. This is true of even smaller parishes, because in them so many more of the routine responsibilities fall upon him. He may at times be his own janitor, secretary, and altar guild. Two of the things which are liable to suffer are the maintenance of parish records and the carrying on of personal correspondence. I cannot overstress the importance of these responsibilities: the first to the Church, which a clergyman agreed to assume in his ordination vows; and the second to his personal relationships.

### Records

There are more important things for a clergyman to do than to keep records: it is much more important to have something worth recording. As we inherit valuable records of the past, we owe it to those in the future to leave even more adequate history, because we have far better facilities for doing so. If all the churches since the days of the apostles had kept good records, and made adequate provision for their safe-keeping, how much more we should know today! At least, we must follow Paul's instructions to the Corinthians, that all things be done "decently and in order."

There is considerable laxity on the part of many parishes in the preserving and adequate safekeeping of important parish documents. Title deeds, contracts for construction, lists of founders and contributors—all should be carefully guarded. Sometimes the Consecration document, signed by the bishop, is hung on the wall until the signature fades, or a new rector decides it is unsightly and puts it out of sight in some closet; then the glass inevitably breaks and the document gets discarded and forever lost.

It is important to have the history of the parish kept from the very beginning, brought up to date every twenty-five years, and stored in a safe place. Is there an adequate fireproof safe? Are the old records kept in it? What is being done to keep the history up to date? Are the bindings firm? Most of the records of the past are in the handwriting of the clerk, and fortunate is the parish with a clerk whose writing was in a script both beautiful and legible. Today it is possible to buy books with loose leaves of good paper which can be typed and then locked in the book. This has many advantages. One great disadvantage is that the separate sheets may get lost before they are locked in. If the vestry has such a book, check to see that all the pages are locked in place at each annual meeting. The minutes of any meeting may prove unexpectedly important at a later date, and care should be taken to see that they are accurate. *Pro forma* approval is a dangerous practice and should not be allowed.

We have already called attention to the fact that the canons require that, "At every visitation it shall be the duty of the Minister, and of the Churchwardens, or Vestrymen . . . to exhibit to the Bishop the Parish Register and to give information to him of the state of the Congregation." The canons also explicitly state that the minister is personally responsible for the keeping of the records.[1] This is the bare minimum of records: baptisms, confirmations, marriages, burials, and the names of all communicants within his cure.

Today, besides the alphabetical parish record, every pastor should have a small loose-leaf list of the parish by streets that can be taken along in the car. (See Appendix) It is almost essential for good parish calling. This list should contain full facts about families—recording not only those who are baptized, but those who are still unbaptized and unconfirmed, and inactive communicants. If the minister is able to secure an efficient volunteer, or is sensibly given an allowance for a part or full-time secretary, these records should be amplified; although there is the danger of trying to keep too many records as well as too few.

## *Parish Communication*

The parish should supply some sort of a duplicator; but it is not worth the time involved to publish a weekly leaflet, if the mechanics have to be done by the minister. Even if done by volunteer labor, I question its value merely as a service leaflet. The hymns and psalms listed on the boards in the church are sufficient. Regular meetings need not be announced every week, but should be conspicuously posted in the vestibule. Special events are better advertised in a brief statement during the notice period. A monthly leaflet mailed out to all on the parish list has much more merit, and can be kept for reference. The local weekly of smaller communities, or a column in a nearby city daily, has more value than the leaflet because the people who are not in church will be reached, and these are the ones who need the information. This should be carefully prepared with date of release, as newspapers prefer, giving "Who, what, where, when," with full names and complete facts. (See Appendix.)

Someone should be appointed to send regular news releases to the newspapers at least once a week. How much of the material sent in is used, depends upon local conditions and on the way releases are prepared. It is certainly worth while for the minister, or someone who knows the city editor, to make him a personal visit to find out what he would like to know, and the exact form and time in which he wants notices to come in. Newspapers are eager to print news when it is news. They are reluctant and resistant to material that is more what should be properly an advertisement. It should be the policy of the church to pay for newspaper advertising for special events, as an indication of appreciation for the service rendered in publicizing the parish. I shall speak more of the importance of public relations in my chapter on "The Parish and the Community."

The minister who is prompt in answering his correspondence wins a treasure of good-will for the time spent in sending short notes of gratitude and congratulations, in keeping close touch with the parishioners who are away at school, college, or in the armed forces, or sick at a distance. He may do some of his best pastoral work through this medium. More times than I can count, I have had men and women years later tell how much it has meant to them to have received a certain letter. The years pass, but they remember.

Few things are more irritating than to have an invitation ignored, so that a long-distance telephone call has to be made to get an answer. It is a poor show of gratitude not to be quick to acknowledge a check sent to the church or rector as a voluntary thank offering. Some such failures are due to thoughtlessness which ill becomes a clergyman; but some of them are due to an untidy desk, a besetting sin of many a priest. For such hapless clerics "work organizers" are a great boon. These classify material in various pockets in which one can put matters for reference in the weeks and months ahead. I have found this of great help in building up traditions, as well as saving the necessity of remembering when to start inviting Lenten preachers or getting ready for the Every Member Canvass.

It is extraordinary how businesslike vestrymen will allow their minister to get along without modern equipment for his office. The parish should certainly provide the rector with an adequate desk and chair, filing equipment, typewriter, stationery and stamps, a fire-resistant cabinet, proper book-shelves, a safe for the permanent records, and, if he is a bachelor, and so difficult to reach, an automatic answering service.

## *The Parish Meeting*

There is one event which is often a matter of dull routine and should be a high point in the life of every parish: the annual meeting. In order to make it an exciting experience, imagination of a high order must be exercised and a thoroughly competent committee set up to prepare for it. Of course, there are some necessary procedures which are difficult to make exciting; but even the signing of the registry of voters can have its drama, if the actual signing is done after services for several Sundays preceding. If a preliminary supper takes place (and this is recommended for the fellowship it affords), the new members should be invited as guests, each one brought by a host and introduced to the parish family.

The rector should spend plenty of time, and use his imagination, in preparing a fresh, newsy, stimulating report. Perhaps he can have live illustrations, or use a flannel-board or slides. "One picture is worth ten thousand words," and the treasurer's report doesn't need to be a list of figures; although figures must be submitted by title, they can be a human interest story in terms of appreciation and accomplishment. The meeting must not drag and, with supper, should end by nine p.m. If children are invited to the supper, a special entertainment should be provided for them. The annual meeting can be varied by holding it on Sunday morning after service, combined with a parish luncheon. The parish by-laws must be fulfilled, however, and this can be done by holding a formally called meeting on the date set, with the necessary quorum present, and then voting to adjourn the meeting to Sunday.

## *Summary*

It is true that ministers have long hours, that their work is not merely from sun up to sun down, and is never done. However, the ministers themselves are partly responsible for this, and for various reasons: (a) unwillingness to delegate responsibility, too many being anxious to keep everything in their own hands; (b) inadequate planning ahead of time so that inevitably they have to run around at the last minute and do themselves many of the things that should have been done—and would better have been done by others; (c) succumbing to the temptation of doing first the things they like most to do, or for the person who presses them the hardest, instead of putting first things first; (d) finally, because they sometimes yield to requests which are far beyond the call of duty and take time they cannot afford to spare. Sometimes they get themselves so involved that they just look at the mass of work waiting to be done, and instead of tackling it piece by piece, wait for a good time to come along—in the meanwhile continuing to be staggered by the pile, and, in self pity, thinking how overworked they are.

But with all the long hours and unrelieved duties and responsibilities which rest upon their shoulders in the care and cure of souls, I have often told my clergy that we are among the lucky people in the world: we get paid for doing the thing we most want to do. If we could afford it, I feel we ought to pay for the privilege of being ministers and priests of the Church, giving our whole time to serving the Lord.

---

REFERENCE

1. Canon 45, Sections 3 (a) and 3 (c)

# 10

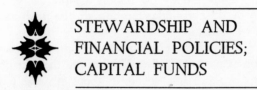

# STEWARDSHIP AND FINANCIAL POLICIES; CAPITAL FUNDS

"Will those who have been putting buttons in the collection basket kindly put in their own buttons and not those from the church upholstery."

You may chuckle as you read this quotation from the leaflet of a Scottish Presbyterian Church; but if you do so with any feeling of self-righteousness, beware—because underneath the humor are fundamental truths that many of us need to take to heart.

## *Not from the Top of Our Purse*

Financing the work of the Church is never going to be adequate until we change our whole concept of giving and put it in its proper theological perspective. The problem is a spiritual one. It goes much deeper, and has far wider application, than merely meeting budget requirements. It is a matter of love, rather than of law. What should be a glad offering to the Lord too often falls to the level of a collection from somewhat reluctant givers who are more likely to think how little they need to give to keep face than how much they can give. Or, they may say "I certainly want to give my share; I don't want to be dependent upon the charity of others," and so seem to look on their giving in the same light as paying their club dues, or remitting for services rendered. We have got to lift the level of church finances from being a collection for the church to being an offering to God. This cannot be done by improving techniques for extracting more money from more people. It will only be achieved by a deeper understanding of the real meaning of money and stewardship.

We may not have been putting buttons into the offering-plate; but many times we have "offered" what we thought of as completely our own, and felt generous about it. We have glibly joined in singing, "All things come of thee, O Lord, and of thine own have we given thee," never taking seriously the principle it sets forth.

In recent years there has been a new interest and emphasis on tithing. Do we succumb to a feeling of pride and self-righteousness when we have given five per cent of our income to the church and five per cent to other charitable purposes? Are we confident that, having done our legalistic share by giving the biblical tithe, we can now spend the other ninety per cent entirely as we wish? Originally, this tithe was in the nature of a tax, and giving did not begin until the tithe had been paid. Ten per cent may be too great a portion for some who have heavy family responsibilities and debts to discharge. In other cases ten per cent may be far too low. We ought not to be thinking in legalistic terms: we cannot buy our way into the kingdom of God on a percentage basis. Rather, we are called upon to be faithful stewards of all of our income, none of which is wholly ours to do with as we please. Even the government will stop us from burning it up! Eventually we are to be called upon to account for our use of the whole one hundred per cent.

Often we hear it said that the clergyman ought not to be expected to speak of finances. Why shouldn't he? It is one of the few things that by rubric we are told to place upon the altar. The mere fact that money has to be "raised" reveals an unhealthy situation. It should flow from hearts full of gratitude for many blessings.

## *Our Selves, Our Souls and Bodies*

There is nothing crass about money in itself, for money represents life and time, ability and energy. It is a medium of exchange and we can spend it in various ways. We can gamble it away, or we can give it to charity. We can offer it to the church to spread the news of the saving power of Jesus Christ. Far from being free from mentioning money, the minister has a responsibility to preach and teach the fundamental principle of the good stewardship of money which lies at the very heart of parish finances and giving. This cannot be done by preaching a sermon once a year at Every Member Canvass time, or by making a special appeal at Christmas and Easter. Nor is it merely a matter of preaching and teaching the stewardship of money—for what is true of our money is equally true of our time and of our abilities. It must be expressed not only in our activities, but in our worship, for it is only as we give that we truly live the abundant life which Christ came to bring us. This idea is supremely expressed in The Holy Communion which, interestingly enough, is the only service at which rubric requires that an offering shall be received. The whole service is an offering to God. First, we offer the alms and oblations; and finally we offer "our selves, our souls and bodies, to be a reasonable, holy, and living sacrifice," that we may be filled with his "grace and heavenly benediction, and made one body with him, that he may dwell in us, and we in him."

The right relationship of a man to his possessions is the subject which Christ taught more than any other. Therefore, the clergyman not only has the responsibility of preaching and teaching the proper stewardship of money, he must see that it is practiced in the active program of the parish as well as in worship. In doing so he must bear in mind that the most sensitive nerve in the human body is the one that controls the pocketbook.

## *For My Sake and the Gospel's*

People must not be allowed to think of the parish as a place merely for the strengthening of their own spirits and the satisfaction of their own needs. One great weakness of our Church today is that so much time, effort, and money continue to be spent in mere maintenance of the fabric and perpetuation of the institution. Christ's teaching, "Whosoever will save his life shall lose it; but whosoever shall lose his life for my sake and the gospel's, the same shall save it," [1] is as true for the Church and with parishes within the Church, as it is for individuals. We give in order that we may live, and when we stop giving, we stop living in that fullest sense to which Christ calls us, and without which life sinks to the level of mere existence.

> "Give to the needy sweet charity's bread,
> For giving is living," the angel said.
> "But must I keep giving, again and again?"
> My peevish, petulant answer ran;
> "Oh, no," said the angel, piercing me through,
> "Just give until God stops giving to you."

All this may seem a far cry from the subject of finances, but the basic weakness in the whole matter of money is due to a false theology by which many of us have been brought up: we have been imbued with the false idea that what we earn is ours. I know that this is a repetition; but it needs to be said again and again. We have devised new techniques of more skillful persuasion, made appeals directed to pride, to sense of duty as good churchmen and have even implied that they will be assured of happiness in this world or gain the reward of the kingdom in the next. None of these is the right answer. High pressure salesmanship may raise more money, but it softens no hearts. It merely speeds up the pump. The real answer is raising the spiritual understanding of the people to a recognition of God as the giver of all that we are and of all that we have, and that he calls us to give "good measure, pressed down, and shaken together, and running over.[2]

## *Meticulous Care and Scrupulous Attention*

Having said all this, we must recognize that it will take a long time to change the thinking of our people to a full recognition of these theological principles. In the meantime, it is well that we should improve many of the practices of the Church in the handling as well as in the securing of funds.

The Church has a canon on business methods[3] which should be read yearly to the vestry and to the treasurers of all parish organizations. In the main, it is a follow-through of what we have been saying. It emphasizes the fact that the Church is merely the custodian of funds, and that it is incumbent upon each parish to see that every penny is accounted for, with meticulous care and scrupulous attention that every provision for the right use of these funds be complied with, and every safeguard be employed so that there is no opportunity for dishonesty. The integrity of the Church, of all institutions, should be above reproach.

Unfortunately, the reverse is often true. The conditions which exist in some parishes in regard to the care of the monies are almost unbelievable. I have seen alms basins left unattended in the sacristy. I have found money and church offering envelopes left in the drawer of an ordinary table, and glass birthday-offering banks in full view on a shelf—an open temptation. I have known of cases where treasurers have mixed the accounts of the parish organizations with their own funds. Time and time again, I have discovered that money given for some special purpose has been used for another. I have known of organizations that have died, with their treasurers holding the funds in their personal accounts for years.

You may think that such things could not happen in your parish. I hope this is true. From a wide acquaintance with many parishes, I can say that such a situation is the exception rather than the rule; and I hope that every parish officer who reads these words will take the time and the trouble to look into the way money is cared for in his parish. First, he should read the canons of the Church, and then should follow through by finding the facts about such matters as what happens to the offering Sunday morning, from the time it leaves the ushers' hands through the processes of being taken off the altar, counted, credited to the proper account, banked, and finally spent. Does the acolyte take it off the altar? If so, has it been put into a bag so that there is no chance of a loose bill being dropped as he takes it to the sacristy? Who handles the church school funds? Are the offering envelopes of the children checked, to be sure that the child who starts to church with an envelope actually puts it into the offering-plate? And if not, is it right to permit such temptation to continue? Are all the Lenten offering boxes given out later accounted for? What about the treasurers of the parish organizations: are the organizations in any way related to the vestry, or is each one a law unto itself; are the treasurers bonded, and who audits their accounts? What provision is made for payment of bills if the parish treasurer is out of town or falls ill? What is the practice of the vestry in handling insurance, and who has the responsibility for checking it year by year, to see that valuations are adequate and all possible liabilities properly covered? What is everybody's business is often nobody's business. Responsibility should be pin-pointed by vestry action. Everything should not be put on the shoulders of the treasurer.

The work of the parish treasurer can be greatly simplified if he uses the standard Parish Cash Book for recording all receipts and disbursements. This can be secured from the National Council. Many dioceses now maintain a blanket bond through which additional coverage can be obtained for treasurers of parish organizations. The auditing of parish accounts should be done by a certified public accountant; however, with parish organizations a person with adequate accounting experience may be certified by the vestry, provided he is in no way related to the organization or particular treasurer involved.

## *Insurance and Salaries*

Fire insurance should be carried in at least a minimum amount of eighty per cent of the sound value (replacement cost less depreciation); and extended coverage is recommended for protection against windstorm and smoke damage. This does not cover breakage of expensive glass windows, and a fine arts policy should be taken out for special windows and art objects of value. Burglary insurance is advisable; and public liability insurance should include medical payment coverage—otherwise nothing will be received in the event of injuries.

Clergy are now eligible for Social Security, and it is a good thing to encourage your rector to apply for it. The premium payments must be made by the clergyman himself, but this can be made up to him by an equivalent increase in salary or allowances. Total salaries paid must be reported to the Internal Revenue Service at the end of the year. Form 1099 is used for clergy, and Form W2 for lay employees, with a copy supplied to the employee. If Social Security coverage is adopted by the group of parish employees (two-thirds or more having voted to adopt it), any new employee automatically comes under the plan.

## *Pledges and Funds*

It is a good practice to send out quarterly statements to all pledgers to verify the treasurer's pledge records as well as to serve as a reminder to those in arrears. It will be discovered that if a weekly pledger falls more than three months behind in his pledge, it is difficult for him to catch up. Often there are good reasons for his doing so, in which case it may be wise to adjust discrepancies before they get too large.

It is desirable for the parish to send to the diocesan office monthly payments on the quota accepted. This is voluntary, of course. But the assessment is an obligatory tax to provide for the cost of running the diocese and the diocesan share of the provincial and General Convention budgets. Usually instructions are sent by the diocese about where the church school Lenten offering is to be sent, and whether it counts on the quota of the diocese. The Good Friday and Theological Education Sunday offerings are usually put through the diocesan books.

The canons of the National Church are very complete and explicit in regard to handling trust funds, and they should be rigidly observed. Failure to take the precautions provided has proved very costly to many parishes I have known; and some cases, where carelessness and dishonesty were involved, have called for action both unpleasant and harmful to the good name of the Church.

If the parish contemplates buying or selling its property, or placing a mortgage on it, be sure you comply with national and diocesan requirements of securing approval before doing so.

## *In Praise of Parish Treasurers*

I have not gone into the detail of conducting an Every Member Canvass or a Capital Funds Campaign because there is so much excellent material available on these matters. A list of suggested sources may be found in the Appendix. But I would like to say that I consider it very important that an every-member visitation, or its equivalent, be made every year. A campaign by mail is not enough. An every-member visitation should be made not merely to maintain financial support; it is even more important that the people should be visited and know that they are remembered. These visitations also obtain the additional information which always comes in such efforts: changes of address, illness, new families in the neighborhood, etc. On canvass or parish calls money for pledges or other purposes should not, except in special cases, be received by clergyman or canvasser.

I have heard over and over again all the arguments against employing professional help in campaigns for capital funds. I hate to think that professional help is necessary, or to part with the good money required to obtain it. All I can say is that unless you are the one exception that proves the rule, you will fail to tap all the potential resources that are in your parish, and will have lost the rich spiritual experience of people working together for a common goal which seems far beyond their reach, and the surprise which comes in attaining it. After all, why should we hesitate to seek professional help in this field, when we consider it essential to employ a lawyer, a doctor, or an engineer when their help is needed?

I have the highest regard and gratitude for the many men who serve the Church in the capacity of parish treasurer with the utmost devotion and integrity. The work is exacting. It takes far more time than one would suppose. It is in many ways a thankless job, for the most part painstaking and demanding; but it is done out of sight, and is rarely properly appreciated. The treasurer is blamed for many things not his fault. He has to "take it" from irate parishioners who object to receiving notice of their delinquency, although he is only acting on orders from the vestry. He is called to account for not paying bills promptly, when he lacks the money to do so. He it is who has to worry when expenses exceed income. To my mind, most parish treasurers are unsung heroes who deserve all the praise we can give them.

In conclusion, I would like to quote two passages from the Bible which summarize most of what I have said:

> "Ye shall not appear before the Lord empty: every man shall give as he is able, according to the blessing of the Lord thy God which he hath given thee."[4]
>
> "It is required in stewards, that a man be found faithful."[5]

---

REFERENCES

1. Mark 8:35
2. Luke 6:38
3. Canon 6
4. Deuteronomy 16:16-17
5. I Corinthians 4:2

11

# BUILDINGS AND GROUNDS

## *An Asset to the Community*

When you first meet a person, you unconsciously and inevitably form some judgment. This judgment may not be correct—probably is not—but it is important. We judge a parish in much the same way, and the outward appearance of church property makes an immediate impression which either attracts or repels. Tragedy lies in the fact that those who see these buildings day by day over a period of time may come to love them so much, with all their imperfections, that they lose any idea of the impression that neglected property makes on visitors and newcomers.

The upkeep and care of the parish buildings and grounds can be a constant witness in the community to how much the parishioners really care about their church, or value their religion. As a tax-free property, the church has the responsibility to see that its buildings and grounds are an asset to the community in which they are located. Sometimes this responsibility is not faced and the parish property compares unfavorably with its surroundings. In many cases the sexton has other responsibilities, and the lawn goes unmowed, or the sidewalks remain unshovelled in winter. The people of a parish do not always take sufficiently seriously their responsibilities of praiseworthy maintenance. Merchants invest thousands of dollars to make their shops attractive and to draw customers while, near by, the signboard of the church may be shabby, difficult to read, and the hours of the services not even up to date. The front doors of many churches are shut, and for all one can tell they may be locked. The whole appearance of the property repels, rather than attracts. It is important, therefore, that the vestry assume its responsibilities in this connection.

## *The Building and Grounds Committee*

The canons are quite explicit in saying that "The Vestry shall be agents and legal representatives of the Parish in all matters concerning its corporate property and the relations of the Parish to its Clergy." [1] For the sake of efficiency, it is well to pick as members of the vestry buildings and grounds committee those who are concerned about proper maintenance of property, as well as other members of the parish who are professionally qualified to give advice. This committee should be charged with the responsibility of overseeing the work of the sexton and of reporting at each vestry meeting on the condition of the fabric of the parish, including the rectory or vicarage, and its grounds. It should have an annual budget, sufficiently large for immediate needs and long-term maintenance, recognizing that roofs and heating and plumbing facilities have to be replaced periodically. In many parishes, if the budget is not balanced, one of the first items cut is the maintenance item. The result is that the parish will be faced with a major emergency situation and no funds with which to meet it.

The rector (as with all vestry sub-committees) should be a member, ex officio, of this committee, because he will sometimes see things missed by members of the committee. He has a responsibility, too, in that the canons explicitly state that "For the purposes of his office and for the full and free discharge of all functions and duties pertaining thereto, the Rector shall, at all times, be entitled to the use and control of the Church and Parish buildings with the appurtenances and furniture thereof." [2]

It is unfortunate that some vestries lack the vision to recognize that the parish is in the community to leaven the community, and is not a "club" made up of those who contribute to it. As a tax-free institution, the parish should serve as far as possible the general welfare organizations which serve the community. No rental charge can be made for such service without endangering its tax-free status. It is reasonable, however, to suggest that a contribution towards expenses of janitor service, lighting, and heating would be most welcome. In small parishes, the buildings and grounds committee may have a list of men qualified in repair and building trades, who are willing to contribute their services, even as the church school teachers, and members of the altar guild and choir contribute theirs.

The control of decorations for weddings, or at Christmas and Easter, although technically under the direction of the rector, may well be discharged (after consulting with him) by the buildings and grounds committee or by the altar guild. Sometimes over-ambitious and unthinking people drive nails which deface walls or furniture. Professionals frequently lack a sense of reverence as they work, and need to be reminded, at times, that they are beautifying God's house.

### Memorials

It is usually convenient to set up a special committee on memorials, which may be a sub-committee of the buildings and grounds committee, to pass upon the appropriateness and design of the memorials which are offered to the church. The rector, or the senior warden, certainly should be chairman of this committee. Sometimes furnishings or vestments are offered which are out of keeping with the architecture or represent a churchmanship which is not generally representative of the parish, and so create an embarrassing situation. It is unwise for the rector alone to make the decision regarding acceptance or refusal. It should be made by the vestry as a whole upon recommendation of the memorials committee. A complete list of all memorials given to the parish should be kept. If none exists, it should be compiled. It is also useful to have a list of things which might be given as memorials, prepared and ready for those who may want to give a special gift to the parish.

### Long-Range Planning

It is also well to have a planning committee, composed of a few vestrymen with some other members of the parish especially qualified by training and interest in this field, to think in terms of the future. It is important to keep in touch with those who are on a similar committee of the town or city, to note trends in population change and growth. This is especially important in fast-growing communities.

### Insurance

Unless there is a special insurance committee, the matter of adequate insurance should also be under the direction of the buildings and grounds committee. All insurance should be reviewed annually. With rising costs, the coverage must be watched constantly. This is a complicated matter, and requires professional guidance. The church, like other organizations, is subject to suit; but until recently precedent has provided a protection by exempting non-profit organizations. This may not always be true. Some damage claims against churches in certain areas have been allowed. In any case, churches should not hide behind such precedent; they should be first to realize their moral obligations to strangers as well as to members, when accidents happen. Indeed, with the number of people who use the church and equipment (often with unskilled hands, and many of them in the older age bracket), the potential for accidents is very real.

### Good Housekeeping

In exercising its responsibility as custodian of the parish property, the vestry, and particularly the building and grounds committee, should be keenly aware of the necessity of ordinary housekeeping practices. For instance, in many churches the condition of the cellar is a disgrace as well as a fire hazard. It is good practice for the vestry to go over the premises, as part of a regularly called meeting, at least once a year, to view all the property at first hand. It is vital that a woman be concerned with the inspection of parish property.

A complete inventory of the property should be prepared and periodically reconsidered. This is especially useful in case of fire, and in checking on loaned property.

The use of keys, to the parish house particularly, should be carefully supervised. It is undesirable for any organization to have exclusive use of certain equipment. All should contribute to the needs of all; although youth organizations ought not to use the best china, nor church school teachers the cooking utensils for mixing of plaster and paint.

A capable and dedicated sexton is a rare treasure. A poor sexton, by having the church too cold, or letting it become dirty and messy, can empty the pews of people as quickly as any rector can fill them. There are men (and women, too) who "would rather be doorkeepers in the house of the Lord" than work in a highly competitive secular field. The sexton can exercise an important ministry by his actions and attitudes. A good sexton should be given more recognition and pay than he usually gets. Encouragement and appreciation mean a lot to a man who puts in long hours which often go unnoticed and unappreciated.

We encourage our people to kneel in prayer; yet it is extraordinary in how many churches this is impossible except under such discomfort as takes our mind off our prayers. Copies of the hymnal and prayer book, with broken backs and missing pages or frayed edges, are a poor advertisement for any parish. It is better to be rid of them entirely, so that people will be compelled to buy new ones. The books should be properly distributed each week. Old leaflets should be removed from the racks and pews, and the hymn numbers should be taken down from the boards immediately after each service. To delay means that they may still be there when special weekday services take place. This is poor housekeeping. Tests of the lighting and acoustics should be made from time to time. Staring at a naked electric bulb is as trying an experience, as is attempting to read with inadequate light.

It is desirable to have a well-lighted and adequate bulletin board outside. The name of the church should be sufficiently large to be read by those passing in automobiles. There should also be a bulletin board in the parish house and vestibule of the church. Many filling-station lavatories have a prominently-placed request that those using them should report any lack of cleanliness or disorder. This should apply to the wash-rooms in the parish house. A "Suggestion Box" might well be conspicuously placed; many minds are better than a few.

Special services in the church, such as weddings and funerals, often require the use of the choir; and the parish house may be needed for a reception following a wedding. The rector and the committee on buildings and grounds should formulate a statement which would include parish policy and costs for such events. This statement should be adequately publicized on the bulletin board, or printed in the parish leaflet.

The parking problem has become peculiarly acute in recent years, and adequate parking space is essential. In purchasing new property, at least four acres should be bought to allow sufficient room for parking. In some cities, arrangements can be made with nearby merchants or parking lots, for special Sunday rates. Many of them are most generous in this respect.

When the time comes for new construction or radical remodelling, serious consideration must be given to the appointing of committees which will have heavy responsibilities. I am including in the Appendix some suggestions which I hope will be of help in undertaking such a project.

## *The Beauty of Holiness*

What I would stress throughout is that the care and beautifying of the church buildings and grounds is an evident and constant witness to the character and devotion of its members. The parish has a civic responsibility to provide adequate landscaping, and, by good housekeeping and repair, make the church an asset to the community. Many buildings may be architecturally mediocre, but I am happy to note a concern which shows that the members love their church and its buildings and give them constant and devoted care. They realize that there is such a thing as "the beauty of holiness." Take a new look, critically, at your property from this point of view, and note if it measures up to this scriptural standard.

---


REFERENCES

1. Canon 13, Section 2
2. Canon 45, Section 1 (b)

12

# RELIGIOUS EDUCATION AND CHRISTIAN NURTURE

The first half of this century has witnessed a revolution in our thinking about religious education. The new approach considers Christian education as a cradle-to-grave process, with all age levels integrated into the life of the Church. The result of this revolution has been a definite upgrading of the task of education to a status second to none in the Church's outreach to save souls.

In this, the Church is following the example of Jesus Christ, who was called "Teacher" and the gospels are full of stories which tell not only how Christ taught, but what he taught about the nature of God and the relation of man to him. "He opened his mouth, and taught them." "Jesus was moved with compassion toward them, and he began to teach them many things."

The Church is very explicit in laying this primary duty and responsibility on the clergyman when it says, "It shall be the duty of Ministers of this Church who have charge of Parishes or Cures to be diligent in instructing the children in the Catechism, and from time to time examine them in the same publicly before the Congregation."[1] During my twenty years as bishop, I had only one clergyman who examined the children in the presence of the congregation; and he did not use the Prayer Book catechism, but another which had no official standing and which, to my mind, contained many questionable answers. The custom of using the Offices of Instruction from time to time has much to commend it, and group teaching of children is given authority and justification especially in very small parishes where good teachers are difficult to find and separate classrooms for different age levels are non-existent. In such cases it is far better for the clergyman, trained to teach, to take the whole school—with the exception of the very little children—into the nave and instruct them all together. Then the few available teachers can be used to test the children in smaller groups, to find out how much of what has been said has taken root. With this kind of teaching, visual aids are helpful, and slides and movies can often be borrowed from diocesan headquarters. Here the clergyman will have to use his imagination to devise ways to hold the attention of the boys and girls.

The clergyman's responsibility for Christian education is not, however, limited to children. The canon goes on to say that the minister "shall also, by stated catechetical lectures and instruction, inform the youth and others in the Holy Scriptures and the Doctrines, Polity, History and Liturgy of the Church. They shall also instruct all persons in their Parishes and Cures concerning the missionary work of the Church at home and abroad, and give suitable opportunities for offerings to maintain that work." [2] The Church is definitely interested in having *all* its members adequately informed about its faith and work. But what is the actual situation? Many members of our Church are destitute of knowledge of the faith that they profess. Chaplains in the recent war were shocked to find out how ignorant the men in the armed forces were about the Bible and the most common teachings of the Church.

This disturbing discovery was one of several forces which finally compelled the Church to strengthen and enlarge the National Department of Christian Education, and led to the development of the Seabury Series. Whatever one may think about the merit of this particular course of lessons, it must be admitted that the Department has accomplished three very important things: first, it has provided a series of books on the teaching and history of the Church, the Bible, and Christian ethics, which offer a semi-official standard; second, it has lifted the whole question of religious education from the narrow confines of Sunday School for children to a lifelong process; third, it has introduced a family service which has so met the needs of many that now, in most larger parishes, where two morning services are held after the early Communion service, the family service at the middle hour is usually better attended than the later service which, a few years ago, seemed to be the only proper time to be saved. A good part of the Department's material seems to have been prepared for use by people with more than a high school education, and is more suited to the larger schools; but the group laboratories for clergy, and the parish life conferences, have helped to bring in a new approach which, with imagination, makes it possible to apply many of the methods of the Seabury Series to other courses and books.

The Church has gained immeasurably by beginning to take seriously the importance of having its members better informed about the faith they profess. There are still far too few who could convincingly refute the information and zealous conviction of a Communist, or even evangelists of religious sects. And it is quite evident that although the primary responsibility may be with the clergy, the task can only be accomplished when the laity share that responsibility. It is heartening to see how eager they are to do so, and what a valuable contribution they make, when the Church provides opportunity for their training and gives them responsibilities to draw out their capabilities. Christian education must follow Christian conversion. We cannot long keep that which we do not share with others. This means that every baptized member is charged with the responsibility of telling others the Good News of Jesus Christ. Why is it that we are so eager to spread the word about a book we have read, or a play we like, or a person we admire, and so shy and reticent about speaking of Christ and his Church? We often bear witness against him by our silence. Whether we like it or not, we must admit that we are inevitably teachers through our influence—by the good or poor examples we set, by the kind of goals we have, the standards we live by, and our attendance or non-attendance at corporate worship. "Each one teach one" is the motto of the World Literacy Movement. It should be that of every Christian, because all that we are or fail to be has its effect for good or for ill on others.

If this is so, what can be said about religious education, especially in the smaller parishes? By virtue of the fact that they are small, and so more closely approximate the family unit, small parishes can make a very special contribution in this field. It is within them that a vital Christian fellowship can best be made real. They must never make their size or less adequate equipment an excuse for less than the best.

## *Some Basic Principles*

We often hear it said, "But my parish is different." Of course, it is different—every person, every tree, every snowflake is different. God makes no duplicates. But there are certain basic principles which undergird all good methods of religious education, and I would like to set down at least a few of them.

### What Are We Trying to Do?

For the Church, religious education is inevitably Christian education, and this calls for a rethinking of the Church's life and purpose. What are we really trying to accomplish in the name and power of Jesus Christ? Why was the parish started in the community? What is it really trying to accomplish, and how best can this be done?

I believe that Christian education takes place in a parish as in a Christian family; and a parish is a place where one expects to find more love and understanding, combined with a program and purpose, than in a secular society, even though it calls itself Christian. All this involves a wide departure from the idea of having a church school which meets on Sunday mornings, when certain willing but often untrained teachers try to impart information about the Bible and the prayer book, the Church and the Christian life, to a group of more or less uninterested boys and girls.

If we really believe that "God so loved the world, that he gave his only begotten Son, that whosoever believeth in him should not perish";[3] and if we believe that our Lord taught us to think of God as our Father and all men as our brothers; and also believe that as one of his final instructions he said, "Go, teach all nations," then certain things inevitably become part of the teaching program of every parish. No one can compel us to love. Love grows as we give ourselves to God and to the service of others.

Every parish needs a core of concerned persons who feel a responsibility to carry the Good News of Jesus Christ to others, who will "leaven the larger lump," by providing the matrix out of which a vision of the power and purposes of God, as revealed in Jesus Christ, will be born. For as our Lord told Nicodemus, except we be born of the Spirit, we cannot enter into the kingdom.

In the early part of this century, there was a general feeling that the world was slowly getting better and better and that, given time, mankind would soon have a wonderful, warless world, with comfort and plenty for all. Two world wars shattered that illusion, and we have since been witnessing a great swing to the other extreme that stresses man's basic brutality and sin, that preaches judgment and defeatism, doom and destruction. Man is nothing. I believe that the truth is somewhere between these two extremes. God needs man to build his kingdom. God's mighty acts can only be seen as God's mighty acts by those who are willing to make ventures of faith. Perhaps the most important thing a minister can do is to gather a small group of deeply committed Christians who, as a very first charge upon their time and interest, will pray, think, and work to make clear the goals and purposes of their particular parish. They must, at the same time, press for changes to bring them nearer to realization, confident that God's Holy Spirit is not working only in the past, but is a powerful force in the present. It will take time and patience to change the thinking of a parish about religious education, to see it as the creation of a fellowship in which the family is the core—with the parish providing a larger family as the Christian core within the community.

### The Word Must Become Flesh

If this is so, the second thing we must do is to make it plain that Christian education is not only a matter of imparting information about Christ and the Christian faith. It is a commitment of love and loyalty to a person—Jesus Christ. A person may know all the facts about Jesus Christ, and be very intelligent and well informed about the Bible and the Christian faith, and yet be very far from being a committed Christian. Christian education is not merely a matter of ethics and conduct. A person may behave in a very exemplary manner well worthy of a Christian, and yet be doing so for all the wrong motives and reasons. Christian education only results when a person grows in the love, as well as the knowledge, of God as revealed in Jesus Christ, and sees all sorts and kinds, colors and creeds, as God's children. It is utterly false to assume that the mere presentation of a carefully structured formulation of the Christian faith will reproduce such a faith. Our concern must not be to impose an authority or a truth on a child or older person, but rather to present it in such a way that the Christian gospel will become an authority and a truth that will win his acceptance. Youth at present finds no vital, soul-satisfying function in the life of the Church.

It is therefore self evident that it is more important that teachers be contagious Christians than merely academic ones. I discovered this the hard way when, in my first parish, I succeeded in persuading a large number of public school teachers to teach our church school. But I soon discovered that the effectiveness of these professional teachers was far less than that of the devoted souls who gave lavishly of themselves, even though they were weak in teaching techniques. Of course, the best teachers are those who are both trained and dedicated Christians.

Generalizations are ineffective if the people are to understand. The faith has to be clothed with facts within the limit of their experience. This does not mean that a student should be given pat and neat answers to all his questions. There are many who would like to have their minister and teachers tell them exactly what to do on each and every occasion. The catechetical method has its place, especially in the years when memory work comes more easily; but it must not be a substitute for the growing of personal Christian insights and convictions. Person-to-person relationship is the means by which the Gospel is spread, and no veneer of Christian knowledge will stand the wear and tear of life. Christian education is not a matter of coating people with information, but of changing them.

### Parents Are the First Key

It is easy to see that if these two points are to be put into practice, a third naturally follows: Christian education must involve parents as well as children, weekdays as well as Sundays, activity as well as instruction. It is basically because of the failure and default of parents in fulfilling their function as parents, that church schools came into existence. Parents did not teach their children at home, so the Church had to take over. But for the most part, I believe that such schools are a temporary makeshift provided for a century of cultural change which has broken down the family unit and exalted the individual. Somehow, parents must be interested. When earnest effort is put into accomplishing this, it is amazing to discover how parents rally to the excitement, responsibility, and opportunity which is theirs. After all, there are few challenges in life which offer the interest and opportunities for creative endeavor as do the challenges of working with growing children. Once you have successfully interested a group of enthusiastic parents, you will find that their response grows readily and rapidly. *Parents are the first key to the solution in any parish that seeks to be a real Christian family.*

We have said that Christian education should begin with the cradle. Perhaps this is too late, because even before the baby is born, expectant fathers and mothers are aware of the responsibility which they are soon to assume, and are especially receptive to a new approach on the part of the Church. Every parish, therefore, ought to have some group, usually composed of parents who already have younger children, who will, by friendly visiting, make up what might be called "The Guild of the Christ-Child." How they will go about the job of making the couple feel that they are part of a fellowship which is concerned about the arrival of this new member cannot be spelled out; but the couple must be made to understand the interest of this larger fellowship.

When the baby arrives, the clergyman ought to be told promptly. He will want to send a message of greeting immediately and soon make a special call in order that parents and priest may have prayers of thanksgiving for God's great gift of life. There is no more propitious moment, than when the wonder and mystery of life are in the forefront, to make God a reality to persons to whom he was formerly only a name or a vague power. We are told that the first years of a baby's life are by far the most important, so no parish should ever be content to have baptism a mere formality. We shall deal more fully with baptism, but we would stress here the tremendous importance of the fellowship of the Church in helping the couple provide the sense of love and security which is so important for the child.

The first three or four years, before a child comes to kindergarten, have been sadly neglected by the Church. She has failed to recognize that this period contains her greatest opportunity to influence the life of both the child and the parents. Appropriate prayer-cards, leaflets, pictures, and symbols of the Church, may be given; there are books to loan; Christmas and Easter baby parties to attend. Ingenuity will be called for how best to meet each situation. A weekday kindergarten may be the answer. Somehow, minister and people must learn how to meet this opportunity which they will never have again. An invitation to attend should be sent to every child when he comes to kindergarten age. If the church provides "baby-sitting" during services, he may already have come to church; and perhaps he may have come to one of the Christmas or Easter children's services. Parents should also be encouraged to bring him into the church when out for a drive or on shopping tours or walks, in order that he may have a feeling of "this is my church."

Much of the activity necessary to implement the instruction given on Sunday must take place in the home as well as in the parish house. Week-day activities should provide valuable experience in the mixing of youngsters from different backgrounds and racial groups, helping them to understand and appreciate those in the wide range of the parish family—and beyond those limits—in the environment which a parish ought to provide before the child goes out to meet the colder and more hostile experience of the world.

## *Organizations Aid Christian Nurture*

The activities program of the parish ought to be an integral part of the educational process of the church school. If the leaders of the boys' and girls' organizations are also teachers in the church school, the fact that they are dealing with the same boys and girls during the week should produce a certain tie-in with the total program. Often this is not true; and even when it is, it should not be left to chance to provide proper and timely expression of the truths and principles that they are learning in the church school classroom. If "The Life of Christ" or "The History of the Church" is being taught, drama definitely connected with these subjects can be helpfully provided as part of the weekday program. If the symbolism or ritual of the Church is a subject of study, experience as acolytes and junior members of the altar guild should be definitely related to that study. If Christian ethics is the theme, illustrations can be drawn from weekday activities, whether it be good sportsmanship in athletics, or proper behavior between the sexes. Obviously such close connection calls for planning and consultation between the leaders in both groups, and points up the fact that parish groups should essentially be Church-centered.

Secular clubs meeting under church auspices on church property are rarely manifestations of the Body of Christ. There is an opportunity for the parish in certain communities to serve by providing accommodations for such groups as the Scout troops; but if the Scout troops include those who are not in the church school, their usefulness to the parish family is greatly limited, and they should be recognized for what they are—a community service and no part of the educational program of the parish. Organizations such as The Order of Sir Galahad, The Order of the Fleur de Lis, The Girls' Friendly Society, lend themselves much more appropriately to our Church's life and work.

I strongly suggest that leaders of youth take advantage of the helpful material now available from diocesan and national offices, designed to aid parish group leaders in implementing new programs which enable their members to join more actively in the wider fellowship of the Church. Sometimes informative material never reaches group leaders. It gets bogged down and pushed aside by a rector under the pressure of immediate business, or he may not take the time to recognize its value. I want to stress that a great deal of very helpful material is available to those who want such assistance.

## *Not in the Church—in the Market Place*

It is one of the tragedies of many parishes that the activity programs provided by their various organizations are so vapid and insipid. There are so many things that so much need doing. We continue to dabble in stagnant parochial puddles, while the mainstream of secular society undercuts the Christian principles and practices of our forbears. We shall have more to say about this in our chapter on "The Church and The Community."

Of one thing I am sure: the organizational patterns of most of our parish groups have become outdated. The first step to an effective parish program is a re-examination of present program and procedures, to discover how relevant they are to present needs and opportunities. When this has been done, let us pray that the plans for next year will be such as to be evident to all that they tie together the worship and work of the Church, the teaching and the living of the Christian faith. At present, there is often a great gulf between the two. We need again to underline the fact that "there is no real impression until there has been expression"; and if there is to be a Christian act, it should be undergirded with Christian motives, conviction, and consecration.

At the national level, both the men's and women's work have recently been reorganized and revitalized. The women no longer are simply an Auxiliary. They are at last recognized for what they are—an important part of the working body of the Church. The organizational activity of the men is also being elevated to a higher and more significant plane. They are no longer to be regarded merely as workers for the rector to direct and use in various necessary but rather routine duties such as ushering, canvassing, and counting the offering. They are the Church in society; and it is being generally recognized that their greatest service is perhaps not within the church or parish-house walls, but in the market-place, in the political field, and wherever they live and earn their daily bread.

This shift in emphasis in the national organizational life of both men and women is much more important, and runs much deeper, than a mere change of name or arrangement. It has a definite theological basis, and the Church has a long way to go in fully recognizing the basic principles which it involves. Eventually, and inevitably, it will mean full recognition for women of their equality with men before God. There may well be difference in function, according to their interests and human qualifications; but there must be no remnant left of their being regarded as second or third class citizens. With the men, too, there must be a complete elimination of any idea that a man who is particularly active and important in ecclesiastical circles is preferred by God over one who has little contact with the ecclesiastical life of the Church, but who nevertheless is a faithful and devoted Christian in other areas of life. This shift in understanding and emphasis should be implemented into the life and activity of every parish in this coming generation in ways which must be creatively thought through. The old programs and patterns no longer have the same appeal as when garments needed to be sewed, when means of transportation and communication were so very different; when nations were far more isolated and self-sufficient than they are today, when some of the ideas of freedom and equality which are creating such a ferment among the underprivileged and dispossessed were either unknown or remote in their realization. Now, however, the Church has a wonderful opportunity to pioneer and lead the way to their fulfillment—but all too often she lags behind.

Groups that are vital and significant in the parish life should be born out of some unmet Christian need. When that need has been met, the group might profitably be disbanded and not continued as, say, the "Mothers' Club," when the members are all grandmothers; or as the "Rector's Study Group," when it has changed into a bridge club. It would be a wonderful thing if every person who reads these words would persuade the various groups he or she may belong to, seriously to consider whether the group hasn't outlived its usefulness and is running along on sentimental inertia, with time and effort wasted trying to stimulate, and keep alive the group for the group's sake. I know there are many rectors who would breathe a sigh of relief, and perhaps even sing a *Te Deum,* if one or more organizations would be content to die gracefully. To expect him to spend his time and effort trying to keep them alive, when there are so many good causes to be espoused and needs to be met, is to force him to dissipate his energies.

### Community Service

As a tax-exempt institution, the Church has a real responsibility to offer its facilities for community endeavors. Indeed, a parish should welcome such opportunities; but let us not fool ourselves into thinking that outsiders are going to strengthen the religious life of the parish. The reverse is often true, when non-members come into a church organization in such large numbers as to change the very character and purpose for which the organization was originally created. In meeting community needs, the parish must be certain that it is expanding the boundaries of the kingdom.

## *Supplemental Activity*

There are many individuals in every parish who are not touched by programs centered around the family—people who have never married, or widows and widowers without children. Adequate provision must be made for their spiritual growth and development. This may be done in various ways, and every parish must devise plans best to meet its special needs with the resources at its disposal. Regular retreats, a parish library, reading groups, short lecture courses with discussion periods, appropriate moving-pictures or slides provided by national or diocesan headquarters, religious art exhibits—are but a few of the many ways possible.

The Advent and post-Easter seasons are excellent for "trial runs" of experimental efforts, and the summer months provide a very good opportunity for reading, pilgrimages to other parishes, and for summer camps and conferences.

## *Camps and Conferences*

It is only fairly recently that the Church has come to recognize the amazing, wide-open opportunity that exists for the growth of Christian character in camps and conferences. The Unit of Camps and Conferences of the Department of Christian Education now has much to offer of help in this area, and I strongly urge that parish and diocesan groups use the material available. Experts with a background of years of actual experience in this field have prepared it and are eager to save others from the difficulties and mistakes involved in learning the hard way.

Two weeks in a good camp definitely centered in Christian purpose is worth far more than two years of class sessions in a church school, because it is in the actual life situations that one can discover far more about the character, habits, and hopes of a boy or girl, than one can ever uncover in the formal, restrained, and unnatural setting of a classroom. Modern miracles are being accomplished in changing youngsters, when they are set in a community where people live together in love, trust, and fellowship, and are provided with understanding leadership. Such an environment of good will and friendliness lends itself to a joyful, creative, and unforgettable experience.

Camping is usually best for youngsters in the grammar grades and first years of junior high. It is activity-centered. Conferences are a challenge to those in high school up through college—and, even when properly adapted, well on into the middle-aged group. In some places, provision is made for family camping. The success or failure of a camp or conference, however, depends very largely upon the leadership provided, and upon the purpose around which it is centered. There are many camps and conferences and they vary from excellent to a few which are a waste of time and effort. No parish or diocese should undertake to operate a camp, or send young people to a camp, unless its program has definite Christian overtones: not merely a service on Sunday, grace at meals, and prayers at night, but a sincere concern and effort made by the leadership of the camp, especially the cabin or tent counselors, to interpret the experience of the day in terms of Christian life and what lies behind the activity. We learn by experience, but we also need reflection on the actual experience to understand why it happened and how it came about. Life in the open—free from the artificialities, inhibitions, and restraints of conventional existence—gives many wonderful opportunities to talk and live on a different level, and to act with a freedom that reveals the real self, sometimes quite different from the "front" ordinarily assumed.

This closely-knit fellowship supplies the atmosphere of expectancy, joy, and willing helpfulness that one rarely finds in ordinary society; and the youngster wants to be a part of it, so almost automatically is absorbed into the group life. Of course, there are exceptions and problems: some are homesick, some are spoiled and selfish, and some are uncooperative. Such difficulties reveal the character under the veneer which hid it, and test the depth of our love, and the reality of our Christian concern for every boy and girl. What were formerly only words about patience and understanding now come alive and are given body in the give-and-take of life.

Also important is that the camping and conference experience be definitely integrated with the church school program. The closer the connection, the better. If some of the teachers can be summer counselors, that is ideal. If the camp or conference is run by the diocese, provision should be made for the staff to know something about the child when he comes. At the close of the camp or conference period the report on the child sent to the parents should be shared with the rector.

What I would stress is this: many are bemoaning our record of juvenile delinquency; parents are wringing their hands over their youngsters' behavior; parishes and missions all over the land are spending large sums of money for more adequate parish houses. Here, in the field of camps and conferences, is a resource and opportunity right at hand but sadly overlooked and it yields amazing results. It needs to be greatly developed and used. Camps and conferences can do what the best church school—even the finest Christian family—can never do, because they deal with life situations rather than words, and because they provide experiences and relationships in similar age groups, which are more true to life than any family can supply.

But a final word of caution: it is not just *any* camp or conference that works the magic. It must have a definitely Christian purpose, a contagious Christian leadership, adequate health and other facilities; and its programs should tie into the life and work of the parish from which the child comes. Under these conditions, I can say with absolute confidence that a camping or conference experience will stay with a child through life, and he will often look back on it as a turning point in his life.

---

REFERENCES

1. Canon 45, Section 2 (a)
2. Canon 45, Section 2 (a)
3. John 3:16

13

# WORSHIP AS A CONVERTING EXPERIENCE

"To worship is to quicken the conscience by the holiness of God, to feed the mind with the truth of God, to purge the imagination by the beauty of God, to open the heart to the love of God, to devote the will to the purpose of God. All this is gathered up in the emotion which most cleanses us from selfishness because it is the most selfless of all emotions—adoration." [1]

If we are to take the above definition of worship as our own, I think we shall have to agree that most of the services we conduct or attend are very inadequate and imperfect expressions of real worship. We all need to make a far more conscious effort to lift them to a higher level. A sloppy or slovenly service is an insult and an abomination to the Lord, and both clergy and laity need to be reminded of this fact.

There are certain definite canonical provisions relating to worship which spell out basic requirements, which everyone should read. The canons state: "All persons within this Church shall celebrate and keep the Lord's Day, commonly called Sunday, by regular participation in the public worship of the Church, by hearing the Word of God read and taught, and by other acts of devotion and works of charity, using all godly and sober conversation." [2] In other words, attendance at church is not an optional matter, as so many people seem to think. It is an assumed requirement of membership. This is particularly emphasized in the Second Office of Instruction. In answer to the question, "What is your bounden duty as a member of the Church," the reply is, "My bounden duty is to follow Christ, to worship God every Sunday in his Church; and to work and pray and give for the spread of his kingdom."[3] Attendance at public worship is not a question to be settled Saturday night or Sunday morning, according to our mood, or our busyness, or the weather.

Another canon provides that the book to be used shall be *The Book of Common Prayer*.[4] In the Preface to this book it is stated that it does not intend "to depart from the Church of England in any essential point of doctrine, discipline, or worship; or further than local circumstances require." The canons do provide, however, for a continuing Liturgical Commission,[5] and for bishops to make such changes, under certain carefully-restricted conditions, as shall make the worship appropriate to the time and the occasion. The canon does not, in my mind, permit the liberties which some clergymen casually assume, of changing the wording and order of the services; and clergy should remember that when they were ordained they solemnly engaged "to conform to the Doctrine, Discipline and Worship of the Protestant Episcopal Church in the United States of America."

This does not mean that services should be conducted without variety or without adequate preparation and imagination. Within the canons and the rubrics there is a wide liberty of choice in psalms and lessons and prayers. I am constantly amazed that so many clergymen fail to make recognition of great events and timely incidents by not using many of the beautiful, optional, and appropriate prayers which are to be found within *The Book of Common Prayer*. They remain content to use the same calls to worship, the same order of service, the same prayers, Sunday after Sunday. For example, in questioning the laity, I find that practically none of them have ever heard the Bidding Prayer found on page 47; that only a few have heard The Exhortations following the Holy Communion, or are acquainted with the general rubrics, on page 85, which precede them. Only a small fraction of our members seem to have discovered the "Forms of Prayer to be used in Families" at the back of the book following the Catechism. This latter also seems to be largely unknown and unused.

Proper timing in leading worship is an important factor. There is nothing, for example, which prohibits a space of silence at different points in the service; and I feel that silence is often very helpful. Contemplation should have a far larger place in our corporate worship. Silences well placed give opportunity for truths to penetrate.

When the words of the service are not read clearly or audibly, it seems an almost inexcusable fault on the part of the clergyman; but it is made all the more blameworthy when the service is hurried and the clergyman rushes along as if the object were to finish as quickly as possible. Unfortunately, as the years go by and he gets more and more familiar with the words of the services, a clergyman increases the pace of his reading almost automatically. It is the responsibility of the laity to speak of this. But congregations get so used to mannerisms that they come to accept them without comment. I was amazed to discover, as I went from parish to parish, to find men with definite speech peculiarities of which both they and the congregations seemed almost unaware, but which to strangers must have been a hindrance and a distraction.

## *Thoughts on Rites and Ceremonies*

A few words may be in place here, indicating the difference between "rites" and "ceremonials." A "rite" is a fixed order of service. "Ceremonial" has to do with the interpretation or rendering of that order in terms of action and conduct. The rite of a simple, early service of Holy Communion should be the same as that of a later choral celebration; but the latter will naturally be more colorful and elaborate. The ceremonial of a parish is governed by custom and tradition under the direction of the rector. There is no exact right or wrong in regard to much ceremonial because, as the prayer book says in the opening words of the Preface, "different forms and usages may without offence be allowed, provided the substance of the Faith be kept entire." It becomes largely a matter of choice and taste in regard to posture, dress, and movements. The priest or rector is, by canon, the final arbiter in such matters; but every rector, whether he personally desires the very simplest type of ceremonial or the most elaborate, does well to recognize that he is not there to indulge his own tastes and desires, but to serve the people, to provide them with services of corporate worship which will "quicken the conscience by the holiness of God, feed the mind with the truth of God, purge the imagination by the beauty of God, open the heart to the love of God, and devote the will to the purpose of God."

The problem which confronts every rector is how he may make the services of the Church such glorious, rich, and moving experiences that they will be real, vital, and full of strength to his congregation. I would like to make a few definite suggestions.

He must remind his people that, although the chief responsibility for accomplishing this is laid upon the clergyman by canon, he is absolutely helpless without the cooperation and support of the congregation. People are essential to corporate worship. If no one appears at a publicly advertised service of Holy Communion, the priest ends the service at the close of the Ante-Communion. For a priest to conduct a service of corporate worship without a congregation is an anomaly. The people should be continually reminded of the importance of their presence, for their own welfare and for the welfare of others. Indeed, the spiritual temperature of a service of corporate worship is usually increased in direct proportion to the number present. Enthusiasm grows by contagion. One of the most moving services I ever attended was at the Anglican Congress in Minneapolis. Here more than a hundred thousand persons joined together in the singing of the great hymns and in praying the Lord's Prayer—each in his own tongue. It is important to impress upon a congregation that every time they stay away from a service of corporate worship they are depriving themselves;

of equal import, they are thereby diminishing the spirit and power of the service for others, because every empty seat is a non-conductor.

The rector must not only impress upon people the importance of their presence at services, but also the necessity of their active participation. And in this connection, he should be careful to give them as full an opportunity for such participation as possible. If you ever catch yourself saying, "I didn't get any good out of that service," ask yourself, "What did I bring to the service, and was my mind prepared to receive anything from it?"

The clergyman must take time and pains in the careful preparation of the service to give it unity and to make it relevant, either to the season of the year or to the activities and interests of his people. I am sure very few clergymen take as seriously as they should this very important responsibility, and I confess that many times I have been guilty of going into a service without such preparation. We take time to prepare our sermons but somehow tend to think that the liturgy needs only to be read. Thus it becomes almost a matter of routine and is completely devoid of the imagination which is so important to its becoming alive and vital.

Many people come to church faithfully over many years. I find that this is often a matter of habit, and that they get so accustomed to hearing certain words and phrases that their minds wander and they do not think about what is being said. I recall one saintly soul who, in his later years, was asked what he would most like to do. He replied, "I would like to be able to say one good 'Our Father'." It is well, therefore, periodically to explain carefully and explicitly the meaning of phrases to the people. For example, we say in the General Confession that we are "miserable sinners," but most people seem to take their sins very lightly. This phrase ought to help impress upon every person how miserable he would be if he realized his true condition. Or, take the General Confession as a whole. This is not the public confession of our sins in specific terms. Rather it is the confession of the sins of society for which no one individual is wholly responsible, but for which all of us are partially responsible—war, juvenile delinquency, dishonesty, class prejudice. Someone has well said that the world is in its present condition not because of a few very bad and wicked persons (although we often try to make them scapegoats), but because there are so many of us who are no better than we are; who pride ourselves on the fact that we have never been caught; who think it is enough to live up to the standards of society; who outwardly are quite respectable and decent, but inwardly nourish hatreds and allow imagination to dwell on things we would blush to have found out.

There are many people in our congregations who remain silent during the saying of the Creed—if not completely silent, at least omitting phrases which they say they cannot believe. They need to be told that the Creeds are not necessarily exact and complete definitions of our personal faith: they are the expressions of the Faith of the Church—the historic statements which each generation receives and may interpret. It is certain that there are basic truths in the Creeds which we are expected to believe. These are made plain in the Offices of Instruction. In answer to the question, "What do you chiefly learn in these Articles of your Belief," we reply, "First, I learn to believe in God the Father, who hath made me, and all the world. Secondly, in God the Son, who hath redeemed me, and all mankind. Thirdly, in God the Holy Ghost, who sanctifieth me, and all the people of God."

Please note that even here it says that we "learn." Throughout our lives new fullness will come into the phrases—a growing experience, not an attained fact. Also, please note that there is no required definition of how or when the Lord made the world, or how long it took him to do it. There is no exact statement how he redeemed the world other than through our Lord's death on the cross; or how he sanctifies us, or who are the people of God. One of the glories of our Church is that beyond this simple, basic minimum, no creedal demand is made in terms of intellectual acceptance. Its emphasis is upon complete commitment to God our Father, to Jesus Christ our Lord and Saviour, and to the Holy Spirit our sanctifier. I might add here, because I believe they are sometimes a stumbling block to sensitive souls, that the Thirty-nine Articles bound into *The Book of Common Prayer* have no official standing whatsoever, other than as an historical document indicating what certain people believed at a certain time. As you will see, they have an entirely separate title page. Both for the sake of clarity and economy, I believe they should be removed when the next revision of the prayer book takes place.

In regard to the Offertory, it is perhaps all too clear that the people have a part in this portion of the service. Misunderstanding comes from the idea that it is a "collection" rather than an "offering"; and there is an inadequate recognition of the fact that it is an integral part of the service rather than a method of securing church support. The rector, then, should take pains to explain the fact that the money representing what we have earned through the giving of time, skill, and service reminds us that we are to give all parts of our life to God, who has given us life and strength. "All things come of thee, O Lord, and of thine own have we given thee." In early days, people actually brought offerings in kind—lambs and vegetables, bread and wine. This is dramatized in some parishes by having lay persons bring forward the bread and wine for Holy Communion for presentation at the altar with the alms.

## *The Sermon—Preacher and Congregation*

Preaching is a very definite part of worship. It is a strange anomaly that has led to the omission of a sermon at many services of Holy Communion—the only service in which the rubrics call for one—and has made it a regular custom at Morning and Evening Prayer where it is not even suggested or required by rubric. The whole matter of preaching, its purpose and practice, needs some rethinking.

It is generally assumed that preaching is the sole concern of the minister: that what he preaches is for him to decide, and how he preaches is dependent upon his ability and training. Actually, however, preaching is a two-way affair: there is the preacher, and there is the congregation. Please note that we use the word "congregation" rather than "audience." There is a definite difference. An audience merely sits and listens to what the speaker says. A congregation has a very definite responsibility in the preaching of a sermon. A former parishioner, in referring to the preaching of one of my predecessors, who was a saintly man but certainly not a great preacher, once said to me, "If Mr. Amory got up in the pulpit and only repeated the alphabet, it would help me." Why? Because she came to church prepared to hear something that would help her, with the result that the contagious Christian character, simplicity, and devout holiness of the clergyman shone through everything he said in a way that enabled her to hear the word that God had for her. Such an ability is very rare, and it should in no way excuse a preacher from sufficient care and thought in the preparation of his sermon; but this story is illustrative of the fact that every member of a congregation has a definite share in the hearing of a sermon.

A preacher needs a congregation in order to preach. I well recall the first time I walked into a radio station to give an address. For some reason I had not thought about what was going to happen, and I had brought with me only some sketchy notes of the points I wanted to make. I was utterly unprepared to be ushered into a sort of padded cell with a stick topped by a microphone. I was aghast and said, "I cannot talk to a stick—you'll have to get me some people." Three persons were rounded up as willing victims and were seated on three chairs in front of me, while I put the stick slightly to one side where it was less obvious, and tried to use my imagination to picture the unseen listeners. I am sure the effort was a "dud." This is why a man usually preaches up to his best ability when there is a good congregation, and is at his worst when there are many empty pews or when those present sit like bumps on a log, apathetic and unresponsive. Attendance at church is therefore the first ingredient in a good sermon.

Eagerness to hear what the preacher is trying to say is the second valuable ingredient in the sermon's effectiveness. The story is told of a man who came up to Dwight L. Moody after he had preached his heart out one day and said, "Mr. Moody, do you realize that you made twelve mistakes in English grammar this morning?" Moody replied, "My friend, I did the best I could with the education I have. What are you doing for the Lord with your education?" A critical faculty of this sort is a devastating detriment to hearing God's word, and it should be parked at the door of the church. This does not mean that a congregation cannot be very helpful to the clergyman by giving him constructive suggestions: telling him what they find helpful, and how they think he might make the sermons even more inspiring and pertinent to the parishioners.

We must recognize that a sermon is far from finished when the preacher leaves the pulpit. Actually, its effectiveness is tested by how far it is translated into action. Every sermon should aim to accomplish something definite in the lives of its hearers; should aim to convert, to bring a new understanding of the presence, power, and purpose of God. Although a hundred people may hear the preacher speak the very same words, they will hear them with different interest and understanding, and if they should be asked to write down what had been said, there would be a hundred different versions. Every sermon, to be effective, cannot be merely an oratorical effort, it must be a living event in the life of the hearer; and this can only be accomplished if both preacher and congregation understand their part in the process. Again I would quote Moody, as he replied to a preacher who, having listened to his moving address, expressed his discouragement over his own feeble efforts. "But," said Moody, "you don't really expect to convert everyone in every sermon?" "No" admitted the discouraged preacher, to which Moody countered with, "That is precisely why you don't." The "Good News" should not be merely pleasant information, it should provide a dynamic for transformation.

It is amazing to me to discover how few people seem to realize the large part they play in the preaching of a sermon; and I am equally disturbed over the clergyman's lack of recognition of the importance of a sermon to the worship of the Episcopal

Church. The fact that we have the incomparable liturgy provided in *The Book of Common Prayer* is no excuse for downgrading the sermon. Rather, it should provide a setting in which sermons take on new meaning and provide effectiveness to the word of God which we would present. Because so many people do not realize how important they are in the preaching of a sermon, it may be advisable, from time to time, to explain their part to them. They can do much to help the preacher by reminding him of the importance of preaching in their lives.

## *The Minister as Worshipper*

The last suggestion I have to make in our effort to make the worship of the Church more vital and real is that the minister himself must join in the worship. Because he is the leader of worship—because it is his responsibility to see that it is well rendered—it is sometimes difficult for the clergyman himself to worship. He retains a certain objectivity as director rather than a sense of involvement as actual participant. Yet I am sure that it is as important for the clergyman to worship as it is for the choir to try to forget themselves in singing to the glory of the Lord. A clergyman must pray, not merely lead in saying the prayers. This is not easy. It requires as continued effort, discipline, and practice as is true of the disciplines of good writing, or good acting, or skill in sports. We must have so completely learned and absorbed the rules and regulations that we do not think of them as we apply them, but rather, we concentrate upon what we want to say or to achieve. Only as we give ourselves fully to worship—without self-consciousness and by our evident personal adoration—do we help to stir the same spirit in others. All life should be worship: it should be an offering of ourselves—our friendships, our activities, our time, our interest, our work—to God. But there is little likelihood that this will happen until we consciously and constantly make time in our lives to remind ourselves of God's presence, and recall ourselves to the fact that it is in God that we live and move and have our being; that from him we come, and to him we go.

REFERENCES


1. Temple, *Hope of the World,* page 30
2. Canon 19
3. Prayer Book, page 291
4. Canon 21
5. Canon 22

# 14

# ADMINISTERING THE SACRAMENTS—OCCASIONAL OFFICES

*Question:* How many Sacraments hath Christ ordained in his Church?
*Answer:* Christ hath ordained two Sacraments only, as generally necessary to salvation; that is to say, Baptism, and the Supper of the Lord.
*Question:* What do you mean by this word Sacrament?
*Answer:* I mean . . . an outward and visible sign of an inward and spiritual grace given unto us; ordained by Christ himself, as a means whereby we receive this grace, and a pledge to assure us thereof.[1]

These two questions and answers are the first of a whole series of questions and answers describing in a brief, simple, accurate, and official way what the Church believes about these two great Sacraments. They are well worth your careful reading. Much that they say is worth learning by heart. For my part, I have found them invaluable in my ministry in trying to explain to people the Church's teaching about the two Sacraments. In this brief manual I do not feel that I can add anything helpful to what they say; nor would I subtract anything from them.

What I would like to do, however, is to make some comments upon their use, our participation, and their place in the life and work of the parish.

## *Holy Baptism*

There has been a very real movement recently to put Holy Baptism in its important and rightful place. In the early years of the century, it was largely a sentimental rite which parents wanted for their children. There was very little appreciation of its deeper Christian significance, nor much awareness of the fact that it cannot be forgotten once it has been done, without definite loss. The service was usually held with only the family, sponsors, and perhaps a few close friends invited to be present. Often it was postponed for various reasons until the children were well along in years. Sometimes it seemed more convenient to the family, if they were not very active church members, to hold the service at home rather than in church. There was no explanation of the real meaning of the service.

The sponsors often were not members of our Church—occasionally, not even baptized themselves, and the people of the parish were usually uninformed and uninterested—this in spite of the fact that the rubrics clearly state that "The Minister of every Parish shall often admonish the People, that they defer not the Baptism of their Children," and that "he shall warn them that, except for urgent cause, they seek not to have their Children baptized in their houses." They also state that "It is most convenient that Baptism should be administered upon Sundays and other Holy Days," and that it shall take place "immediately after the Second Lesson at Morning or Evening Prayer." The rubrics provide that there shall be two Godfathers and one Godmother for every male child; and for every female, one Godfather and two Godmothers.[2]

While it does not spell out the fact that these sponsors are to be communicants, or at the very least, baptized members of the Church, it does imply that this should be so when it says in the Offices of Instruction that infants are received into Christ's Church "by the faith of their Sponsors" by whom they "are trained in the household of faith." Many times, ministers will be confronted with the problem of parents wishing to have as sponsors intimate friends who may have no connection with, or interest in, the Church. We believe that no firm rule should be laid down in such cases, but that every situation must be met and decided on its own merits. In making his decision, the minister must be careful to keep in mind both the expectation and demands of the Church; and also, he must never forget the opportunity such borderline cases offer to teach and to win people by pointing out the inconsistency of trying to remain neutral in a world in which it is perfectly evident that, as Christ himself said, "He that is not with me is against me." If sponsors are to assume responsibility for a child's learning "the Creed, the Lord's Prayer, The Ten Commandments, and all other things which a Christian ought to know and believe to his soul's health," it is certainly important that they be properly informed as to that faith themselves. The conscientious minister should therefore welcome the opportunity to do some very important pastoral work, telling the sponsors in detail what their duties are in the upbringing of the child. Parents, of course, will do all they can; but the friendship, example, and influence of someone outside the family circle can often accomplish what parents cannot.

It should be made clear that the responsibility of being a sponsor is not simply to give an appropriate gift at the time of baptism, but is something to be taken seriously and discharged conscientiously over the years. It can even be suggested that the sponsor remember the child each year on the anniversary of his baptism—his spiritual rather than his physical birthday. I used to have a series of gifts appropriate for each year on display near the baptistry for sponsors to see. Certificates given to sponsors as well as to the baby baptized are also useful. (See Appendix) In any case, every effort should be exerted to make sponsors more responsible, and members of the parish more aware of the importance of their part in surrounding the child with the strengthening influence of Christian fellowship and love which are so vital to the follow-through of baptism.

In the baptism of adults, it is plainly stated that they are to be "sufficiently instructed in the Principles of the Christian Religion."

One of the most memorable services I ever participated in was at a summer camp when three campers and a counselor were baptized by immersion in the lake by the chaplain. Coming out of the water, they knelt before me on the beach and received "the laying on of hands." The occasion, I am sure, was unforgettable to all who were in camp. Everyone was keenly interested and concerned, in a way that every parish ought to be concerned about those baptized.

Blanks should be secured or printed which give proper space for the information required in the parish register. A blank should be filled out by the parents when the date and time of the baptismal service is arranged. The number of baptisms each year will determine the number of Sundays on which this service will be included in Morning or Evening Prayer; but it is desirable to limit them to every other month, rather than tax the patience of the congregation. If more services are needed, baptisms could take place at the church school service, or after the morning service, the congregation being invited to attend.

The altar guild should be instructed, in regard to desired preparations; the person who is to answer the first question, the one to hold the child, and the sponsors who are to make the replies, should be advised of their duties. Before the service, it is well to say a few words to the congregation in regard to their part.

Last, but very important, the priest should be sure that the baptism is completely recorded, and that he signs his name to the record in the official register which is admissible legal evidence of birth.

## *Holy Communion*

The Administration of the Lord's Supper, Holy Communion, or Holy Eucharist—which are the only three terms used in *The Book of Common Prayer*—has received increasing attention in recent years by clergymen who emphasize the supreme importance of this service by greatly increasing the number of times it is provided. But I raise the question if one cannot appreciate the Holy Communion as being of first importance without having it become the only service every Sunday. The criticism to which the Daily Offices are so often subjected is due, in part at least, to the fact that many ministers fail to use and develop the drama contained in these services by not giving adequate background information to their people about the psalms, lessons, canticles, Creed, prayers, and general structure. The Daily Office is an excellent basis for a growing knowledge and love for the Bible and the Christian Faith and heritage. It seems to me that there must be room for both the Catholic and Protestant traditions—a recognition that they are not mutually exclusive. It is not a matter of either/or, but of both/and; and the Church must have different services to meet different human needs. I feel this is especially true where a parish tries to serve the community rather than merely its own members, and is endeavoring to reach out to those who, having left their own communion, are looking for a church home which is more satisfying to them.

### Who May Receive Holy Communion?

It is plainly written that "It is required of those who come to the Lord's Supper to examine themselves, whether they repent them truly of their former sins, with stedfast purpose to lead a new life; to have a lively faith in God's mercy through Christ, with a thankful remembrance of his death; and to be in charity with all men."[3] This is repeated in other words in the Invitation: "Ye who do truly and earnestly repent you of your sins . . ." just before the General Confession, and in The Exhortations. It is true that the rubric following Confirmation says, "And there shall none be admitted to the Holy Communion, until such time as he be confirmed, or be ready and desirous to be confirmed."[4] "At the Lambeth Conference in 1920 and again in 1930, the bishops passed resolutions affirming that the rubric does not 'necessarily apply to the case of baptized persons who seek Communion under conditions that in the Bishop's judgment justify their admission thereto.'"[5] I feel it is only a very presumptuous priest who would pass over a person who has come to the altar with uplifted hand and heart to receive a Sacrament which is our Lord's to give much more than it is ours. Are there not many confirmed persons who come regularly to receive the Lord's Supper who we have good reason to think fall far short of the other requirement by failing to be "in love and charity" with their neighbors?

On the other hand, it is a mistake for a priest to allow a person who has not been confirmed to come frequently to Holy Communion without calling his attention to the rubric, which clearly indicates that there is a practice and discipline of our Church; and if he appreciates the privileges of the Church he should also assume its responsibilities. In case of doubt, it should of course be referred to the bishop of the diocese, as suggested by Lambeth.

### Conduct of the Service

Also, I am often disturbed in my worship when a priest arbitrarily changes a word or a phrase of the prayer book. Our communicants have a right, as well as a justified expectation, to have a service read exactly as it is provided in the prayer book, rather than with embellishments (even though they may be sincerely offered as in the long tradition of the Church), or shortened because of the necessity of meeting certain secular demands. What right has an individual priest to alter the language of the official prayer book of the Church to suit his taste, when at the time of his ordination he solemnly engaged to conform to this book?

I should like to state a few of my convictions about the conduct of The Holy Communion.

The first is that the service should be read distinctly, as the rubric provides, so that everyone in the congregation will hear what is being said. To meet the needs of those unfamiliar with the service, it may be helpful to announce the page numbers of the Collect, Epistle, and Gospel.

I also feel strongly that the rubric providing for the monthly reading of The Decalogue should be observed.

The receiving of the alms should be done with a dignity which befits an offering to the Lord: neither casually nor with ostentation.

The Exhortations should be used more frequently. Some priests seem to forget that they "shall be said on the First Sunday in Advent, the First Sunday in Lent, and Trinity Sunday."

I shall say something about Intinction in the chapter "The Parish and the General Church." Suffice it to say here that, in all churches, every communicant should be given the right to receive in the manner prescribed in the prayer book. The parish priest should instruct his people to receive the bread in ungloved hands and to steady the base of the chalice lightly when they receive the wine.

## *Occasional Offices*

In Confirmation we receive a new infusion of God's Holy Spirit through the laying on of hands by the Bishop, and in the presence of our fellows and before God we ratify and confirm the promises which were made by us or for us in Holy Baptism; and we do openly promise "to follow Jesus Christ as our Lord and Saviour." The three promises at baptism were to renounce that which is evil, to believe that which is true and, "by God's help," to do that which is right. That phrase, "by God's help," is very important, as we cannot do it by ourselves, in our own strength. We must face that fact. Our desire for Confirmation shows that we have reached the essential stage of humble maturity; because it is only as we recognize our need for God's help that we are open to receive the renewing strength of the Holy Ghost, which is his gift in Confirmation.

That the promises of Confirmation are not simply a once-and-for-all affair, but vows requiring a follow-through demanding patient perseverance, is clearly shown not only in the phrase used—"daily increase"—but by the wording of the rubric at the close: "The Minister shall not omit earnestly to move the Persons confirmed to come, without delay, to the Lord's Supper." [6]

This leads me to emphasize my personal conviction that, although most ministers and people emphasize the importance of adequate preparation for confirmation, I feel that a faithful follow-through after both by the minister and the person confirmed is perhaps even more important. I do not wish in the least to minimize preparation, especially in its emphasis upon adequate commitment rather than hoped-for improvement through learning certain facts. The minister should see to it that every person confirmed starts to come regularly to Holy Communion, and is made a part of the parish fellowship through some of its activities and interests. For this purpose members of the previous year's class, or some special group, should be given the name of each individual in the new confirmation class, and charged with responsibility for them. The minister alone cannot do this. The sacrament of Confirmation is tested not by the words of the confirmand on a certain day, but by his life in the days and years that follow.

## *Recruiting and Instruction*

Recruiting for Confirmation should be a year-around affair. On every call made there should be a search for possible candidates. When one is discovered, the name should be noted on the parish file card (see Appendix). Then when the bishop notifies you of his visitation, there will be a nucleus of possibilities with which to work. New families in the community are a fruitful source of candidates. Mixed marriages offer an opportunity to bring unity to a divided family in a most important relationship.

There are various opinions as to the best age for Confirmation, and it is well for each clergyman to give some thought and study to this in relation to the members of his own congregation by checking former confirmation classes. If the age of ten to twelve seems best, teaching of what Confirmation actually means must be adapted, because children at this age will have a limited appreciation of what the decision they are making really involves. On the other hand, if fourteen is the standard age, the herd instinct—of wanting to be confirmed when Johnny is—is a strong factor, and may outweigh the real seriousness of the step they are taking. But if you wait until they are sixteen, you may lose them. Each priest must come to his own decision, recognizing that even at twenty-one many are still not yet mature enough to understand all that is inherent in this commitment.

This leads to more questions. What should be taught before Confirmation? How important is knowledge of the history and the faith of the Church, unless one is ready to make a commitment? In the long run, is it not better to insure that confirmands have established habits of private prayer, regular Bible reading, and attendance at church services, than that they should know certain facts beyond the Creed, the Lord's Prayer and the Ten Commandments? (See Appendix.)

With regard to the service, if the bishop has not indicated his wishes, information should be requested of him. He may prefer to have the candidates come to the altar rail as a group, or singly, or in pairs; he may prefer to stand or sit at the Laying on of Hands. He may wish to speak to the class in addition to his sermon. The architecture of the church sometimes affects his decision: the choir stalls may make it impossible for the people to see the confirmands at the altar rail, and confirmation at the front of the chancel, where all can see, is to be preferred. If such limitations exist, it would be helpful to call them to the bishop's attention, and to make suggestions, and to remind him what the procedure of the parish has been. All arrangements should be well planned in advance, so that on the Sunday before the bishop comes, the class can rehearse the proceedings. Some clergymen like to have the bishop use the Christian name of the person in the Laying on of Hands. This is not provided for in the service and complicates matters considerably, and would seem to be unnecessary if the confirmation takes place where the person being confirmed is known and can be seen. It seems to me to be a sentimental addition—like the blessing of children when they come to the altar rail with their parents at Holy Communion—introduced by a priest who happens to like it. However, this may create a problem for the next rector who may not. This is also true of the growing custom of having the sponsors come forward with the confirmand. Certainly it is advisable that sponsors be notified of the event by the child or his parents, and invited to attend. To have them come forward seems to me to do little more than create confusion.

The dress of the candidates usually takes on far greater importance than it deserves. It is true there is appropriate symbolism in having the girls and women dress in white, or wear white veils. The latter is usually preferable by allowing less distinction, especially if the veils are alike and provided by the parish. This avoids individual expense. Some of the older women may be reluctant to wear a veil, and it may be well to limit the veils to the girls. The boys and men and women will wear the clothes they would ordinarily wear to church. However, the women must be warned ahead of time that they are to remove their hats before they go forward for the Laying on of Hands.

All those confirmed should be notified well ahead of time when they will be expected to make their First Communion; and as a matter of assurance that they do so, the confirmation certificates usually provided by the bishop may well be held for distribution at that time.

Again I would press home the necessity of following up the persons confirmed, both in regard to their attendance at church services and in their participation in the fellowship of the parish. The first three to six months are all-important. The results of Confirmation are not automatic. Like everything else that is worth while, they call for work.

## *Holy Matrimony*

The Church assumes that the Solemnization of Matrimony takes place when people are gathered together "in the sight of God" to unite a man and a woman in Holy Matrimony, "which is an honorable estate, instituted of God . . . not by any to be entered into unadvisedly or lightly; but reverently, discreetly, advisedly, soberly, and in the fear of God." The congregation is confronted with the responsibility of testifying. "If any man can show just cause, why they may not lawfully be joined together, let him now speak, or else hereafter for ever hold his peace."

This should make clear to all that marriage is not merely a matter of agreement between two persons, but has social overtones which affect the whole community. Not only has the community a definite interest in it, as is evidenced by the fact that a marriage license is required by the State, but the Church as a whole has a concern for it by setting forth its requirements. One of these is that the two who are getting married, if they are to receive the blessing of the Church, must make evident their serious intention to make it a Christian marriage, by signing a statement which runs as follows:

> "We, A.B. and C.D., desiring to receive the blessing of Holy Matrimony in the Church, do solemnly declare that we hold marriage to be a lifelong union of husband and wife as it is set forth in the Form of Solemnization of Matrimony in the Book of Common Prayer. We believe it is for the purpose of mutual fellowship, encouragement, and understanding, for the procreation (if it may be) of children, and their physical and spiritual nurture, for the safeguarding and benefit of society. And we do engage ourselves, so far as in us lies, to make our utmost effort to establish this relationship and to seek God's help thereto." [7]

The responsibility of requiring that this promise is signed and fully understood is laid upon the clergyman who is to perform the ceremony. The canon says that every minister of this Church shall ascertain "the right of the parties to contract a marriage according to the laws of the State, and according to the laws of this Church;" that he shall ascertain "that at least one of the parties has received Holy Baptism;" that he shall "have instructed the parties as to the nature of Holy Matrimony;" that he shall have had at least three days' notice except under very unusual circumstances; and that "it shall be within the discretion of any Minister of this Church to decline to solemnize any marriage." [8]

In the course of the preparation which the minister should give every couple, he should certainly emphasize the fact that marriage, although a very intimate relationship between two persons, is also very definitely a matter of deep concern to the members of the parish and the Church of which they are a part. When the ceremony is over, and they walk down the aisle together as man and wife, they are married, legally and spiritually. Yet, in a certain sense, it is not a completed fact. It is only the beginning of a lifelong relationship in which they will need the help of God and the support of others. I used to suggest that as a definite expression of the partnership of God in this great enterprise, the couple come to Holy Communion together the morning of their marriage (with their attendants, if they so wished). Holy Communion was formerly an integral part of the service of Holy Matrimony; but with the large number of people often present who are not Church members, and would have to witness it under a measure of duress, the Eucharist is not usually part of the marriage service. It seems more appropriate, in our present secular society, to have it as a special preparation for the participants.

My brother prepared a list of questions for those contemplating marriage (Appendix), which he used to give the couple when they first came to see him. He would ask them to talk over the questions together and come back at a later date, thus making the second conference far more effective. A request which I used to make of the couple at our last conference has proved helpful, and many have thanked me for it. I gave them a copy of Bishop Slattery's prayer, read it to them (Appendix) and asked them to use it together on their wedding night. It is tragic to find how many couples never have prayed together, except in church, and the best time to begin is the very first night.

Actually, preparation for Christian marriage should be of far greater concern to the church than it usually is—in the child's teen years, in the church school, in Y.P.F., and in confirmation lectures. This is beginning to be recognized, but it must be stressed still more, because it is through the associations a child has that he finds the special person who leads him to marriage, and determines the values, standards, and goals which are such important ingredients in the make-up of a happy union. Very little can be done after the engagement has been announced, and still less after the marriage date has been set.

The canons also provide, and the minister should make this perfectly clear (even though every couple will regard their marriage as the exception), that "When marital unity is imperilled by dissension, it shall be the duty of either or both parties, before contemplating legal action, to lay the matter before a Minister of this Church; and it shall be the duty of such Minister to labor that the parties may be reconciled."[9]

There is one more act which every pastor should regard as of very first importance. When the couple return from their honeymoon, he should make a special point of calling on them at a time when they are both at home; and if they are going to live in another community, he should leave no stone unturned to see that a priest in that place is informed and urged to call upon them (a return envelope enclosed will notify you that he has done so). Responsibility may be further discharged by writing them a letter on their anniversaries.

There is so much material on arrangements available, and there are so many variants in procedure, that I will only say that each priest should outline his own procedure. This may vary according to the architecture and tradition of the particular church; but he should be sure that the couple and their attendants are completely familiar with what is expected of them. To this end there should be at least one rehearsal; and it is well to begin the rehearsal with prayer.

### Some Important Procedures

One of the customs that is growing in the Church is the publication of the Banns of Matrimony. This is done in the English Church and has much to commend it in helping the congregation to realize their stake in the marriage. It also gives protection from the hurried weddings which are usually ill advised.

Priests of our Church are fortunate in being protected by the canons from being expected, as an officer of the State, to perform marriages of persons unknown to them.

And here let me inject one lesson I learned by hard experience: be sure that the parents of the couple are invited to the wedding, or that you know a valid reason why they have not been.

Marriages should be solemnized in the church. There will be some families who will hesitate to ask for this, fearing the expense involved. Therefore, it should be understood that when the priest feels it desirable, arrangements may be made to have a church wedding at no extra cost.

The priest should have the marriage license in hand *before* the wedding day. It is best to ask for this at the first conference in order to be assured that there are no complications. The record in the official parish register should be filled out from the information given on the license, and this should be done before the ceremony, ready for the signatures of the bride, groom, and the two witnesses, before they leave the church. The sexton, if there is one, should be charged with responsibility for seeing that this is done; or it might be delegated to an usher.

Another very small matter is that the couple should be told to face each other as they make their vows. So often they make them to the priest rather than before him.

It is well to have a typed sheet stating parish procedures, with full instructions, including the regulations in regard to flowers, photographers, organist's and sexton's fees, etc.

## *Absolution*

No one in the Episcopal Church is required to seek sacramental absolution. For many, the General Confession in Morning or Evening Prayer or Holy Communion may be sufficient; but there are some who seek a peace of mind and a quieting of conscience that these opportunities do not meet. They are among those referred to in the Second Exhortation which states, "If there be any of you, who by this means cannot quiet his own conscience . . . but requireth further comfort or counsel, let him come to me (his priest), or to some other Minister of God's Word, and open his grief; that he may receive such godly counsel and advice, as may tend to the quieting of his conscience, and the removing of all scruple and doubtfulness."[10]

There is, also, in the Order for the Visitation of the Sick[11] a rubric which says, "Then shall the sick person be moved to make a special confession of his sins, if he feel his conscience troubled with any matter; after which confession, on evidence of his repentance, the Minister shall assure him of God's mercy and forgiveness." The experiences of modern times, and the rapid rise of psychiatrists in the world today, testify to a widespread need for confession—not only in a general way to God, but also in a more particular way to a human person. The Church has perhaps been neglectful of her special ministry in this latter field. Public confession to God can often be helpfully particularized through personal confession to a priest, with the consequent pronouncement of absolution.

There are three forms of absolution: (1) that used in Morning and Evening Prayer (declaratory), declaring that God forgives the penitent and bidding the people to pray for repentance; (2) precatory, in Holy Communion, reminding the person of God's forgiveness when accompanied by penitence and faith; (3) authoritative, the more direct absolution found in the services of the Visitation of the Sick, The Communion of the Sick, and as an alternate in Evening Prayer, in which the priest speaks more authoritatively. In all cases it should be made perfectly clear that the priest has no power of himself to forgive sins, but that he is acting in behalf of the Church which has given him the authority to promise God's forgiveness under certain definite conditions.

The giving of spiritual counsel and the promising of absolution is a great responsibility, and is not to be undertaken lightly. Those expected and authorized to do so should be adequately prepared both by study and experience.

With regard to auricular confession in the Episcopal Church, someone has said, "All may, some do, none must."

## *Unction*

The last in the list of sacraments, for which provision is made in the prayer book, is Unction of the Sick.[12] In the Roman Church, this is administered as a preparation for death, when hope of recovery has gone. But from apostolic times until about 800, unction was the Church's healing sacrament. That it should be used only in this context is made plain in the introductory rubric which says, "When any sick person shall in humble faith desire the ministry of healing through Anointing or Laying on of Hands, the Minister may use such portion of the foregoing Office (Visitation of the Sick) as he shall think fit." Then follows the prayer for release from sin and all pain of soul and body, and for the restoration of health, and a sentence to be used with the anointing with oil, and/or the laying on of hands. The latter is at present the more common because, as almost everyone knows from personal experience, the actual human contact between one person and another has a definite effect in producing comfort and strength; and because the familiar practice of anointing with oil is carried over from the Roman Church which associates it with death rather than with life and healing.

In recent years there has been a new interest in the close connection of body and mind and spirit. Much has been done to restore the healing ministry which played so large a part in the practice of the early Church and to bring it back to its rightful place. Both doctors and clergy are coming to a far deeper understanding of their special ministries—and the need of one for the other—as well as to a wider acceptance of the fundamental unity of the human being. In a recent study made by the Outpatient Department of the Massachusetts General Hospital in Boston, it was discovered that more than eighty per cent of the patients had no organic illness related to the symptoms they reported, but that eighty-four per cent of them had psychiatric or emotional problems. We know now that we must deal with body, mind, and spirit, not as separate parts of a person, but rather as inextricably interwoven so that they act and react upon one another. Pastor and physician have a joint ministry.

### Visitation of the Sick

There are some portions of the Order for the Visitation of the Sick which are formal, stilted, and theologically outdated; but the rubric gives wide permission when it says the order should be used at the discretion of the minister, and that parts may be used separately. Here, it may be that informal prayer is more helpful and appropriate. The one infallible rule for all ministers is that when a person is seriously ill, the call should be brief. Sick persons tire very easily and very quickly. Special provision for brevity is made in The Communion of the Sick. The minister must also be extremely sensitive to the fact that people who are often said to be unconscious have a peculiar power to hear what is being said. I have often offered prayers over such persons, and have had them tell me later that they remembered very well my coming and were grateful for the prayer. This sensitivity is also true in regard to remarks made in the sickroom, and special care should be taken in conversing with the nurse or doctor so as to avoid anything which would give the patient undue cause for concern about his condition.

The comfort and mood of the patient must react upon the minister. To one feeling weak and ill, the showing of over-exuberant vitality is often irritating and depressing. The smell of tobacco is often offensive. The minister will be careful to stand or sit in a position where he can be easily seen; and he will move about the room quietly and slowly. With experience he will learn how to lead the conversation to a point where prayer can occur as a natural thing. He will never introduce it abruptly, in a way that might scare a patient into thinking he is sicker than he is. On the other hand, as ministers, I think we are sometimes overtimid in this direction, and more than once I have been ashamed that a patient has had to ask for prayer. We should remember that we are in the sickroom for a purpose not simply to cheer, but also to help channel God's healing powers to an ailing patient.

## *Burial of the Dead*

There is no service which needs so much to be rescued from an overlay of pagan principles and practices as *The Order for The Burial of the Dead.*[13] There is no occasion when a minister can mean more to those who are left behind than in these hours of sorrow and loneliness.

A service which should be one of triumphant confidence is all too often a dreary and dismal formality. We believe that both clergy and laity can do much to change this. Already, we see hopeful signs that change is on the way—the increased use of the pall, and the custom of making memorial gifts in the place of a wicked waste of money on flowers and funeral pieces. I know, too, that there are many fine Christian funeral directors who want to do the right thing but find themselves caught in a vise of commercialism and vulgar sentimentality.

I believe very strongly that such changes as are made should be accomplished not by setting up unbreakable rules of procedure which surprise and hurt people who are in a peculiarly sensitive mood, but, rather, should be effected through constant teaching in the pulpit, parish leaflet, and in pastoral calling. Memorial Day, All Saints' Day, the Easter season—all provide special opportunity for teaching. And a clergyman should be continually teaching because all the people are not in church at the same time, they do not all read the weekly leaflet, new people are continually moving in, and we all easily forget what is not immediately of interest to us. More than this, thought of death is something our minds tend to reject.

What can any one of us do to change the burial service from a pagan rite to a Christian experience? First, the parish can provide leaflets on this subject, available to everyone in the tract rack of the church.

Second, while we are in full health, we can discuss these last things with the rector. In talking with him, we can decide what hymns we would like, what prayers and lessons. We can select the funeral director. We can then write down our wishes, including such matters as the omission of flowers, our favorite charity, as well as the details of the service. One copy should be filed with the rector, another put with the will, and a third given to the nearest relative. The Church wishes to provide for the reverent care of the body which for years has housed the spirit; but once the spirit has departed, we must free ourselves from the association. Therefore the practice of "viewing the body" must be discouraged and, certainly, the coffin is to be closed before the service. It is not opened again. This should never astonish members of our Church: they should have been taught this long before.

If we are asked to bury one who has never been a member of the Church, the rubric at the end of the Office provides for variation from the rules of the Church to be used with pastoral discretion; always mindful of the fact that people are unusually upset at such times, and that Christian charity and understanding are sometimes more important than general rules. A lack of knowledge of Church customs is our fault as well as theirs.

## *Ordination*

The canons of our Church clearly spell out the requirements a man must fulfill before he is ordained, and the rubric which precedes services of Ordination says, "When the day appointed by the Bishop is come, there shall be a Sermon, or Exhortation, declaring the Duty and Office of such as come to be admitted Deacons (or Priest); how necessary that Order is in the Church of Christ, and also, how the People ought to esteem them in their Office." [14] The services are impressive in the responsibility which they lay not only on those to be ordained but also upon those present—and, indeed, upon all members of the Church.

Because the service is so truly a service of the Church, I feel it is important to have as many members of the parish present as possible. Sometimes the service takes place in the cathedral with all the candidates for ordination present. The impact of a church packed with people gives a sense of the presence and power of the Church of God; but I feel there is much to be said for having an ordination in the home parish of the ordinand, both for its teaching value and because the total attendance is liable to be greater when the service is in the home parish. Ordination is a very unusual service, not likely to occur in a single parish more than once in ten years, and in all too many parishes, scarcely once in a lifetime. Therefore, if the bishop is pressed for time, an ordination would seem to take precedence over the annual visitation for Confirmation—which sometimes may be combined, or more often postponed a year. Of course, this is more possible in the small diocese where the ordinands are fewer; but even in dioceses which have eight to ten ordinands a year (which happened to be true in Western Massachusetts), it is possible, by using Saturdays as well as Sundays and Holy Days, to have all the ordinations in local churches within a month's time. This was helpful in making the service more personal to each ordinand, by giving him opportunity to suggest to the bishop the men he wanted to participate in his ordination. The parish, in presenting him, is made to feel in a dramatic way its role as part of the whole Church.

---

REFERENCES

1. Office of Instruction, Prayer Book, page 292
2. Baptism, rubric page 273
3. Office of Instruction, Prayer Book, page 293
4. Prayer Book, page 299
5. *The Oxford American Prayer Book Commentary,* page 299.
6. Prayer Book, page 299
7. Canon 17, Section 3
8. Canon 17, Sections 2 and 4
9. Canon 16, Section 3 (c)
10. Prayer Book, page 88
11. Prayer Book, page 313
12. Prayer Book, page 320
13. Prayer Book, page 324
14. Prayer Book, page 530

15

# THE BEAUTY OF HOLINESS: THE ALTAR GUILD

The altar guild is a group of women selected by the rector to perform his wishes in regard to the housekeeping of the sanctuary. The women should be carefully chosen, communicants in good standing, interested in such service, and willing to give more of their time and of themselves than is usually asked by the Church. They should never be pressed to serve as a matter of duty. The guild should be helpful to the rector in suggesting members, but it should never be allowed to become self-perpetuating or a select group in which membership might be considered a social asset. Altar guild service provides a unique opportunity for growth in the devotional life, and will often result in a wider knowledge of the history, function, and meaning of the Church. The head of the altar guild is, technically speaking, the rector of the parish, and it is a wise rector who recognizes his guild as one of his most important and helpful groups. The rector can expect, and should receive, the complete cooperation of the members, and he should set them an example by his own respect for, and use of, holy things.

Individual parishes have their particular needs and conditions, in that there are varying degrees of ceremonial in the Episcopal Church. Therefore, there cannot be a specific set of rules that will apply to the organization and procedure of every parish altar guild. The number of members depends partly on the size and equipment of the church building, partly on the number of services of Holy Communion, and the richness of the ceremonial.

The requirements for membership should be kept high, as altar guild work is a vocation. A guild of six to twelve devoted members, in the average size parish, is far superior to one composed of twice that number of only mildly interested, undependable, and less highly motivated members.

The rector should ask one of the guild to serve as director and to act as his deputy in the calling and conducting of regular meetings, in assigning work according to the schedule of services, and in the general oversight of the upkeep and replacement of linens, array, vestments, and adequate provision of supplies. It is very important that this person should have the ability to lead others, and to work with all kinds of people; to receive suggestions with an open mind, and to be absolutely loyal to her rector.

## *Decently and in Order*

The rector should make a point of meeting frequently with the group—especially when it is first formed or when he comes as the new head of the parish—in order to see that the members are fully informed, and understand what he desires. While they can be of the very greatest help to him in the smooth and reverent functioning of the services, any failure on their part is liable to be a conspicuous interruption and a distraction in the devotions of the parishioners. When, however, he is sure they are well instructed and understand his wishes, it is a mistake for him to keep continually interfering. Additional instructions or suggestions should be made through the director.

It should be recognized by the altar guild members that there is of necessity a variety of tradition, custom, and practice within our Church; and the wishes of one rector may be very different from those of another. The present rector's orders are "the orders of the day." His authority in these matters is final.

Whether simple or elaborate, the ceremonial may be equally right and helpful to the devout soul. Local conditions make for necessary adjustments. Different manuals give different procedures. There should be no effort to standardize customs beyond what may be helpful in each particular parish. As rectors change, customs and practices will also inevitably change; *but parish customs and traditions should be respected and as a rule continued.* Constant change is an irritation and tends to confuse the important with the inconsequential. The really important thing is that the work should be performed reverently, "decently and in order."

## *The Sacristy*

If possible, a special room, or sacristy, should be provided by the vestry and designated as the working area for the altar guild. This may not be possible in some of the smaller parishes; but even when make-shifts are necessary, the place should be as well equipped as possible, and, whether simple or elaborate, should be kept as scrupulously clean and neat as the sanctuary itself. Making the best of conditions and circumstances, even under difficulties, should be a matter of joy and pride.

The sacristy should contain a safe or locked cabinet for the sacred vessels, properly sized drawers for the altar linens (all carefully labeled), a chest or closet for altar hangings, and some arrangement for heating water. It is also desirable to install a drain without a trap, connecting directly with the ground. This drain is called a "piscina" and is used for the disposal of consecrated water and the first rinsing of vessels after their use at the altar. The vestry should be impressed with the fact that the provision of some properly equipped place for the altar guild is as essential as the providing of hymnals and prayer books for the worshippers; and it falls within their canonical duty to make this provision.

## *Finances*

It is desirable to have the financial support for the altar guild come from the parish budget, and there is good basis for this in the canon. In some places it comes through the parish council. Additional equipment and ornaments may well come from other sources, such as endowments, special gifts, or the raising of funds by the guild through appropriate special efforts.

## *Altar Flowers*

Altar flowers are usually memorial gifts, or may appropriately be given in thanksgiving on some anniversary or for some special event. Larger churches need more formal arrangements, with flowers purchased from a florist; but for medium-size and smaller churches, garden flowers and sprays from flowering bushes and trees may well be used in season, and often have added significance for the donor. Some people have unusual ability in arranging flowers, but this should never become the responsibility of one person. The privilege should be shared. As a matter of policy, it is never a good practice to have one or two women monopolize altar guild work. Over a period of years they are inclined to develop a possessive attitude; and this exclusiveness denies to many members of the parish opportunities that would help in their spiritual growth.

## *Composition of the Guild*

Although the number of members in a parish altar guild will vary according to the amount of work required, the most satisfactory arrangement in the average parish seems to be a rotation of groups of two or three to serve each Sunday. This gives opportunity for most of them to serve twelve times a year, keeps them active in the work, and provides for substitutes in case of illness or absence. More satisfactory than having each group take a whole month at a time, the rotation system permits each member to keep her "hand in," and guarantees an even distribution of the work throughout the Church Year.

Guild members should regard their service as an offering to God: work done for him, and presented to him. It is an act of praise and thanksgiving, and it should be done with reverence and quietness of mind—especially within the sanctuary—and with a humbleness of spirit which gladly accepts work which is often unseen and unrewarded, except in results. The wearing of smocks or veils while doing altar guild work has no religious significance, although there should be some head covering. Distinctive dress may help, however, in adding a sense of dignity and reverence to the work. For the same reason an admission service for members is desirable.

Guild membership can be divided, if the parish is large enough, into (a) active members—those doing the actual work; (b) associate members—those interested and who contribute through gifts, training of junior members, and cooperating in other ways; (c) junior members—who should not be a separate organization, but should work under the supervision of an older person, assigned to their particular tasks on a particular Sunday, and helped to learn how to do the work by example and instruction, and by doing the work themselves under close supervision. Junior members may also be very useful on special festivals and other occasions when the work load is increased. The young people of the Church should not be thought of merely as "the Church of tomorrow," but should be given a share in the work of the Church today. Working as a junior altar guild member can be a significant educational opportunity, and the training given in discipline, order, reverence, cleanliness, and punctuality, is of great personal value.

The altar guild should be adequately informed about special services. The decoration and special preparation as are needed for baptisms, confirmations, weddings, or funerals, although under the control of the rector, may well be handled by the altar guild under his direction.

## *The Guild Is a Part of the Parish and Diocese*

It is tremendously important that the altar guild should not be "sufficient unto itself," but that it should take its part in the life and work of the parish. It should also have a concern for the other parishes and missions in the diocese and in the general

Church. Very often there is an accumulation of unused equipment which other parishes might be able to use—altar vessels, hangings, linens. In consultation with the diocesan altar guild, real service can often be rendered in the reconditioning of these materials so that, instead of cluttering up shelves and taking space in a limited area, they may be of further service to the glory of the Lord in other places where they may be greatly needed and appreciated. When they are memorials, and there is hesitation about making an outright gift, they may be loaned indefinitely, with a careful record kept.

We have referred to the diocesan altar guild. If there is not one in your diocese or district, it might be well to propose the formation of one to the bishop. Such an organization can be of help in terms of fellowship, inspiration, cooperation, and in the exchange of information among people who have special interest in this form of service. If there is one, the parish guild should plan to send representatives to all diocesan meetings, and take part in its work and worship. The diocesan altar guild will probably have a resource library; but in using and reading such books members should never forget that, whatever may be done in other places, their job is to perform their task according to the wishes of their rector. The success or failure of an altar guild depends very largely upon how ready the members are to serve the rector, how seriously they take their duties, how faithfully they perform them, and what they teach through their performance.

## *Conclusion*

Indeed, the work of the guild is a projection of the rector's ministry, and because of its special spiritual significance, it can well set the standard for other groups and make a great contribution to the devotional life of the parish as the members reflect reverence, joy, praise, and the spirit of thanksgiving.

If no other parish organization does so, the altar guild might well help the rector to sponsor devotional pilgrimages through the parish church, as well as quiet days and retreats for all parish groups.

An altar guild prayer should be used before each occasion of service. The following may be found useful.

> O God of beauty, love and peace; make us thankful for the privilege of adding beauty to thy sanctuary, growing in love through thy service, and gaining peace from thy presence; through Jesus Christ, our Lord. Amen.

After work, or at the end of meetings, the following prayer may be used:

> Blessed be our God, who hath shared with us the joy and the work of angels. O God, we thank thee for thy wondrous love, and for thy marvelous beauty; for thy mighty acts, and for thy tender care; above all, we thank thee for thy most precious gift of thyself in the blessed sacrament of the altar. Hold us fast, O God, that we may always be close to thee. Amen.

# 16

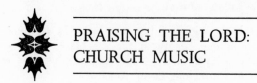

# PRAISING THE LORD: CHURCH MUSIC

O come, let us sing unto the Lord; let us heartily rejoice in the strength of our salvation.

Let us come before his presence with thanksgiving; and show ourselves glad in him with psalms.

With these words at Morning Prayer we are called to rejoice and give thanks; but Jesus pointed out the danger of mere noisiness when he said, "This people draweth nigh unto me with their mouth, and honoureth me with their lips; but their heart is far from me."

According to the canons of our Church, "It shall be the duty of every Minister to see that music is used in his congregation as an offering for the glory of God and as a help to the people in their worship . . . To this end he shall be the final authority in the administration of matters pertaining to music with such assistance as he may see fit to employ from persons skilled in music. It shall be his duty to suppress all light and unseemly music and all irreverence in the rendition thereof." [1]

This is a large order. He is a wise priest who sees the unique opportunity it affords for making the music so spiritually uplifting and so contagiously joyful that the people will look forward to coming to church "to sing unto the Lord and heartily rejoice in the strength of our salvation," will want "to come before his presence with thanksgiving," and show themselves "glad in him with psalms."

Music plays a tremendously important part in our worship. There are some things that cannot be expressed in words, and we feel impelled to burst into song. Unfortunately, however, I am afraid that in church we too often only mouth words and do not feel joyful or thankful at all. What can we do to change this? Here is an area of opportunity which is often neglected. We are too content to leave things as they are. Much more time and thought should be given to lifting the people to the level of the words they sing, and making musical worship an integral part of the service, filling it with life and meaning. This requires the very closest of team-work between the minister and the organist. A basic consideration is timing. Certainly there should be no sense of haste. The organist should be allowed time for unhurried transition. Hymns should not be arbitrarily stopped when the choir reaches the door; nor should the ushers start forward with the offering before the anthem is finished. The worship of God calls for the very best we can offer, and essential is the cooperative attention and effort of minister, organist, and people.

To accomplish this demands careful planning, unending patience, and a steady pursuit of different ways in which this may be brought about. Fortunately, the minister has certain helpful forces working with him in that people generally love to sing together. Community-sings were especially popular during the war days, and helped greatly to lift the morale of people and country. Also, there are always people in every congregation who are especially interested in music and want church music to be worthy of God.

## *Technique Is Not Everything*

This book is being written with the smaller parishes in mind, and it might seem that really good music is beyond their reach for lack of funds to engage the necessary talent. Actually, however, the small church has some advantage over the large, well-endowed parish, in that there is not the same temptation to emphasize the professional side of a choir. In the small church, much more must be left to the congregation, and this is as it should be. It is difficult, if not impossible, to worship by proxy. One of the great assets of our church is the large place the people have in common worship. Whether the people participate musically or not is largely dependent on whether the organist measures his timing so as to encourage congregational singing, goes so fast as to leave people breathless, or so slowly that they get bored. Too often, professional choirs put on a show in which pride in their ability and technique completely overshadows the humble and happy spirit of worship which alone can bring the congregation to a new awareness of the glory of God in whose name and for whose praise the singing takes place. Often, just because the congregation does not have the means to provide paid singers, the spirit of devotion and willing eagerness to give what they have unto the Lord bring a quality of spirit and adoration which is the very heart of worship. What they lack in quality is more than compensated for by the fact that it is a service given humbly out of loving and full hearts, and not paid for or subordinated to professional supply. As a result it is contagiously joyous. The choice of hymns is also important, as some are suitable only for trained choirs; and the hymns should be pitched to suit the congregation.

Although the final authority for the music is placed in the hands of the minister, thus emphasizing its spiritual nature and its spiritual importance as an integral part in the worship, the canon suggests that he should seek help and counsel from "other persons skilled in music." This implies that it is the duty of every member to see that the music is a worthy offering to God by rendering it with reverence. Participation in the various aspects of the worship of the Church is a first requirement and responsibility of every member of a congregation. It is not enough simply to be present each Sunday: one must join in the singing of the hymns, in the reading of the psalms; and be attentive to the lessons and to the message of the sermon, joining himself to the historic continuity of the Church by repeating—out loud for all to hear—the Creed, the General

Confession, and the General Thanksgiving. It is wonderful when a congregation makes the "Amens" and responses a culminating chorus. Such hearty participation will inevitably help to lift the service to the level of the words we sing and hear. Strangers can quickly tell whether the parish is an alive and vital one and a leavening influence in the community, or if it is merely a respectable and smug congregation of people who attend church as a conventional habit and are quite content with things as they are. This difference is made evident by the number of people who wholeheartedly participate in the worship.

Another advantage of a small parish is that it is far easier to secure such general participation than in a large one. A crowded church, as we well know by experience, adds greatly to the inspiration and spirit of a service. This is equally true in reverse. A scattered congregation produces a deadening effect. This self-evident fact emphasizes the responsibility of each member "to worship God every Sunday in his Church."

## *The Organist*

In securing the help of persons skilled in music, probably the key people are the organist and the choir director. These offices are more often than not combined in the same person. In a small community, this choice is severely limited, and often the best obtainable is someone who is skilled in playing the piano. If this is the case, steps should be taken to provide lessons on the organ. The parish may well assume the expense of such training in view of the service to be rendered. Also, there are summer conferences with courses designed to help such persons; and many books are available. The training of organists ought to be taken far more seriously than it is. If a parish expects an organist to be available when it needs one, it certainly has a responsibility in the recruiting and training of men and women for this important service. This means that the church organ should be made available to responsible persons who wish to develop their skill in this field. Of course, there should be some intelligent control to prevent its promiscuous use; but the idea that it will be worn out by such use is absurd. Reasonable use is far better for an organ than disuse.

When an organist has been engaged, both the rector and vestry should recognize that the organist has certain rights. These include: adequate notice from the rector of what he wants played; the right to play at weddings and funerals; the right of a vacation with pay, and of a substitute when ill. These should all be talked over at length; and when mutually agreed upon, the understanding should be written down in full detail, specifying exactly what is expected in terms of rehearsals, extra services, relation to choir and church school. If this has not been thoroughly thought through, it is astonishing how many questions may arise as time goes on. Much misunderstanding and many heartaches will be prevented if everything is fully clarified to the three parties involved—rector, organist, and vestry—with a copy of the agreement given to each.

Certain portions of this agreement, such as apply to church funerals, weddings and rehearsals, and the charges for the services of the organist and sexton, may well be printed, or published in the parish bulletin so that the people may be adequately informed about the practices of the parish. This will help to anticipate and avoid situations which may arise and precipitate unfortunate issues: a bride wanting her best friend to play the organ, to sing *O Promise Me,* or to use other sentimental and uncanonical music at her wedding. When these parish practices have been decided upon, the rector should see that they are carried out. If they are well known, he will not be so liable to be subjected to personal pressure, but will be protected by being able to say, "I am sorry, but this is not simply my decision; this is the practice of the parish, adopted after due consideration for the benefit of all concerned; and I have no personal authority to change it."

What has been said of the organist applies equally to the choir director. If the person is well qualified, the rector may wish to assign certain responsibilities to him. If the rector should sing in the choir, he should realize that as a choir member he is under the director. It is desirable, in any case, for the rector to have constant conferences with the choir director for the advance planning of the music. There are few things more irritating to an organist or a choir director than sudden requests for changes.

## *New Hymns*

The question of the introduction of new hymns may well be discussed. When a rector first comes to a parish, he should find out what hymns are familiar, and also discover what favorite hymns of his are not known by the people. But it is best that he abide by parish preferences at first. No congregation likes to have new hymns introduced without warning, and the high frequency of unfamiliar hymns is sometimes resented. There are six hundred hymns in our hymnal, and most parishes rarely use (except for special seasonal hymns) more than a hundred. Therefore, they should be led to recognize that every hymn was a new hymn at one time, and some of the unfamiliar ones may become even more greatly beloved in the course of time than the "old" ones they now know. This has happened over and over again. Careful thought should be put into their proper presentation. For example, a new hymn might be used first as an anthem. The rector will call attention to it, explain something of its history and why it has been chosen, or put something about it in the weekly leaflet. He may ask the congregation to stay a few minutes after the service once a month to hear and sing new hymns. If the people recognize that he is trying to give them a richer experience and not imposing his favorites upon them, he will be gratified at their willingness to give new hymns a fair try. When one has been introduced, it is good practice at first to use it fairly often.

## *The Choir*

It is the privilege and function of the choir to lead the congregation in worship. This should be distinctly understood.

They are to *assist* in the praise and worship of God. They should be leaders, not only in praise but in the other parts of worship, giving leadership in standing, kneeling, and in full participation in the reading of the psalms and in the saying of "Amen," the General Confession, the Creed, and General Thanksgiving. This may be difficult to accomplish as choirs seem to think they are only to sing. The minister has a responsibility to show them the importance of their example.

In order to hold the interest and sustain the morale of the choir, they may be given the opportunity to sing an anthem during the receiving of the offering; but we question the spiritual value of this practice. All settings of the canticles which prevent participation by the congregation should be definitely discouraged: such arrangements take worship away from the congregation, who then can only stand up and listen. A long choir-setting of the *Te Deum* may easily serve to wear out the spirit of the people, rather than to uplift it.

The family service is bringing a new problem into the picture, where the choir is a volunteer one. The difficulty arises because the young adults, who would normally be the backbone of the late service choir, are parents of the junior choir members and wish to attend service with their children. We know of no simple solution to this problem. In some churches there has been a compromise and they have only one service, for both children and adults, at ten o'clock. This helps with the transportation problem for choir rehearsal, which is held in the early evening, as well as for the service itself. In other parishes a special effort has been made to recruit additional persons to strengthen the later choir. An unvested group, gathered to sing in the rear balcony, is another possibility. In a few cases, the interest and support of a men's choir has been enlisted, and this has served as a stimulation to all. The gathering of a junior choir of boys and girls has the added advantage of service as an excellent training and recruiting ground for the future.

This matter of enlistment is important. It is much better to invite people who are known to be musical and to have good voices than it is to make a public appeal; although the choir director should always be glad to try out the voice of any member of the parish. It should always be considered a privilege to be a member of the choir. Even those with good voices should not be allowed to sing without attending rehearsals, and soloists should be led to realize that they are part of a team. They should never turn towards the congregation when they sing, since they are not singing *to* the people but *for* them to the glory of God.

## *The Organ*

When the parish is buying a new organ, the best professional advice should be sought. Every church should have its needs hand-tailored, and infinite pains and time are well spent in order to secure the very best. The reed organ is still the ideal for every parish having the space to house it. Electronic organs are at best a measure of last resort. Whether reed or electronic, the console should certainly meet the standard specifications of the American Guild of Organists. A good, secondhand reed organ may cost no more, and give better music, than an electronic makeshift. I would also remind you that you are buying a church organ and not a concert organ. Fancy stops are a temptation rather than an asset. This is a tremendously important decision, and one that the people will have to live with the rest of their lives. The fact that you have to buy a new organ should make you aware of the fact that a "cheap buy" is a poor investment, and that all organs need proper installation and continuous care.

I have known excellent organs to be ruined in a short time by being subject to dangers caused by inadequate ventilation. The life of a good organ can be continued over many generations if it is properly cared for. An adequate item should be put in the parish budget each year for this purpose, and should not be subject to elimination or reduction for the sake of economy. Economies of this sort are, in the long run, false economies.

## *Additional Suggestions*

Some additional miscellaneous suggestions may be helpful. For example, the congregation will only be able to start singing with the first word if they are taught to stand up promptly when the organ begins to play. If they rise casually as the hymn or canticle is about to be sung, they will start raggedly in the first or second line.

If the choir comes in by a processional, the members should start singing when they are well within the church, so that the congregation will be given courage to begin with them; and in the recessional the singing of the congregation should not be allowed to dwindle off into nothing, but should be maintained in full volume to the close. Here, it should be pointed out that some stanzas are units in themselves while others carry over the meaning to the next stanza. Certain ones can be omitted and sense maintained; but it is wrong to cut a hymn simply because the preacher is ready, or the choir has reached the end of an aisle. Indeed, this whole matter of processionals and recessionals as a convenience to get the choir in and out has recently come under judgment. The number of appropriate hymns is limited. It is more difficult to sing while walking, and certainly the endeavor to try to keep step disconcerting and undesirable, and the stilted and awkward carriage of the crucifer often is a major distraction rather than a help.

If it is kept firmly in mind that the music of the church is the natural and inevitable response of the people to express their joy, their praise and thanksgiving; and if it is made clear that the purpose of the organ and the choir is to give body, life, and leadership to the music, and so make the worship of God a thrilling experience; if every effort is made to make it real, by careful planning and general participation, I feel that the details will take care of themselves. Every service will then help to nurture the spiritual life of the parish.

---

REFERENCE

1. Canon 24

17

# RELEVANT RELIGION: THE PARISH AND THE COMMUNITY

Every community is different from every other community. To a certain extent we can classify them into groups; but even within these groups the differences are very great. Every community is an admixture of all sorts of factors having to do with its history, its geography, its industry, its residents; it has a personality all its own. Moreover, every community is constantly changing. We are told that about thirty-one million Americans change their residence every year, and three-quarters of the population have moved during the past twenty years. Anyone who has anything to do with keeping parish lists up to date does not find this hard to believe. Those who have been born since the beginning of the twentieth century may have difficulty in realizing the newness of our present culture or the uprooting effect of the industrial revolution on our lives —mentally, emotionally, and spiritually. Family life and parish programs have been subjected to a new set of circumstances and pressures which have drastically altered their character. Our inherited Christianity must be rephrased and reformed to meet the industrial age. It grew out of small communities with an agricultural or pastoral background and must be reshaped to serve cities with industrial and merchandizing cores and sprawling suburban areas.

Under the circumstances it would be foolish for me to make definite suggestions as to what a particular parish should do in its community. All I can hope to do is to encourage more creative thinking about the purpose and future of your parish in terms of your community, laying down certain abiding principles which I believe hold good under any and all circumstances; and at the close, giving a few definite suggestions to test and implement your thinking.

## *The Parish Must Serve the Community*

The first of these principles would seem self-evident, but is far from being generally accepted. It is: the parish exists for the community and not for itself. It is there to minister to community needs and not merely to its own membership. While it is unfair to say that most parishes in the Episcopal Church are introvert parishes, we do need to face hard facts. I think it is often true that a parish measures its program and progress not by the gauge of its service to the community but according to its size, its fabric, its activity, and its financial strength. If it is growing in numbers with its services well attended, and its financial condition is good, people are satisfied. They are apt to be too satisfied. The parish repeats this same fallacy when it measures the usefulness of its members not by their helpfulness to the community, but by the service they are rendering within the parish itself as officers, workers, and worshipers. This limited point of view unfortunately is as common with clergy as it is with laity. The goal of service to others is often intellectually accepted but not practically applied. If you do not believe me, check your own parish and see if it is not more generally true than you had thought: that the members look to their church to minister to them and not to others. They are far from ready to have it give its life a ransom for anybody but themselves. The two great commandments of our Lord, "Thou shalt love the Lord thy God . . . and thy neighbor as thyself," have no such narrow parochial limitations. If we are to accept Christ's commandments as our standard, the relevance of a parish must be judged solely on how fully it is leavening the life of the community with its love, reaching out to all who are in need.

When Archbishop Temple said that the Church is the only organization that exists to put itself out of business and that the role of the Anglican Church was to render herself unnecessary, many were shocked at the low estimate he seemed to place on what they held so dear. The job of the Church is to bring in the kingdom of God, not merely to perpetuate itself. If Christ himself could tell his disciples, "it is expedient for you that I should go away," those who follow him should have no less a standard. A local parish church is planted in a certain area so that the surrounding community will be affected and uplifted by its Christian influence in the same way that yeast lifts dough. But what all too often happens, as the Abbé Michonneau dramatically notes, the average parish spends about ninety-five per cent of its time, energy, and effort in providing services for its membership, and only five per cent to win and serve the outsider. This, of course, should be reversed. The parish is where it is in order to serve all those who need its ministrations. How does your parish measure up in this respect? How much would it be missed by the community if it did not exist? How pertinent is its program to the needs of your community? What percentage of its time, energy, and effort is put into reaching those who are living without God?

## *On Their Own Level, in Their Own Language*

The third principle, "One does good with people, not to people," is summed up in this brief statement by Jane Addams of Hull House. "The do-gooders," of the early twentieth century have been rightly condemned because they made the fatal mistake of being tainted by the idea that they were superior people, reaching down to help their inferiors. Their work had a patronizing quality. Many of them were busy-bodies. You can find nothing of this in Jesus as he walked among men. He did not hold himself aloof, or reach down to pull others up. He went in and out among all sorts of people, talked to them on their own level and in their own language. He so identified himself with them that his enemies accused him of being a winebibber, of associating with sinners. In striking contrast, our parishes are often insulated from the market-place and the underprivileged. An ordinary person may feel strange and uncomfortable when he attends one of our churches. It has been well said that "a bar-room provides a far more receptive fellowship and therefore is better attended." We can profitably take a leaf out of the book of the fundamentalist sects in this connection. If they start work in an agricultural area, they first establish relationship with the farmers by working with them. Unless we are familiar with the kind of problems facing a machine-operator, or an unskilled worker, or whoever he is to whom we minister, he will find it very difficult—perhaps impossible—to understand what we are trying to say to him. We must learn to talk in terms our people understand, as our Lord so clearly showed us by his homely illustrations and simple parables.

## *Between Church and World—A Bridge*

The Church is beginning to pioneer in this field, in its rural work, its inner-city program, and through its Division of Citizenship. But when I read of the eighty-three billion dollars being spent by the Federal Government, by industry, by medicine, by engineering, and by others, I discover that our Church, in comparison with any one of these, is spending only piddling pennies in the far more significant area of human relationships and spiritual values. Dr. Steinmetz, a research man for the General Electric Company more than a generation ago, challenged the Church by saying, "When the Church has created laboratories for the study of prayer and the people of God, we will see more advance in one generation than we have seen in the past five."

Our failure, however, is not only in lack of research but in the lack of awareness as to how far short we are falling in our efforts; that there is so little deep concern about the fact that we are missing the mark—which is the meaning of the Greek word for sin. Winifred Kirkland in her book, *The Great Conjec-*

*ture,* tells the story of how, one night before Christmas, there suddenly appeared in neon lights on billboards and subway stations of a certain city this simple statement, "Christ will preach in this city tomorrow." This was indeed news. City editors rounded up the available reporters and sent them to all the churches and synagogues. But none of them heard Christ preach. One free-lance reporter went off on his own; and when he did find Christ, he found him on the waterfront talking to the longshoremen—talking to them in their own terms about the Church as a great ship sailing the stormy seas.

There is practically no meeting of minds between those who are immersed in the work of the world and those who are building the programs of our parishes. Somehow this great gulf must be bridged so that traffic can pass between the two, not as from a superior, spiritual group bringing help to an inferior, worldly group, but as two groups seeking together to build the kingdom of God.

## *Identification with the World*

It is an interesting fact to ponder that holiness in the Old Testament is deeply concerned with cleanliness, with keeping apart from contamination of all kinds; while holiness in the New Testament, as set forth by Jesus, emphasizes identification, entering into the suffering of the innocent, bearing the burdens of the weak and afflicted, sharing the gifts that God has given us. Many parishes live in isolation quite apart from the seething problems and pressures that exist in their communities. Juvenile delinquency, or race relations, they read about, discuss, and theoretically are concerned with, but do little about until a youngster active in the life of the parish gets involved in some mess. Then the parish may become deeply concerned. It is greatly handicapped, however, because it was not awake, or aware of the problem until its own self-interest was involved. Under such circumstances, those who have worked long and hard to solve the problem may well wonder how real our concern is, and how deeply we will be interested once the threat to our parish has been removed. And how right they often are, as they note the long history of our short-lived enthusiasms in other fields such as national emergency, or political corruption, or even adequate playgrounds. As soon as the danger has been removed from our doorstep and we have been served, we are satisfied, and return to our petty parish affairs.

## *God Is Not in a Hurry*

Service to others, holiness as entering in to create wholeness —and finally, everlasting patience and persistence. Someone has said, "The trouble is that we are in a hurry and God is not." We Americans especially are impatient. We chafe at a traffic light that slows us down for less than a half-minute, only to squander a half-hour in some silly indulgence; we are irritated when we are not waited upon immediately in a store. We are restless for results. It may be well for us to realize that some things take time to mature; that Rome was not built in a day; that it is going to take time to accomplish some things that we want to accomplish overnight.

One of the handicaps of the Church today is the way the younger clergy move about. The average length of stay in the smaller parishes of my diocese was less than three years. What can a man expect to accomplish in three years? On the surface, he can step up activity; he can make quite a splash in terms of increasing attendance; he can start to build the fabric and then leave some other man the job of paying off the debt. But no man can do much more than scratch the surface of the real work of changing people in three years. Roots of confidence, of mutual understanding, and appreciation take time to grow. Faith needs time to mature. The spirit cannot be developed on a time-clock schedule. One clergyman who had stayed more than twenty years in his parish preached at an ordination service on the subject "If you stay." Then he told most effectively about the joy and satisfaction of a long ministry in a single community, of marrying those he had baptized years before, having watched them grow up; of slowly becoming the father confessor to the whole community.

The matter of timing is far more important than most of us think, not only in allowing time for things to mature, but "cashing in" at the right time. There is a time when the fruit ripens and must be picked; and this is just as true of spiritual fruit. One afternoon I called on a woman who had an inordinately jealous husband. He unexpectedly returned, and I had to make a hasty and undignified retreat before his angry words and threats. I hardly dared to go near the house again. But a little more than a year later he called me. The wife he loved so much had died. Then it was that I had my chance to reach him —a chance that would never come again and could not have been hurried. It is important to lay groundwork in normal times by making friends with people in strategic positions, by coming to know personally city officials, social workers, politicians, and so on. Then when an emergency arises, you will naturally be turned to for advice and assistance. Quiet, behind-the-scenes suggestions, friendly letters, especially of approval to men in public life when they stand for the "hard right against the easy wrong," usually accomplish more in the long run than front-page publicity of condemnation or frantic telephone calls at the last minute.

## *The Parish and Other Churches*

I believe there is the possibility of far greater cooperation than now exists in joining the efforts of other Christian bodies in small towns, without contradicting our faith or compromising our witness. Indeed, we shall receive strength through fellowship with others who worship the same Lord and Master of us all. We pray that we may be given grace seriously to lay to heart "the great dangers we are in by our unhappy divisions," and that we may be delivered from "all hatred and prejudice and whatsoever else may hinder us from godly union and concord." We talk seriously about these problems in the abstract at the upper levels; yet we are terribly backward and fearfully hesitant, and sometimes stubbornly unwilling, to venture forth in the creation of new patterns of cooperation in Christian fellowship at "grass roots."

I am reminded of the woman who was asked how her little mission was faring, and she replied, "The vicar is pathetic, the music is terrible, the congregation has dwindled to about a half-dozen, we are badly in debt—but thank God we are better off than the Baptists!" This is not as absurd as it sounds. In small communities especially, there is very often a competitive spirit between Christian groups which is anything but Christian. Our attitude toward the Roman Catholics is more often antagonistic than not, yet they also are baptized members of Christ's Church. They, too, are trying to extend his kingdom. They, too, are followers of our common Lord and Saviour. There are missions of our Church that are over a hundred years old, and they are still missions. We should be ashamed of such a situation. Too often, we are perpetuating a selfish, ingrown group with no sense of the mission of the Church—spoiling them, as parents sometimes spoil their children, by over indulgence. I feel that one may well call in question the continuing of any mission that has not reached self support within a generation. There are some exceptions to this rule—work in depressed areas, college campuses, work with foreign-born persons—but such work should be the rare exception which proves the rule.

## *Practical Procedures*

These principles which we have been considering should be pinpointed by presenting some practical procedures which I think apply generally to all parishes.

(1) The clergyman should have a regular routine of visiting certain places within the boundaries of his parish, places sometimes forgotten by others—nursing homes, jails, county institutions, state and general hospitals—even if no person on the parish list is known to be in them. Many people there are

lonely, sometimes they are friendless and unchurched. A chaplain who had served for more than ten years in a state institution said there were several hundred patients who had never received a single visitor from outside during his tenure. A new rector came to the local parish and this was quickly remedied, not only by visits, but by transportation to church services and the involvement of the parish in providing fellowship in other ways to these forgotten people.

(2) The clergyman should be willing to spend some of his time on community functions of all sorts—veterans' activities, service clubs, public school graduations, athletic events, United Fund drives, Grange affairs, social agency, and community boards. Sometimes this may seem a waste of time, and this involvement may decrease when the parish priest is well established. But it should be definitely regarded as part of the Christian ministry and understood by the vestry as good public relations for the parish.

(3) By intercessory prayer, by his sermon illustration, and by his general conversation, the pastor must demonstrate that he is genuinely interested in community life.

(4) He should recognize his responsibility to the unchurched in his willingness to share in burial services, hospital visiting, and taking care of the homeless and wanderers; but he should be careful to use all community resources in the way of referral, and cooperate with all welfare agencies to the full. If there is a confidential exchange of information, he should be as ready to provide it as to ask for it.

(5) He should participate in every way possible in all interchurch efforts, and should seek to have friendly relations with Roman Catholic as well as with Protestant clergy.

(6) The laity will make their chief contribution by participation, as Christians and church members, in politics, social agencies, educational affairs, fraternal organizations, service clubs, as well as by the example and witness of regular attendance at church services. The more our church members can involve themselves in the Scouts, Little Leaguers, the Red Cross,

the local hospitals, and the many other interdenominational activities of the community, the more they advance the time of the coming of God's kingdom.

(7) As a tax-free institution, the parish should feel special responsibility for being a community asset by concern for the appearance of parish buildings and grounds. In times of catastrophe, it should open its doors and offer its facilities. It must serve the community in every possible way by lending its buildings to such community organizations as parent-teacher groups, Alcoholics Anonymous, Boy and Girl Scouts, and welfare boards, etc. It must help reach the unchurched through vacation Bible schools, weekday kindergarten, playground with public programs, and an open church on weekdays. It must work with social agencies for the better welfare of the community. The parish should give the rector complete freedom in his service to community needs.

Whether we like it or not, the image of the Episcopal Church in the minds of most communities, especially among the unchurched, is that of a refuge for the economically and socially elite; and there is often too sound a basis for this picture. Most of our parishes do live for the benefit of their membership. This is heresy. The parish must somehow convince the community that it cares for all of them. This will not be easy, because in all too many parishes it simply isn't true. The change can take place only as the leaders of the parish, both clergy and laity, come really to believe that Christ died for *all* mankind. In the last analysis, it is not merely a practical program, it is a matter of theological conviction. Christ came, as he himself said, to minister to the sick and the needy, and not to call the righteous but sinners to repentance.

# 18

# RELEVANT RELIGION: THE PARISH AND THE DIOCESE

As a bishop charged with the responsibility of a diocese, I often have wondered why there was not more protest from the parishes about the payment of their annual assessment. Actually, there was less "griping" about this than there was about the amount of the missionary quota. It is true that the diocesan assessment, if unpaid, has the penalty of disenfranchisement in most dioceses, and so it is considered a tax. Yet, when I looked at the amount of money the larger parishes were assessed for the salary of the bishop and general administrative expenses of the diocese, I asked myself the question, "What is that parish getting for all it pays?" It is true that this is not a Christian standard of measurement, but for many a hard-headed, New England-bred vestryman this was the standard used. Let us look at some of the benefits a parish of the Episcopal Church reaps by belonging to a diocese.

## *Benefits of the Diocesan Assessment*

First, I want to point out that the diocese is the basic unit of our Church. We are an episcopal church with a bishop in charge of each of the dioceses and missionary districts. In addition we have extra-continental missionary districts, and overseas missionary districts—making a grand total, this year, of one hundred and three. Moreover, when I speak of the complaint about the diocesan assessment I would stress the fact that every baptized member of the diocese is a part of the diocese, and through the democratic processes of representation provided, it is decided how much that assessment shall be each year. There can be no just complaint if one believes that the democratic process, with open discussion, is the best government. In our case, the government of the country almost exactly parallels the government of the Church. This was because the majority of the Founding Fathers were Episcopalians. So we have a Presiding Bishop, to match the President; dioceses which in many cases are identical with state boundaries; bishops instead of governors; rectors instead of mayors; advisory boards—the National Council instead of the Cabinet; the Diocesan Council for the Governor's Council—with varying methods of local control, depending upon the size and character of the community. Our loyalty to the Church is in part measured by our loyalty to the group which represents the next higher level of our organization.

At the annual meeting of the parish the delegates to the diocesan convention are elected. These delegates serve as the parish representatives in the legislative body which, under the leadership of the bishop, determines the plans and policies of the diocese, sets the budget and, by canon, provides the machinery by which the work of the diocese may be carried on. This is your means of making effective such suggestions and criticisms as you may have for the conduct of the affairs of the diocese. The convention is a representative body through which the wishes of the parishes and missions are made effective by means of their vote. (It is good practice to have delegates report to the parish on the Sunday following the convention.) This would seem to me to be the first great advantage in the payment of either assessment or quota. It is taxation and apportionment of responsibility through the democratic process with open discussion.

### The Anglican Communion

The second benefit will be less widely recognized and is more intangible—membership in the Anglican Communion. The Anglican Communion is made up of eleven autonomous national churches similar to our own. These reach completely around the world. The Church of England is, of course, the Mother Church, and its history goes back to the very early days. Before the third century there were bishops in England who traced their authority back to the apostles at Jerusalem. When the two small Provinces of Canterbury and York severed their ties with the Roman Church in the middle of the sixteenth century by refusing obedience to the Pope and ridding themselves of many of the abuses in ecclesiastical affairs and ceremonial which had accumulated over the centuries, the Church in England stood alone, reverting to the principles and practices of the Church in the early centuries. Today it remains unique—the only Church in Christendom which is Catholic and yet reformed, constitutional as well as apostolic, national yet world-wide. From the small seed, planted in England, it has expanded to a total of three hundred twenty-one dioceses, and a baptized membership of almost thirty-five million people. These eleven national churches, while autonomous, are held together by: (1) a common faith, the Apostles and the Nicene Creed; (2) a common worship, *The Book of Common Prayer;* and, (3) a common fellowship.

### The Lambeth Conference

This common fellowship is brought into focus, and dramatized approximately every ten years, in the calling of the Lambeth Conference by the Archbishop of Canterbury. The most recent one, in 1958, was attended by more than three hundred bishops from all over the world—black, brown, yellow and white. If you were to have the privilege of attending one, you would understand why I put this first. I was given a new vision of the strength, the diversity, and the world-wide character of our Church. This experience would be hard to secure in any other way than by discovering oneself to be physically a part of so great a fellowship, in which men of widely different points of view, coming from the far corners of the earth, discussed matters of common interest to the Church and to all mankind.

The enlightening report of the Lambeth Conference is published for all to read.

### Support of the Bishop

Third, the assessment helps to pay the salary and expenses of the bishop. Actually, of course, the average parishioner sees his bishop only once a year, when he comes for his visitation. He may not be impressed by this contact and may not feel it is worth the price. The confirmation service may be tedious, the sermon poor, and the bishop somewhat aloof. But what about the intangible benefits of Confirmation with all its historic implications and helpful relationships, together with the gift of God's Holy Spirit which the Church authorizes the bishop to convey through the Laying on of Hands in Confirmation and Ordination? Beyond this, the assessment supports the bishop in many worthy activities about which parish, and sometimes priest, can never know.

### Support for the General Church

Fourth, the diocesan assessment also includes the share of the diocese towards the general administration expenses of the General Church. This part of the assessment is based upon the number of clergy canonically resident in the diocese at the first of the year. This pays part of the expenses and salary of the Presiding Bishop, his travel, and certain other well defined expenses connected with the administration of the Church at headquarters, including the cost of General Convention every three years. It reminds us that we are not simply separate parishes facing the world-wide forces of evil alone, but are a part of a great Church which brings to us spiritual resources and a strengthening fellowship, so that we may stand together to face the destructive and evil forces all over the world.

### Support of Provincial Work

Fifth, the diocesan share of the expenses of the province are usually included in this item. The size of the provincial budget varies greatly from province to province, and they function rather differently in the United States of America from the rest of the Anglican Communion. Our Church here in the United States is divided into eight provinces. This enables dioceses which are close together to work on projects that are of mutual interest and responsibility in particular areas, such as seminaries, radio programs and college work.

### Professional Services

Sixth, the assessment often helps the diocese to employ professional services which are beyond the reach of most parishes —for example, professional help in Christian education, Christian social relations, in publicity and promotion, and the conducting of the Every Member Canvass.

### Direct Services to the Parish

Seventh, there are certain other claims upon the bishop which it is important to note, and which, on special occasions, are worth a great deal to the parish.

(a) When there is a vacancy in the rectorship, the first thing the canons require is that the wardens are to notify the bishop. The parish gains greatly by having his expert advice available. His long experience and wide knowledge in this field can be extremely helpful. He may well save the parish from costly mistakes. The parish, of course, has the last word, as it is they who ultimately choose and elect their rector, but the bishop is ready with resources at your disposal which are beyond price.

(b) When there is disagreement between the rector and the vestry or the parish, again the canons provide that the bishop may be called to help settle the differences and resolve the problems involved. His deep concern and objective judgment can be invaluable in helping to heal parish differences.

(c) The bishop and diocese usually have resources for the borrowing of money. There is often a non-profit holding corporation for the investment of funds. This body usually has on its board of directors men who are able, objective, and often far beyond the ability of a small parish to secure.

(d) In matters of acquiring property and buildings, the diocese has had experience far greater than that of any single parish. The results and resources of these experiences are at the service of any parish. Indeed, as a protection to all (for in the diocese we are one corporate body), it is canonically required that the diocese be consulted in such matters.

(e) Then there is the question of the status of a communicant who has broken some law of the Church, or is "an open and notorious evil-liver," and has wronged "his neighbors by word or deed, so that the Congregation is thereby offended." Such cases of doubt and discipline must be submitted to the bishop, who is to take into consideration the "Godly discipline both of justice and mercy," and who "shall give his judgment to them in writing."

(f) There is usually a diocesan magazine with the subscription charge set below cost in order that people of the diocese may be better informed about diocesan activities. Also, there are tangible resources—books, slides, movies—which few parishes can afford to own but which can be bought by the diocese for the benefit of all. In the Episcopal Church, no parish can be an island unto itself. What happens in one parish is the definite concern of all parishes. We are all part of a team.

## *Summary*

These few facts I would make plain by reiterating them. Everything that happens in any parish in the diocese is of consequence to every other parish and mission in the diocese, just as anything that happens to any member of a family is a matter of deep concern to the whole family. Every parish, therefore, has a stake in who is called to a vacancy, as his coming will either raise or lower the tone of the diocese. If some parish has a destructive fire or other calamity, it should make a difference and be felt in all the parishes. Many parishes will want to make a contribution towards the rebuilding; messages of sympathy will be sent; prayers will be offered. One parish, leveled by a tornado, has an offering every year, on the Sunday nearest the anniversary of the event, in gratitude for the help they received from other parishes near and far. This offering is given to some parish which, during the year has suffered a similar calamity. Thus are we bound closely together in a family.

In this family decisions are made under the leadership of the bishop, the "father in God" of the diocese, on a democratic basis for the good of all. The stronger and more privileged parishes will want to help their sister parishes; the weaker will want to become self-supporting in order to show their appreciation of the help they have received, and will want to help start new work to help people and parishes less fortunate than themselves, not only within the diocese but all over the world. As in every family there are obligations to be met, and advantages and opportunities provided. This is especially true of a diocese, and it is as much the responsibility of the rector and parish, as of the bishop of the diocese, that these should be made known.

19

# RELEVANT RELIGION: THE PARISH AND THE GENERAL CHURCH

It may be a surprise to some who read this that when I began my ministry there was no National Council such as we have today, and the Presiding Bishop was the senior bishop of our Church in order of consecration. I can well remember old Bishop Tuttle, who was bishop from 1867 to 1923, taking part in General Convention when he was well along in his eighties, and so deaf he could not hear anything that was said. It was not until 1919 that General Convention set up the National Council and authorized the election of the Presiding Bishop. For many years he continued his diocesan duties in addition to those of the general Church. This was changed, however, when several bishops in quick succession died while performing this double duty. It was during Bishop Tucker's time that the position was made full-time; and with the election of Bishop Sherrill the Presiding Bishop was elected to serve until his compulsory retirement at seventy years of age. With the election of Bishop Lichtenberger, the General Convention voted to provide a full-time assistant to the Presiding Bishop, to aid him in administrative detail which has grown apace.

## *The National Council*

The National Council is composed of sixteen persons elected by General Convention—four bishops, four presbyters, and eight laymen. Half are elected at each Convention to serve for six years. In addition, there is one representative from each province in the Church, elected by the synod of the province, and four women elected at the Triennial Meeting of the women of the Church. The president, vice-presidents, and treasurer are *ex officio* members of National Council.

This national body is the group which, under the Presiding Bishop, has charge of the "unification, development, and prosecution of the Missionary, Educational and Social Work of the Church."[1] It "exercises the powers conferred on it by Canon, and such further powers as may be designated by General Convention, and between sessions of the General Convention may initiate and develop such new work as it may deem necessary."[2] It also directs "the disposition of the moneys and other property of The Domestic and Foreign Missionary Society," the corporate body before the formation of the National Council. The Council is charged with the responsibility of preparing the budget for each General Convention, which is presented in joint session but is acted on separately by the House of Bishops and the House of Deputies.

The total amount of this budget is then apportioned to the dioceses and missionary districts according to a carefully prepared formula adopted some years ago by General Convention. The formula is based upon "current expenses" carefully defined and slightly weighted to favor the smaller dioceses and missionary districts. In their turn, the dioceses and districts apportion the share assigned them to the various parishes and missions within their jurisdiction, by methods which vary from a flat fixed percentage of "current expenses," to the completely voluntary method of allowing parishes and missions to set their own objective. In recent years there has been a growing recognition of the responsibility not only of giving to the regular on-going work of the Church to meet obligations already assumed, but of providing for advance work. This new work is often dramatized by the selection of some area or person, thus creating personal ties and more intimate understanding of the work being supported.

## *Missions Are Not Extras*

I mention all this because it is important that vestry and parish should know that what is called the "apportionment" or "quota" is not a figure taken out of the air, but is a democratically-determined responsibility to provide that the work of the Church goes forward. The figures assigned represent human beings and institutions which are carrying on the work for us, following the command of Christ to go unto all nations and to all peoples. They are not doing something extra that has been thought of by some bright person. They are the Church at work, and this work lies at the very heart and core of the Christian faith. Everybody who has Christ in his heart is a missionary. Everybody who has not, is a missionary field. It is as simple as that. No one is really a Christian unless he has an evangelistic and missionary spirit. I recall Bishop Slattery telling me of a very rich member of his parish who gave generously to parish support, but not a cent for missions. Her daughter got married and her husband was sent to a small midwestern town. There was no Episcopal Church within twenty miles. The woman came to Bishop Slattery indignant over such a situation. "What was the matter with the Church?" she asked. He simply replied, "The difficulty is that you and others don't give anything to missions." Her generosity was all-inclusive after this personal experience. Christian missions are not something extra.

It is not only that their needs must be met. Our own spiritual health is at stake, because a person or a parish which is not reaching out and growing is inevitably dying. We cannot stand still. Phillips Brooks, asked by a discouraged member of a small and struggling mission how he thought the mission might be revived, replied with the suggestion that they forget themselves and their problems and have an offering for foreign missions. It was sound Christian advice.

## *The Every Member Canvass*

This mention of Phillips Brooks reminds me of a story my father often told. When Dr. Brooks was rector of Trinity Church, Boston, the weather on a certain Sunday in February determined the amount of work the Church could do in China or Japan. In those days, the work of the Church was supported entirely by pew rents, voluntary offerings, endowments, and special efforts such as bazaars. Offering envelopes were unknown. If it happened that a blizzard struck Boston on this February Sunday, and the attendance at Trinity Church was small, the amount of the offering would be equally slim; but if it happened to be a warm, sunny Sunday, the offering would be correspondingly large. All this seems absurd to us today, but it was not until 1919—when The Reverend Robert Patton put on the Nation-Wide Campaign—that the Every Member Canvass came to be a part of the machinery of the Church. In that campaign, which officially introduced this new means of raising funds, the giving of the Church took a great step forward. It was many years, however, before its use became general, and there are still some parishes that have never used it.

In recent years the nature of the Every Member Canvass has been slowly changing. What started as an intensive one-day effort preceded by considerable publicity—with canvassers who were little more than collectors of pledges already prepared—is now in some places an every member visitation which is constant throughout the year, with qualified men and women working on uncommitted Christians, trying to present the work of the Church and the parish in a way that will make the individual want to carry his financial share and give more generously of his time and talents. In recent years, also, there has been a tendency to discard the duplex offering envelopes which would seem to divide the work into two parts—at home and abroad—and have a single envelope and pledge to emphasize the fact that the mission of the Church is one. In this case, however, the minimum obligation, as expressed by the quota, should be the first item on the budget and of first importance, and the last item to be cut if there is a shortage. It is always easier to undervalue those we have never seen, rather than those close at hand. A thousand Chinese are apt to mean less to us than one person in our community. But this is not so in our Lord's eyes. It seems incredible, and is equally shameful, that after 1900 years, forty percent of the world's population still have not heard the name of Christ. The need for missions is not lessening, it is growing. "The state of the world is such that evangelism is the Church's greatest responsibility and privilege. Evangelism is not the task of the few. It is for every Christian." [3] I recall the story of a vestryman who was passing the plate at a missionary rally and who came to a man who refused to put anything on the plate. "I don't believe in missions," he said to the vestryman, to which the latter quickly replied, "Take some then, it is for the heathen."

As a member of the National Council for six years, and for a time chairman of its Department of Finance, and also having served as secretary for the Program and Budget Committee of General Convention, I have had close and intimate relationships with the financial practices of our Church, and am glad to testify that I know of no parish that watches the use of its funds more carefully than the National Council. Of course, mistakes are occasionally made. Inevitably there is some wastage. The larger the undertaking, the more difficult it is to watch every item. Special expenditures are sometimes authorized, which often are a matter of judgment on the value of which people may disagree. But the people of the Church should know there are few more devoted laborers than those who serve in the executive administration of the general work of the Church, or more self-sacrificing and intelligent Christians than those who are elected members of the Council. I wish that clergy, vestries, and people would come to a better understanding of what the apportionment or quota really is, and not regard it (as so often they do) as an obligation to be paid if convenient or as a matter of duty.

## *Apportionment Means Opportunity*

I wish that everyone could see the apportionment as an opportunity expressing the bare minimum, rather than the maximum, that the parish should do. I wish everyone could follow their dollars to their destinations—into the homes, schools and hospitals, and far-flung parishes from Alaska to Liberia, from the Philippines to the West Indies. I wish everyone could see the hardships which men and women are enduring, and the real heroism of many who serve in hard and distant places, carrying on the spreading of the "Good News" (which is our responsibility as much as it is theirs) without which our Church would soon wither and die.

## *The Parish and the World Church*

There are many ways in which the parish relates itself to the work of our Church throughout the world. The Overseas Department of the National Council, and the Overseas Missions Society with offices at the National Cathedral, Washington, are eager to help the clergy and laity know more about and understand more fully the personnel as well as the places of our work at home and abroad. They have a speakers' bureau, literature, slides, and many suggestions for special needs; but they are all of little use unless lay people and clergy make use of them. From time to time, tours are arranged especially to see the work of our Church in various countries. It would be a good investment for a parish to make a practice of subsidising the travel expenses of some faithful parishioner each year, in recognition of devoted work for the parish and in anticipation of the return of added knowledge and broadened horizons.

There is a continuous demand for professional lay workers in the mission fields—teachers, doctors, nurses especially, but occasionally architects or business executives. Lists of such openings are published from time to time in the Church magazines, or can be obtained by writing the personnel officer at National Council.

Prayers for missions, both in public and in private, are effective means of helping this enterprise. Missionaries have often told me how much it has meant to them to know that they were being remembered in prayer at home. A Calendar of Prayer for Missions is available at national headquarters, and its contents, in part or in full, might well be published in the parish bulletin in order to be more readily available.

Lay persons have often said that they have never heard their rector preach a missionary sermon. If this is true, it is tragic. Every sermon should be a missionary sermon in that it should be preached to convert and to win more fully the loyalty and allegiance of the hearer to Christ. The identification of missions with the program of the Church in distant places is a very common misunderstanding. Missions are the very essence of the Gospel. The Church is in the world to carry the "good news" of Jesus Christ everywhere.

## *Our Witness to Others: Abroad*

It is good to know that there is a growing awareness of the great importance of the missionary work of the Church. This is being shown in many ways—by the new approach in the adoption of missionary districts; in the fact that there is a growing exchange of men and women between home dioceses and missionary districts, and that vacation travelers are taking the time and opportunity to see the missionary work of our Church in its various areas. Missionary bishops are laying themselves out in an effort to give these people a chance to see the work in actual operation.

We have been told that there are about 160,000 travelers each year, and that 2,000,000 more represent our country abroad in service or commercial enterprise. In the past, the travelers have gone pleasure-seeking in ways which, for the most part, were a poor advertisement not only for the United States in their common disregard of other people's interests and heritage and by their general attitude of superiority, but more especially in their profession as Christians. A new sense of responsibility in both groups is growing, and is helping to redeem the unworthy image of the United States previously created. Laymen's International, a new organization, has been created to assist all those who go abroad officially by supplying the background of culture and customs in each country. Also, The Episcopal Book Club of Eureka Springs, Arkansas, has a directory of Episcopal churches overseas, as well as one for the United States. Members of our Church ought to take their responsibility seriously by making a special effort to come to know what our Church is doing in the various areas where we are at work, and attending church faithfully on Sunday, wherever they may be. Too many still leave their Church at home when they go on vacation.

This opportunity to witness for our Lord can also be thought of in reverse. There are some forty-thousand foreign students in our midst, and government plans are in the making to push this number up to four-hundred thousand in the near future. They should be given a Christian welcome, invited into our homes, made to feel at home. There are many groups and organizations working on this in the larger centers. Yet I recently received a letter from one of our missionaries saying that some of the young people who had returned to their native land, after three to five years of study in the United States, had never entered a Christian home while they were here.

It is amazing to discover how many of the leaders in the various nations coming to birth have had their education in Christian schools and colleges. They may not have become Christians while there—indeed, many have not. Nevertheless the influence of the teachings of our Lord has made an impression on their lives, and many of the goals they are striving to reach are Christian goals that the Church has failed to achieve in action. These are now being brought about—sometimes in ways of which we greatly disapprove and which contradict the Christian faith; but advances have been made in education, in health, and in land reform, and we must admit they represent achievements which, over the long years, we have failed to realize.

### At Home

There are many other areas where the parish must cooperate with the general Church in the discharge of its ministry. For instance, we have our ministry to those away from home in the armed forces and in colleges. Both are most important and strategic areas where the Church must do its utmost to provide a Church home. Our Anglican Communion has a special advantage here because of its world-wide use of *The Book of Common Prayer*. Wherever our Church may go, the stranger at once has the comfortable feeling of being at home as he recognizes the familiar features of altar, pulpit, lectern, and nave; as he listens to the same prayers in which he was nurtured and joins in the responses and hymns which he has said and sung so often. It is true that there may be some differences, but those differences may be no greater than those between two parishes in the same town back home. Behind and beneath them, one cannot help but know and recognize the fundamental unity of the Church.

These are but a few ways in which the parish has a part in the life and work of the General Church, and in which the General Church is dependent upon the people of the parish. Rector, vestry, and people may profitably spend time in learning about other areas.

## *Conclusion*

All these fields of service, and a great many more, should be common knowledge to the clergy and people of our parishes, but they are not. The ancient and long outgrown image of the missionary being fed to the cooking-pot by the savages still remains, only perhaps slightly modified by the fact that most of the places where we work have been partly westernized so that the pot has been displaced by more polite forms of hostility. Where our best work is being done, however, this is far from true because there are many people who are hungry physically and spiritually, who plead for more men and women who will train and teach their own people so that they may have their own Church. Indeed, the whole understanding of "Missions" is changing, so that no longer is it thought of as "privileged people" being helpful to underprivileged people, in a "do-good" attitude, but rather as an exchange by which we receive as much from them as they from us. It is the "Mission of the Church" wherever it is, to spread the Gospel; and there are missionary opportunities and unconverted people in every parish of this land—and, indeed, within most vestries.

Just what your part and place in this whole scheme of affairs is, I cannot tell you. You alone can discover that by prayer and thought and counsel. In this connection, I am reminded of a story told about George Washington Carver, the great scientist who, at a time when the cotton crops of the South were being plowed under as unmarketable, gave to the South a new crop which helped to save the economy of that area. Born in direst poverty out of wedlock, so it is said, as a boy he had little or nothing of this world's goods or opportunities. He did, however, have an insatiable curiosity. One day he went off by himself and climbed a hill, and because no one was with him, he began to ask God questions. The first was, "God, why did you make the world?" There was silence at first, and then the answer seemed to come to him, "You're only a little boy, George Washington, and that's too big a question for a little boy like you." So he offered a second question, "God, why did you make me?" Again there was silence, and then an answer came to him again. "You're only a little boy, George Washington, and that's too big a question for you." So he tried a third time. "Well," said he, "why did you make the peanut?" This time the answer came more quickly. "Now that's just about your size, George Washington; why don't you try to find out?" So George Washington Carver became a distinguished scientist and discovered more than a hundred new uses for the peanut, and it became the chief industry of the area where he lived and helped to provide more stable work for his people.

The problems of the present state of the world are too great for any one to solve alone—even too great for any one nation—but each one of us has been given a part in the solution. It may be a very small and humble responsibility, or it may be one of considerable influence. What we have to do is really quite simple—just give our very best to our "peanut" in the sight and service of our Lord.

---

REFERENCES

1. Canon 4, Section 1 (a)
2. Canon 4, Section 1 (c)
3. Lambeth Conference Report, part 2, page 75

20

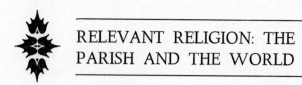

# RELEVANT RELIGION: THE PARISH AND THE WORLD

In the past twenty years we have entered a completely new era. During the second world war the United States exploded two atomic bombs which put every other explosive out of date. For the first time in history man has within his hands his own self-destruction. This power is not limited to a single person or to a small group of responsible people. It is widely spread so that irresponsible people, people of different goals and values than ours, can push a button causing devastating destruction. It is even possible that, quite unintentionally, a chain reaction may be started through human error. We all live under a world-wide threat of extinction in any hour, any minute.

What the angels sang at our Saviour's birth—the preservation of peace on earth and the spreading of good will among men—is now a "must" item with entirely new dimensions. War has become obsolete almost overnight, and no nation can ever again win one. Scientists and generals and statesmen are all agreed on this. The Church has an unequalled challenge and opportunity to meet this issue and provide the spiritual force which is the only answer to our plight.

## *Three Stars of Hope*

In this dark and uncertain hour I see three bright stars in the sky. The first is that we are coming to recognize that the strong church is the missionary church. "The light that shines farthest shines brightest at home." We are, St. Paul tells us, "ambassadors for Christ." We represent our Master, Jesus Christ, and are plenipotentiaries of His Church. It is a tremendously exacting and demanding responsibility. We are on the growing edge, in the front line. It may seem strange to say, but I firmly believe that one of the greatest handicaps to the growth of the Church in these days is its fabric and its endowments. Today we have become largely a maintenance organization often living on the bounty of the past, rather than a great spiritual fellowship of world-wide dimensions. Look back to the early days of the Church during the time of the apostles, and a century or two later, when the Church was at its strongest, when it was "turning the world upside down." Then it was hated and persecuted by those in authority, because they feared it. The Church had no fabric or endowments then, its membership was chiefly among the underprivileged and the dispossessed; but its influence was great and its witness bright. The apostles and their helpers were on fire with the Good News of Jesus Christ, and nothing could stop them from spreading it wherever they went. They were contagious Christians. They were bold beyond belief. They were not afraid to confront those in high authority. They were loving—so loving that others remarked "Look how these Christians love one another." They were missionary-minded and there was no difficulty or hardship which they were not willing to endure in order to spread the Gospel. It is heartening to see this resurgence of a real missionary spirit moving within the Church. Our sights are being lifted and once again the Church is on the march. The Anglican Communion is coming to recognize its world-wide task.

After the second world war, *Fortune* magazine carried an editorial which was based on the result of a questionnaire sent out to hundreds of men in positions of high responsibility, asking them what they thought was the solution of the world's ills. *Fortune* then summarized the general conclusions of the replies in an editorial from which we quote:

"So long as the Church pretends, or assumes to preach, absolute values, but actually preaches relative and secondary values, it will merely hasten this process of disintegration. We are asked to turn to the Church for our enlightenment, but when we do so we find that the voice of the Church is not inspired. The voice of the Church today, we find, is the echo of our own voices. And the result of this experience, already manifest, is disillusionment. There is only one way out. The way out is the sound of a voice, not our voice, but a voice coming from something not ourselves, in the existence of which we cannot disbelieve. It is the earthly task of the pastors to hear this voice, to cause us to hear it, and to tell us what it says. If they cannot hear it, or if they fail to tell us, we, as laymen, are utterly lost. Without it we are no more capable of saving the world than we were capable of creating it in the first place." [1]

It is good to have a secular magazine provide us with an editorial of this sort to tell us that hard-headed businessmen, matter-of-fact industrialists, materially-minded bankers, recognize that the answer is not to be found in physical force; that the ancient truth is as true today as when it was written of old—"Not by might, nor by power, but by my spirit, saith the Lord of hosts" [2]; that the ultimate answer is not massive retaliation but massive redemptive love which reaches out and out, and proves its concern by its provision of food for that half of the population of the world which every night goes to bed hungry; by opening doors of freedom to those who have been enslaved by the primary demand of keeping alive from day to day; and by bringing light to those who sit in darkness.

The Church needs prophets these days who will call men to rise to their best and who, like people of old, "out-thought, out-lived, out-loved and out-died" their contemporaries. The great "expeditionary force" of this century is made up of the lay and ordained missionaries who are carrying the Gospel into far lands and hard places. They represent the forces of the Spirit, the front line of attack which in the long last will be victorious. There is no justification for a parish which is not projecting the Faith far beyond its local boundaries; and the truest picture of its spiritual health is revealed in how fully it is accomplishing this. "The world for Christ in this generation," the slogan of a generation gone by, may seem naive in the present time, but it showed a passion and a vision which is coming alive again today.

### Unity and Cooperation

The second star of hope which I see upon the horizon is the drawing together of the Churches in cooperative endeavor and in common unity. The late Archbishop Temple summarized this when he said, "As though in preparation for such a time as this, God has been building up a Christian fellowship which now extends into almost every nation, and binds citizens of them all together in true unity and mutual love. . . . It is the great new fact of our era." [3]

May 12, 1938 is a date to remember. On that day representatives of the League of Nations met in Geneva, and bowed to force in the exclusion of Ethiopia from the league—thus beginning its ultimate dissolution. But on that very same day, representatives of the Churches met at Utrecht, Holland, and gave birth to the constitution of the World Council of Churches. This was the result of almost a century of preparation.

After the Reformation in the sixteenth century, it looked as if the Church was to be split into smaller and smaller fragments; but about a century ago the tide turned. A spirit of outreach toward cooperation between Churches and union of Churches was born, and the ecumenical movement started on its way. The original meaning of "ecumenical" was "the whole family of God throughout the world." To many, the most important thing that is happening in the world today is that, while the nations of the world have been fragmentizing through nationalism, racialism, and economic and cultural tensions, the Churches have been growing together. As Temple says, "This is the great new fact of our era." I believe it is one of the ways in which God is trying to speak to us in this generation.

By 1854, the growing foreign missionary work of the various Churches had reached a point at which it was important to have cooperation take the place of competition, and there was a meeting in New York which resulted eventually in the formation of the Union Missionary Convention. This was the first of a series of Conferences which led to the calling of a World Missionary Conference in Edinburgh in 1910. At the opening service, our own Bishop Brent pointed out that "the world is too strong for a divided Church," and continuing committees were appointed which brought about subsequent conferences which followed three general lines. The first, and most swiftly moving, was that of missionary cooperation which produced the International Missionary Council and National Christian Councils in many countries; and its great landmarks are the meeting in Jerusalem in 1928, and the one in Madras in 1938. The second is known as the Movement of Faith and Order, resulting in the conferences held at Lausanne in 1927, and at Edinburgh in 1937. The third is known as the Movement of Life and Work which was responsible for the conference at Stockholm in 1925, and at Oxford in 1937. After the 1937 conferences, the two latter streams flowed together, and at the meeting in May of 1938 agreed on a constitution for a World Council of Churches.

War broke out before a meeting could be held to organize, and it was not until 1948 at Amsterdam that the World Council of Churches actually came into being. During the war it proved its vitality and worth. Throughout the turmoil of this period, in spite of the barriers of censorship and travel, there was a fellowship and concern which undergirded the common bond uniting the Churches in Christ, and transcended man-made barriers. "Strangely enough," said Bishop Berggrav, "it was precisely in our isolation, when all legal communication with the outside world was forbidden, that we in Norway really learned for the first time the meaning of "ecumenical," which is the living, inner fellowship of Christians in the world." It was a peasant woman who, bringing him a bottle of milk one day, whispered to him, "My husband listened yesterday to the forbidden radio and he heard the Archbishop of Canterbury pray for you." Martin Niemoeller also told of his father visiting him in prison and saying, "Be of good hope, Martin; Christians all over the world are praying for you. I myself heard the Archbishop of Canterbury pray for you," over B.B.C.

In 1948, at Amsterdam, when the World Council met for the first time, they said, "We intend to stay together. We call upon Christian Congregations to endorse and fulfill this covenant in their relations one with another."[4] When the World Council of Churches was born, there were one hundred and forty-seven holding membership. Today, the Council unites one hundred seventy-eight Anglican, Orthodox and Protestant communions in fifty-three countries. That this movement is not merely a "flash in the pan" in the upper levels, is seen by the fact that here in the United States at the present time there are more than one thousand local Councils of Churches and two thousand interdenominational groups of Church women.

Federation of this sort, however, is not the same thing as organic unity, the ultimate goal. Progress is being steadily made in this area, and from 1938 to 1953 there were thirteen organic unions within family groups. For example, Methodists have united to found the largest single Protestant communion in the United States, with over eight million members; two million more are still divided among nineteen smaller Churches. One can foresee in our lifetime the possible merging of the largest of the present two hundred and fifty Protestant Communions into six or eight major Church bodies. There were six mergers that crossed family grouping, and there are sixteen negotiations now in progress. How "live" a subject this is can be shown by the fact that a national radio hook-up asked the question, "Is a united Protestant Church possible now?" They expected at best only average interest in terms of replies. Instead, they received the heaviest mail of any broadcast that season, and ninety-four per cent of the answers were a resounding "yes."

There is one weakness impeding the movement which the local parish can help to correct: although ecumenicity draws the Churches together at the top, it has failed to draw them together as fully at the local level. The 1958 Lambeth Conference had this to say, "We call upon all clergy and people to break out of the isolation and introversion of much of our church life and seek by every means to establish brotherly relationships and contacts, and to share perplexities and burdens, that we may be one with our Christian brethren of other traditions in Christ's mission to the world." [5]

A recent Conference of Youth at Geneva was attended by fourteen hundred young people from fourteen countries all over the world. These young people stated, "As long as we have self-centered local churches we must not expect to advance toward a Christ-centered universal Church, living in fellowship and rendering a united witness to the world. We must fight the ecumenical battle where that battle is hardest—in the ordinary life of the ordinary congregation."

The World Council long ago adopted the general principle that they would do together everything except what irreconcilable differences or sincere conviction compelled them to do separately. The time has come when we should ask ourselves on the local level if this is what we are doing. Is your parish fully cooperating in every Christian endeavor with others in your community, except when deep theological convictions, and not merely traditional practice or personal prejudice, prevent? Is your parish aroused and concerned about the fact that a divided Church can hardly witness effectively in bringing about a united world? It may well be said, "Physician, heal thyself." Is your parish *really* troubled over the fact that Christ prayed that we all might be one, and yet we are so far from being one in Christ? These are questions which every parish—and every person in every parish—should seriously take to heart!

### The Failure of War

The third guiding star of hope which I see is man's new effort to discover a moral alternative to war. For more than a generation now the great Christian conferences have proclaimed: "War involves compulsory enmity, diabolical outrage against human personality, and a wanton distortion of the truth.

War is a particular demonstration of the power of sin in this world and a defiance of the righteousness of God as revealed in Jesus Christ and him crucified."[6]

"War as a matter of settling international disputes is incompatible with the teaching and example of our Lord Jesus Christ. We believe that as the Christian conscience has condemned infanticide, slavery, and torture, it is now called to condemn war as an outrage on the Fatherhood of God and the brotherhood of mankind."[7] We say these things. We adopt these resolutions in our highest representative assemblies, and then we proceed to forget them, on the basis that war seems the lesser of two evils. But what greater evil is there than the enmities which war breeds when it calls for the wholesale slaughter of innocent men, women, and children; when to lie is patriotic, killing common, and hate methodically taught. Some claim that war is a necessity in a world that is bristling with military might, that it is the only language our enemies can understand. Can't we realize that every step we take to strengthen our own security is a threat to their security? Air bases all over the world can never contain Communism. They serve merely as an illusion, like the famous Maginot line.

The Church is not the State. The State has responsibilities quite different from the Church. The state may perhaps justify its resort to force in a way which the Church of Jesus Christ can never do. It is the State's responsibility to preserve the nation and to protect its citizens. It is the Church's responsibility to follow the life and teachings of Jesus Christ, and to trust in God for the consequences. The Church should be the agency which gives the dynamic to civilization, that helps to shape it anew. We are called to live in the world and yet not be of the world. Our responsibility is to "live with our heads in heaven" and yet keep our feet firmly on the earth; to live by faith, not beset by fear. As Diognetus said long ago, "What the soul is to the body, Christians are called to be in the world. The soul is distributed in every member of the body, and Christians are scattered in every city in the world. The soul dwells in the body, and yet is not of the body. So Christians live in the world, but are not of the world." We are called to lift and leaven life, not to preserve the *status quo*.

It must have seemed to the disciples that all had been lost, that everything they had hoped, and dreamed, and lived for had been swept away on that first Good Friday; but on Easter Day their faith was restored, their hopes fulfilled, and their lives filled with supernatural power and strength. They went out—a small band of simple people without influence, wealth, or position—and changed the whole direction and current of history.

I get very irritated about the present-day emphasis upon adjustment to the ways of the world, of "peace of mind" as a desirable quality, of acceptance of things as they are. The Church is called to be *different,* Christians are called to be different. The Church must set itself against the ways of the world. When the Church really fulfills its task, it will inevitably be persecuted; but didn't Christ say "Woe unto you when all men speak well of thee?" [8] Somehow, the Church must disentangle itself from the war system. The State has its special function, and the Church—the Body of Christ—has its function, and they are not the same. It may not be possible at the present moment for the State to completely disarm itself, in that we have entered into commitments which cannot be disregarded—although a surprise approach of this sort, even on a unilateral basis, might prove to be a moral jujitsu which would throw our enemies off balance and produce a new and much more peaceful climate for peaceful negotiation. The Church, however, has quite a different function, and should make clear that Christ said "Love your enemies . . . pray for them that persecute you . . . for if ye love them that love you, what reward have ye? do not even the publicans the same? What do ye more than others?" [9] But you reply, "This is a counsel of perfection; this doesn't, cannot work in a world such as ours." How *do* you make the world better—by striving after perfection in spite of its seeming impossibility, or by yielding to its standards and being satisfied with imperfection? How else can the pattern of hate being met with more hate—armaments being met by stronger armaments—be broken except through ventures of faith beginning in more limited areas and eventually developing from them into wider spheres, as happened in the early centuries?

The House of Bishops, in its Pastoral Letter of 1930 said, "We urge upon you, the people of the Church, to dare to do some of the things that Jesus Christ died to make real in Christian daily living. If it is a question of compromise between honesty and anything else, dare to do the honest thing. What if it is costly? Are we followers of Christ or not? That is the final question. Let us not be misled by the false slogan of 'my Country right or wrong.' Dare to meet intolerance with good will. Christ's way is the only way for the Church, the only way for a world in need. Stand alone if we must; become a fool, if it is necessary. Let us dare to do the thing that counts . . . Let us practice what our religion stands for." These words are not mine, they are the words of the bishops of the Church. Are they to be merely words, or will we as individuals accept the challenge they set before us?

## *Tension in the Christian Life*

When it comes down to what the Christian, who is also a citizen, is to do at a particular time and place, there is bound to be tension. It is not a clear case of black and white, good and bad; there are innumerable shades of gray. Every man must decide for himself. Is it more Christian for us to allow people to be ruthlessly attacked and do nothing to protect them, or to go to war to beat back the enemy? How about self-defense: Shall we do nothing to protect ourselves? Rather, should we not prepare by being so fully armed that the enemy will not dare to attack? And if he does, is it Christian to retaliate in revenge and to wipe him out? Can a man love and, at the same time, kill his enemy? And why is this man I do not know, my enemy, and I, his enemy?

There are no easy answers. There is no final authority other than that which comes to each individual as he wrestles in his inner chamber to discover Christ's answer for him. But this is very different from merely following popular opinions or yielding to outward pressures. It takes courage to face the enemy in the field, and it takes courage to have different opinions and convictions from those about us. We need to do some very new thinking on some very old problems, and the hopeful factor is that this has actually begun to take place. It is no longer a question of war or subjection and submission.

## The Way of Non-violent Resistance

There is a third way—the way of non-violent resistance. A fact pretty well accepted by historians is that for the first three centuries no Christians served in the military forces. The early Fathers also bear testimony to this. And the pagan Celsus, in 178 A.D., reproaches Christians for their unwillingness to join the army. The great change came with the conversion of Constantine in 312; and in 314 the Council of Arles reversed an early position by enacting a canon which actually brought a censure on those who refused to serve. Yet, through the centuries, there always have been small groups of men and women who have clung to the interpretation of the early Church. It remained for George Fox, a Quaker of the late seventeenth century, to restate the case of non-violent resistance when he said, "I told them I knew from whence all wars arose, even from lust . . . and that I lived in the virtue of that life and power that took away the occasion of all wars." Since that time other groups such as the Mennonites and the Brethren have held the same position. However, it was not widely recognized until Gandhi—himself never baptized as a Christian but quoted as saying he would have been, if Christians had lived more like their Master—brought it to public attention all over the world by his actions in South Africa and more especially in India when he used non-violent resistance as a protest against the rule of the English. Still more recently it has come into prominence in this country when Martin Luther King and his followers succeeded in using it to break segregation in busses in

Montgomery, Alabama, and even more recently in the large number of sit-down demonstrations in restaurants in many communities.

To regard this as a new technique is a mistake. If it is to rest on sound foundations, it must be based upon our own conception of God as the Father of us all, and of Jesus Christ who chose the cross rather than lead a rebellion against the Romans, as he was urged to do, to restore the Jews to their rightful place and heritage. It must also be based upon firm belief in the Resurrection and in the power of the Spirit as greater than worldly power. Today the fear that the cold war will suddenly erupt into a shooting war, which in turn will lead to a world cataclysm, is all about us. We live in an age which, as I have said, has opened up new dimensions of power, and of opportunity; and we need to learn to think in entirely new dimensions. In the olden days war was on a limited scale. There were even some rules by which it was conducted. Now all is changed. There was a day when wars could be won by one side or the other. This is no longer true. War is total. The difference between defense and aggression has become hairline. Some new approach is demanded.

## *New Methods for New Conditions*

Centuries ago men were convinced that the world was the center of the universe; and when Copernicus announced that this was not true he was denounced as a heretic. Now men wonder how human beings could have been so stupid and the Church so bigoted. The same thing might be said about other evils which the Church has accepted and even supported—child labor, slavery, colonialism, torture. Now the Church has openly declared that war is contrary to the teaching and example of Jesus Christ. Now professors and military authorities are recognizing the futility of using old methods to meet new conditions. Professor C. Wright Mills, professor of sociology at Columbia University, in his book, *The Causes of World War Three,* says, "We are at the very end of the military road. It leads nowhere but to death. With war, all nations will fall . . . War has become total. And war has become absurd . . . Retaliation has become massive nonsense." General Omar Bradley has said, "Our knowledge of science has already outstripped our capacity to control it. We have too many men of science; too few men of God. We have grasped the mystery of the atom and rejected the Sermon on the Mount . . . The world has achieved brilliance without wisdom, power without conscience. Ours is a world of nuclear giants and ethical infants. We know more about war than we know about peace, more about killing than we know about living." [10] And Commander Sir Stephen King-Hall, in his book, "*Defence in the Nuclear Age*" writes, "Defence has been revolutionized materially but remained mentally stagnant . . . We must break through the thought-barrier in defence thinking, a thought-barrier represented by the centuries old idea of most people that violence is the only practical means of defence against violence." Then he goes on to recommend that England abandon the use of nuclear energy for military purposes, gradually reduce its armed forces, and develop "a comprehensive scheme for the defence of our way of life by non-violent resistance and positive psychological action against Communism." His reasoning is that we cannot defend human personality by destroying other human personalities; we cannot defend the sanctity of life by killing; we cannot remain as Christians while we act as beasts.

These frank, bold statements put to shame the weak words of Christians and the Church. It is true that, as Christians, we do not assume that the kingdom of God depends upon the preservation of our present civilization, or even that the essence of Christianity is the elimination of war. But neither can we accept the conclusion that the extinction of the human race is better than to be subject to the Soviet or any other tyranny. Christ scorned the suggestion made by his followers that he call down fire from heaven on his enemies—as we would by massive retaliation. Christians down through the ages have faced the harsh reality of evil without despair precisely because they have always regarded evil as an intruder in God's universe, not originally built into the world's creation. The deaths of the martyrs have been the seed-corn of the future.

What I am trying to say is not that we should all immediately become pacifists. That might indeed bring on a calamity—although it might produce reactions and results which would be unbelievably positive and creative. What I do say is that we should free ourselves from the thought-patterns of the past, by which violence was always met by violence. We must do some original and creative thinking and acting more in line with Christ's teaching. Thus shall we help to create a new climate in which relationships would be established on the foundation of faith rather than on fear, on concern for others rather than on selfishness, on good will rather than on ill will. Just how this can be implemented into the international sphere, I am not prepared or competent to say; although I would point out that the Quakers and the World Council of Churches are doing much to embody such a program. However, we can begin in our churches, our parishes, our homes, to try to develop this spirit of good will which the angels tell us is the essential condition of peace on earth. Parishes in which contention exists will drive away many more than modern techniques can pull in. Divided homes are a poor example for those who are looking for a Christian family. Perhaps you have heard the prayer of the little girl, "O God, please make all bad people good, and good people easier to live with!"

Just what your part is in the building of peace I cannot spell out; but these two things I know. If our Church fails in our time, it will not be because our leaders have been stoned, but because our culture has so domesticated and softened our Christianity that we worship its idols of power, popularity, and possessions—while in our liturgy we continue to worship God the Father of our Lord Jesus Christ. We have failed to put our liturgy into our life. Secondly, what we profess in theory is far from what we actually practice. The American Institute of Public Opinion recently concluded a poll in which they asked: (1) whether a person considered religion of first importance; and then (2), taking those who answered "yes," asked a second question, "Would you say your religious beliefs have any effect on your ideas of politics and business?" Fifty-four per cent said "No!" At least we have fifty-four per cent who are honest, because I am afraid that a large proportion of the other forty-six per cent are falling far short of their Christian profession in their daily relationships.

In the face of all the fears and uncertainty that surround us, I would leave the words of the wise man who, when asked if he was afraid, said, "I have loved the stars too long to be afraid of the night." Let us remember that above these three stars of hope —missionary endeavor, ecumenical growth, and the approach of non-violence—there is the Star of Bethlehem which led wise men to their Lord.

---

REFERENCES

1. *Fortune,* January, 1940
2. Zechariah 4:6
3. Temple, *Daily Readings* (1948), pages 212-213
4. First Assembly Message, World Council of Churches, 1948
5. Lambeth Conference Report, 1958
6. Oxford Conference
7. Oxford Conference
8. Luke 6:26
9. Matthew 5:44,46
10. Gen. Omar Bradley, Address to Boston Chamber of Commerce, Nov. 10, 1948

# EPILOGUE

I mentioned in the preface that one of the reasons why, as a boy, I did not want to go into the ministry was because I wanted to make my own way and not be simply a pale reflection of my father, who was a bishop. I have learned many things since then, not the least of these being that as life goes on, with individuals as well as in society, not only are the sins of the fathers visited upon the children unto the third and fourth generation, but also the blessings of our fathers—their influence, example, and inheritance—pursue and encompass their descendants from generation to generation. I want to acknowledge my very real gratitude for all the blessings I received from my mother and father.

## *God Is Here and Now*

The first and most important blessing I received was the truth that God was not an abstract being and power of the past, but is a very vital reality in the present. As he was at work in the time of the Hebrews, so he is at work here and now; and belief in him should make a very definite difference in our lives. My father had little patience with the hypocrisy of people who went regularly to church but who didn't pay their bills. For my father, and so for me, God inevitably reveals himself in the way a man lives his everyday life. Religion seeps down to such simple things as a man's manners. My father had no more respect for the hypocrites of his day than the Lord had for those of his day, who made long prayers but who bound heavy burdens on men's shoulders—whose actions contradicted their words. Religion was for him, and has been for me, a "down-to-earth" affair. Of course, there is also a place for the mystical and supernatural. God is indeed in his heaven, to be worshipped and adored. But things definitely are not all right with the world, and his kingdom cannot come until his will is done on earth as it is in heaven.

## *People Are Important*

Secondly, my father taught me that people are all-important, far more important than wealth or popularity or position; that people are intensely interesting, challenging, and exciting because every person is different from every other person. He felt that by listening to what people said, and loving people, one can usually learn as much as, if not more than, by reading books. Not that books should be neglected—for it is important to know what people thought and taught through the ages—but knowledge only becomes relevant as it serves as a background for our understanding of people today. Reading biography was, for him, the best way of learning history. At every great crisis in history one finds an outstanding personality who embodies in his life and teaching new principles which only take root as they spread from person to person. One of the primary requirements of a useful and successful ministry was for him, as it is for me, a love for and an understanding of people as individuals.

## *Thankfulness*

Thirdly, he taught me that thankfulness for God's blessings is a very important cornerstone of Christian living. In the sermon which he preached at my consecration he said, "I believe that the strongest and finest motive of a worthy life is that of gratitude to God, in the name and life of his son Jesus Christ, for his goodness. 'A life of grateful service' was a favorite phrase of

Phillips Brooks. 'Bless the Lord, O my soul, and all that is within me, bless his holy name' [1] is a happy morning song. Thus in the midst of heavy labor, distress or confusion, the heart is calm, the life confident and serene, and the undertone is one of joy." Then, again, when he came to the close of his sermon—where it is customary for the preacher to speak to the ordinand personally, and he usually prefaces this portion by saying "My brother"—he said "My son, My father used to say to me again and again, 'no man has ever been blessed throughout life as I have been.' Of all his blessings, this one stands high—that you were able to take up this refrain into your life. With the confidence of the people of the diocese which will, I know, ripen into affection, you will go in and out amongst them, carrying the gospel of joyful, grateful service, singing to yourself, 'Bless the Lord, O my soul, and all that is within me, bless his holy name.' "

## *Serenity*

Fourth, my father retired from the active ministry while he was still in vigorous health. He felt that he could exercise his ministry in other ways—less active, perhaps, and not so subject to the compulsion of the daily routine of scheduled duties—set at a slower pace and at a deeper level. This later ministry was a tremendously significant one as he effectively perpetuated the wisdom he had accumulated over the years by transmitting it to those who constantly came to consult with him on all sorts of matters. His last years were permeated with a security and serenity which can only come out of the distillation of a long life which has weathered the many storms and come through victorious. This quality of life is greatly needed during this disturbing era. The concluding words of his address at the time of the celebration of his thirtieth anniversary as bishop, as given in his book, *Harvest of Happy Years,* gives a wonderful summary of his deepest convictions. "To me, as I get older, life is more and more a venture; and the secret of that venture is that I am living; that I have spiritual forces within me as well as a material body; that I am a man; that he whom we call God . . . has given me a touch of his spirit. How do I know this? Can I prove it? No. I know it by faith, and a faith that has been tested by experience: millions on millions of people have tested it by experience, and hold to it as their very life . . . The real thing is that life has a meaning, an aim and a source of power untold . . . I know that my Heavenly Father is Love, Justice and Truth. I believe that Jesus Christ lived that I might learn of him, follow him, pass through the gates of death with him . . . With this clear and final, what have I to fear from man, misfortune, disease, or sorrow? In perfect faith one may live on toward the setting of the sun, tranquil and in perfect serenity."

## *More Wise Words*

There were other wise words which he passed on to me, far less important than these four great foundation-stones already mentioned, but they have stood me in good stead and I am glad to pass them on to others.

The first is, Never make an important decision in the middle of the night, when perhaps you have laid awake worrying about some problem or person. He pointed out how, at that time, one's vitality is apt to be at a low ebb. When the morning comes with its sunlight, and the refreshment of sleep has revived our powers, we are in a much better position to make the right decision. The explorer Nansen, I am told, had a similar phrase when he said, "Never make an important decision when you are afraid." A lesser reflection of the same principle, although somewhat in reverse, was his injunction that when you have written an angry letter, or committed yourself to a responsibility which may be long and hard to discharge, put the letter aside and "sleep on it." The next day you will look at it afresh, and probably be glad you didn't send it. Second thoughts are usually better than immediate reactions. More than once, when I have failed to heed this, I have regretted my impulsive words or action. You will find, too, that sometimes the mere writing of a letter, putting your resentments down in black and white, will relieve the pressure of resentment and draw away some of the bitterness that has gathered within you. Persons who speak quickly, before they have had a chance to think the matter through, almost always get into trouble. I think it was Lincoln who said, "Better remain silent and be thought a fool, than to speak out and remove all doubt."

More wise advice was contained in his counsel, "Never move on small margins." By that he meant, if there should be a division of opinion in the vestry or the parish, and the matter comes to a head in a vote that is close, it is far wiser to be patient and postpone proceeding with the action authorized, than it is to go forward on the basis of the small margin of endorsement. This is but an adaptation of the wisdom embodied in the more familiar phrase which counsels that "a leader should never seem to get too far ahead of his troops." Yet this is precisely what so many clergymen appear to do, leaving a great gulf between themselves and the laity. There are few things more apparent in most parishes than the two quite different worlds in which clergy and laity live. The clergy have a consuming interest in intangible values; their thoughts are often set in abstract terms, and they live in a world of relationships and deal with supernatural things. They even talk a different language, assuming that the laity know what is meant by "redemption," "ecumenical," "incarnation." The laity live very definitely among material things; they deal with statistics and hard, cold facts. They are daily confronted by secular standards and values. The philosophy which underlies a private enterprise is based on the theory of "the survival of the fittest"—the fittest being the successful, the rich, the powerful, and those in high positions, rather than contagious, radiant Christians. This is almost a complete contradiction of a faith which tells us to bear one another's burdens, to help the weak and the handicapped, to give oneself for the sake of others. It is for this reason that I have continually stressed in this book the importance of open and free discussion in order to bridge this gulf; of thinking and planning together; of developing a greater understanding of these diametrically different goals. Clergy and laity must come to recognize the fact that each has a special contribution to make to the total picture.

A different aspect of the same principle of not moving on small margins, revealed itself through the besetting sin from which I have never wholly freed myself—trying to cram too many engagements into my schedule so that there is no margin for the unexpected, or proper time for reflection. The result is that life sometimes becomes very hectic, quality is sacrificed to quantity, and depth is sacrificed by the pressure to spread oneself too thin over too many activities and responsibilities.

Another bit of advice that I treasure comes from a time when he told me, after I had failed to get a contribution from a man I knew was amply able to make it, "If you present a worthy cause to a man and he does not respond as you think he ought to, don't blame him, blame yourself for not having presented the cause in the way he would understand, or with an attractiveness that would win his approval." Christ called his disciples to be "fishers of men," and men are far more elusive than fish: they have the power not only to run away and hide, but to rationalize their failures by blaming others, and fail to see themselves by looking in the wrong direction. We need to be far more skilled than most of us are in this art of winning men. I am reminded of the man who, falling sick while traveling, was reached and converted to the Christian faith by the clergyman who visited him while he was in the hospital. When he returned to his home, full of the enthusiasm of a new convert, he couldn't help but chide his regular golfing partner (a vestryman of his parish) for never once having spoken to him about his religion, or even asked him to attend his parish church. How many of us are equally blameworthy?

In closing, I would like to contribute three suggestions. My first is to the clergy. *Pray without ceasing.*[2] I do not mean merely to say your prayers. I mean that you must have that "soul's sincere desire" which penetrates every aspect of our life. Some people think that action is the important thing, and prayer helps. Actually, prayer is the important thing and action is the result. In the appendix of this book there are five prayers which I have found most helpful, and which I asked the clergy of my diocese to use with me, one by one from Monday through Friday. I hope you may find them useful, too.

My second suggestion is to lay people. "*Go your way into his gates with thanksgiving, and into his courts with praise.*[3] Ours is a world which is in the grip of great forces, mass movements, rising tides; and as we face these forces a feeling of frustration and futility sweeps over us. What can we do? Again we quote Archbishop Temple. "There is one thing, and one thing only, that can save this world from political chaos and collapse, and that is worship." Of course, he did not mean merely the repetition of certain rites and formulas. He meant a coming into the bright light of God's presence; that there we would realize his greatness and glory, and know that as we give ourselves to him, we put ourselves in the current of a power greater than all the rest.

My third suggestion is to parishes: *Ye are a colony of heaven.*[4] This is from Moffatt's translation. A colony is a group of people who go into a strange land to establish a settlement according to their beliefs and desires. So Christians go out into the world in groups to colonize the world in the name of Jesus Christ, and to build his kingdom. Every parish must be a Christian fellowship where one can expect to find an understanding and loving reception; where onlookers may say, as they said of old, "Look how these Christians love one another!" and where, by the contagion of our love, we help others to know more of the love of God as revealed in Jesus Christ.

---

REFERENCES

1. Psalm 103:1
2. Thessalonians 5:17
3. Jubilate Deo, Prayer Book, page 15
4. Philippians 3:20 (Moffatt)

# APPENDIX

# PRAYERS OF PREACHERS AND PRIESTS AND RECTORS CALLED TO BE PROPHETS AND PRIESTS AND KINGS AND FISHERS OF MEN AND SHEPHERDS OF SOULS

## *The Prayer of Preachers*

O God, the Holy Spirit, who hast called us to be prophets, and who shewest to them that love thee the things that were and the things that are and the things that shall be hereafter; Before we dare to speak of thee to others, reveal thyself to us. Breathe into our hearts the mysteries which no man can learn except by prayer. Take every faculty which thou hast given and make it servant to every trust which thou dost reveal. Give us thy message, save us from our own; then help us to utter, without fear and without favour, each word of thine. Give us grace so to preach that we may build, not destroy; guide, not bewilder. And add, O God, thy gift of sympathy, without which no man can be thy prophet. Give us power with souls. Help us to forget ourselves in remembering thee. O Spirit of Holiness, inflame our hearts and inspire our lips, for the sake of Christ our Lord. Amen.

## *The Prayer of Priests*

O God, who hast called us to be thy priests, to live in heaven, yet on earth, to talk with thee and to speak with men; Make us, we beseech thee, deeply sensible of the sacredness of our work. Turn our thoughts from titles and robes to love and sacrifice. Save us from the poison of self-conceit, in which all priesthood dies. Give to us the vision of thyself which thou didst give to Peter, James and John upon the mount, and to Saul upon the plain. When we stand at thine altar, when we walk in the highway, when we counsel men in darkness, when we go among the sick, the dying, and the dead, grant us always so plainly to see thy heaven that we may shew it upon earth. We ask of thee this priesthood, O God, through Christ our Saviour, to whom be honour and worship for evermore. Amen.

## *The Prayer of Rectors*

O Lord of hosts, who hast called us to be kings and rulers in thy Church; Make us rulers of ourselves. Give to us day by day the mastery of our own hearts, which shall make us prevail with others. Strip us, if need be, of our honours, that thou mayest clothe us with thy righteousness. Grant us wisdom in the ordering of thy worship and in the guidance of thy work. Bring the rich and the poor together under thy roof, O thou Maker of them all. Keep us and all thy people diligent in the study of thy law, thy love, and thy sacrifice. O thou, who dwellest among men and makest thy home with those who do thy will, abide in our parishes, be known to us in breaking bread, meet us in our Master's work, that ministers and people may be thine own for ever, in Christ our Lord. Amen.

## *The Prayer of Fishers of Men*

O Master of thy disciples, who, at the sea of Galilee, didst cast thy net for souls, bringing four fishermen into the captivity which set them free, and sending them forth to fetch men to the eternal shore, for life and not for death; We ask to have our part in this great work. Give to us the eye to see the soul which hides itself. Then give to us the word that wins it. In every man may we behold God's Son, and call him forth, till all the waves of this troubled world shall have no power to hold him back from thee. So, when this age is past, and when again thou standest by the sea at the morning watch and callest us to bring what we have caught, may souls that we have won live in thine everlasting light, O Christ our Master and our Saviour. Amen.

## *The Prayer of Pastors*

Almighty God, who hast sent us to be shepherds of thy flock, guide us to thy still waters. Shew us where thou feedest souls.

Never may hearts that hunger, coming to us, depart unfed. Make us faithful leaders of thy sheep, going before them, finding their pastures, meeting their dangers, and, if need be, laying down our lives for their sakes. Give us the patience which goes forth in long quest for wanderers. Teach us how to bear the weight of those that are torn and bruised, and to bring them home, blessed Lord, to thy flock, that they may be saved by our Good Shepherd, Jesus Christ. Amen.

The prayers above were written by the Rev. Dr. Cornelius Bishop Smith.

## *Prayer to Be Used by Parishes Seeking a Clergyman*

O God, our Heavenly Father, who watchest over all thy sheep, bless, we pray thee, the members of this Parish (Mission) with thy love and favor. Fill with thy wisdom those entrusted with the choice of a new Rector (Vicar). Endue us with true insight that we may choose a leader who will, both by his life and doctrine, "set forth thy true and lively Word and rightly and duly administer thy holy Sacraments." Bind us closer together with cords of friendliness and understanding while we await his coming. Inspire us all with the spirit of willing helpfulness, and give to each one of us a vision of our special task. And grant that all things whatsoever we do in word or deed may be done in the Name of Thy Son, our Lord and Saviour, Jesus Christ. Amen.

# ESTABLISHED POLICIES OF —— PARISH
## Regarding the services of the Church adopted by the Vestry ——

In order that we may avoid misunderstandings, the following policies are set forth as binding on all communicant, confirmed, or baptised members.

### *Holy Baptism*

The provisions of all rubrics of the service, *The Ministration of Holy Baptism*, shall be adhered to strictly.

Since Holy Baptism is a sacrament of the Church, the service will be read in the church (except as otherwise provided for in the rubrics).

Since Holy Baptism is our initiation into the fellowship of Christ's Church, it is only proper that the service be read in the presence of the Church.

In the case of the baptism of a child, the parents and sponsors (godparents) shall meet with one of the clergy, at a time agreed upon, before the service for instruction in the sacred responsibilities of their obligations. If, for any reason, this is not possible, the parents and the sponsors (godparents) shall meet with the officiating priest as soon after the service as practical.

Only baptised persons may be admitted as sponsors (godparents).

In the case of the baptism of adults, it is required that the person(s) to be baptised shall receive such instruction as may be required by the officiating priest.

There are no fees connected with the service of Holy Baptism. It is the privilege of the clergy to receive souls into the congregation of Christ's flock. If parents so desire, they may make a designated gift to the work of the parish.

## *Holy Matrimony*

All provisions of all canons of the Protestant Episcopal Church shall be met.

All provisions of the rubrics of the service, *The Form of Solemnization of Matrimony,* shall be adhered to strictly.

Except for weighty cause, the service shall be read in the church.

So far as communicant members of the Church are concerned, there are no fees connected with the ceremony; an honorarium may be given to the organist, sexton, and officiating priest.

In the case of non-communicant members of the Church, the organist's fee is $_____, and the sexton's fee is $_____. Should the parish hall be used for a wedding reception, the fee for the sexton shall be $_____.

The taking of photographs in the church while the service is in progress is absolutely forbidden.

All music used at the ceremony, before or after, shall be as directed by the organist (he being delegated by the rector to exercise such authority).

The use of decorations in the church is under the direction of the parish altar guild, acting under the authority of the rector.

The use of alcoholic beverages of any kind is absolutely forbidden at receptions held in the parish hall.

## *Burials*

The provisions of all rubrics of the service, *The Order for the Burial of the Dead,* shall be adhered to strictly.

*The Order for the Burial of the Dead* shall be read in the church proper, except for exceptional circumstances and with the consent of the rector.

The casket of all persons buried from the church shall be covered with a pall.

All music used at the service, before or after, shall be directed by the organist (he being delegated by the rector to exercise this authority).

The use of flowers in the church is under the direction of the parish altar guild, acting under the authority of the rector.

If there is a Lodge Service, it should be read at the home or at the funeral parlor prior to the service at the church.

There are no fees connected with the service of the *Burial of the Dead.* If families of the deceased so desire, they may make a designated or memorial gift to the parish.

(The only intent of the above stated policies respecting *Holy Baptism, Holy Matrimony,* and the *Burial of the Dead,* is that all men may be treated equally as God has so created them.

## SUGGESTED ESTABLISHED PARISH POLICIES

*St. Mark's Church, Venice, Florida (adapted)*

### Established Parish Policies

*(concerning buildings, finances, organizations, etc.)*

In the interest of efficient operation, the following policies have been established by action of the vestry.

#### *Use of Church Buildings*

The parish buildings are under the direction of the rector, acting in cooperation with the vestry committee on properties. Application for use of the same must be made to the rector or his authorized agent. (Date of action:_____)

#### *Property Committee Expense Fund*

The Property Committee may spend up to $_____ without the prior approval of the vestry. Should an emergency arise calling for an expense greater than this, the Property Committee is authorized to deal with it immediately. (Date of action:_____)

#### *Bids on Goods and Services*

Bids are required on the purchase of all goods and services the cost of which is more than $_____. Bids are to be let out to the lowest bidder consistent with the bidder's ability to perform necessary services or supply goods. (Date of action:_____)

#### *Bills to be Paid without Prior Approval of Vestry*

The following bills or expenses may be paid by the treasurer without the prior approval of the vestry: all salaries, insurance premiums, pension premiums, alms, utilities, Diocesan Assessment, Missions Quota, and other monies due the Diocese or National Church. (Date of action: ____)

## *Payment of Bills*

All other bills for goods or services, for more than $____, except as otherwise provided, must be approved by the vestry, certified for payment by the rector and wardens; or, in the absence of either warden by a second officer of the vestry; or, in the absence of both wardens by another officer of the vestry and two vestrymen. (Date of action: ____)

## *Payment of Assessment and Quota*

Missions Quota and Diocesan Assessment shall be paid____. (Date of action: ____)

## *Treasurer's Expense Fund*

The parish treasurer is authorized to spend up to $____ for expenses incidental to his office, without the prior approval of the vestry. (Date of action: ____)

## *Pledge Statements*

The parish treasurer shall send out to all persons who make a stated contribution of record to the parish a quarterly statement of said contribution. (Date of action: ____)

## *Counting of Offerings*

Offerings for all Sunday services and for all services held during the week preceding shall be counted by at least two persons, as provided by canon. The treasurer or his duly authorized agent shall make the bank deposit on the first banking day following Sunday. All funds shall be kept in the safe provided for that purpose. No funds shall be removed from the church property for any reason other than for deposit in the bank. (Date of action: ____)

## *Committee Reports*

All committee reports shall be made in writing; a copy of the report to be submitted to the clerk of the vestry.

## *Records*

If, for any reason, an officer of the parish or an organization of the parish, who in his (or her) official capacity holds records, shall find it necessary to leave the parish for a protracted period of time, said officer shall deposit all records in his (or her) keeping with the rector for transfer to duly authorized person who will be responsible for said records in the absence of the elected officer. The rector will give receipt for the records given to him, and the person in whose temporary care the records may be entrusted will, in turn, give the rector receipt for said records. (Date of action: ____)

If, for any reason an officer of the parish or an organization of the parish shall resign his (or her) office; or, for any reason be removed from office, said officer or someone designated by him (or her) shall deposit all records in his (or her) possession with the rector for safe keeping until said records have been transferred by the rector to a person authorized and qualified to hold said records. The rector will give receipt for all records deposited with him; and the person to whom said records are entrusted shall, in turn, give the rector receipt for all records entrusted to him (or her). (Date of action: ____)

Old bank statements, cancelled checks, deposit slips, etc., shall be held for a period of five years. Church School records shall be kept so long as a child lives in the community and is under eighteen years of age. All correspondence shall be kept so long as it is active or of any historical value. Real estate contracts, mortgages, etc., shall be held for the life of the contract plus five years. Deeds shall be held permanently. It is understood that the above applies to all parish and organizational records. It is further understood that no records of historical value shall ever be destroyed. (Date of action:_____)

### *Historiographer*

A parish historiographer shall be appointed by the vestry, whose duty it is to preserve all historical records—a proper place for safe-keeping being provided by the vestry—and to see that each year a summary of the year's parish activities is added to the permanent records. (Date of action:_____)

### *Audit of Books*

All provisions of canon law respecting an annual audit of the treasurer's books are to be met. Accounts of parish organizations may be audited by a committee of the vestry, providing income of organization does not exceed $_____. The rector shall appoint the auditing committee. (Date of action:_____)

### *Combination to the Parish Safe*

The rector, wardens, clerk, treasurer, and parish secretary, are authorized to have the combination to the safe in the parish office. (Date of action:_____)

### *Ushers*

It shall be the duty of _____ to prepare a schedule of ushers for all services of the church; the schedule shall be made up from male members of the parish. There shall be an usher at the 8:00 a.m. service on Sunday; not less than two ushers at the 11:00 a.m. service on Sunday. Ushers as may be needed shall be assigned to weekday services. The wardens shall usher at the 11:00 a.m. service on the first Sunday of the month, the Easter and Christmas Eve services, unless either, or both, may be otherwise engaged, in which event two other officers of the vestry shall usher at these services. (Date of action:_____)

### *Church School Attendance*

The only absences that will be excused are those with written excuse presented, resulting from illness, or travel on Sunday morning by plane or train. (Date of action: _____)

# SUGGESTIONS FOR CHOOSING A NEW RECTOR

First of all, authorize a small committee to be responsible for bringing in nominations to the parish body authorized to elect a new rector. This committee should be representative, and include women as well as men. It should be given power to co-opt additional persons for the purpose of visiting and looking up suggested men.

The committee should consult the bishop, the present rector, and other men in whom they have confidence, for suggestions.

Dependence should be placed far more upon the judgment of people whom he has served, who know him well, or under whom he has studied, or with whom he has worked, rather than on a single conversation or sermon.

A great deal can be learned about the clergyman from the general appearance and attentiveness of his congregation:

(1) What proportion of the congregation are men?
(2) Is the congregation reverent while waiting?
(3) Does the service begin on time?
(4) Do people take part in the responses, hymns, and the Creed, etc.?
(5) Are there many young people?
(6) Do the people arrive on time?
(7) Are people attentive or listless?

The attitude and actions of the clergyman sometimes are as important as what he says:

(1) Does he *pray* the prayers?
(2) Does he read the Lessons with meaning?
(3) Does he give out the notices interestingly?

(4) Does the service seem to have life and lift?
(5) Can he be heard plainly?
(6) Is he reverent in manner?
(7) Is the sermon helpful?
(8) How about his voice?

A good sermon is important, but the character and habits of the man are far more important:

(1) Does he have a friendly manner? A firm handshake? Look at you when talking? (2) Is he known for his pastoral calling and interest? (3) How about his church school? (4) Does he seem shy or outgoing? (5) Does he cooperate in community affairs?

If you are favorably impressed, it is well to stop after the service and talk with him—perhaps even indicate your errand. If you get into the sacristy, or the rectory, look around. Is it neat and tidy? What books and magazines are about? What about his wife? A wife can make or break a man's ministry.

It is far more important to get the *right* clergyman than it is to secure a man quickly. It is not easy to get rid of the wrong man. A man's record and references should be checked very carefully.

For your part, a man will be looking for a place with opportunity for growth. With most men, salary is of secondary importance, so long as he is assured of enough to get by without worry.

The Canons provide that before any election is held, the bishop must be notified, and given opportunity to express his opinions and give his counsel and approval.

# SAMPLE CONTRACT FOR A VICAR

Date _____

The Rev. _____

My dear _____

Upon the recommendation of the Department of Missions and Church Extension and with the approval of the Diocesan Council, and after consultation with the Executive Committee of _____ ________________, the following understanding will prevail until further notice.

(1) Your appointment as {Priest / Deacon} in charge will be effective _____, and you will become Vicar of _____ when you are priested (or, on _____).

(2) Your salary will be at the rate of $_____ per year while Deacon, and $_____ when priested.

(3) You will be entitled to one day off per week and a vacation of one full month out of every twelve.

(4) Travel expenses will be paid on the basis of $_____ per year.

(5) Church Pension Fund payments will be made by the Mission, and Blue Cross coverage will be paid for by the Diocese.

(6) A suitable house will be provided by the Mission, including heat, electricity, and the telephone expenses incurred for business purposes.

(7) Your moving expenses will be paid from _____ to _____.

I wish you success in your ministry at _____ and trust that, under your leadership, the Mission will grow quickly and achieve self-support at the earliest moment.

Faithfully,

________________ Bishop

(N.B. If a mission calls a deacon, he is called "Deacon in charge," with the amount of salary adjusted accordingly, with an increase in salary provided for when he is made "Priest in charge" or "Vicar.")

# SAMPLE CONTRACT FOR A RECTOR

Date _____

The Rev. _____

My dear _____

This is to let you know that the vestry, meeting on _____, unanimously voted to call you as Rector of ——— Parish. We earnestly hope that you will give favorable consideration to this call, as we feel that you are the man for this particular position.

It is our understanding:

(1) That your salary will be at the rate of $_____ per year;
(2) That you will be entitled to a vacation of one full month out of every twelve, and one day off per week;
(3) Travel expenses will be paid on the basis of _____;
(4) Your Church Pension Fund payments will be made by the parish (and Blue Cross coverage will be paid for by the diocese);
(5) That the rectory is provided, including heat, electricity, and the telephone expenses incurred for business purposes;
(6) Your moving expenses will be paid (a) up to the amount of $_____; or, (b) from _____ to _____.

The Bishop's consent has been given to this call.

We hope you will let us know as soon as possible of your acceptance so that arrangements may be made to release the announcement simultaneously in both parishes—preferably at a Sunday morning service, with the general news appearing in the Monday morning newspaper.

We feel that under your leadership the parish will go forward, and we look forward to your acceptance.

Yours faithfully,

____________________

Clerk of the Vestry

# SAMPLE FAMILY CARD

| | | | | |
|---|---|---|---|---|
| PHONE | CHRISTIAN NAME: M-F | | FAMILY NAME | |
| HOME ADDRESS | | | GROUP OR DISTRICT | |
| OCCUPATION: BUSINESS ADDRESS | | | RACE OR NATIONALITY | |
| PARENTS | FATHER | MOTHER'S MAIDEN NAME | | |
| | | DATE | REGISTER VOL. | PAGE |
| BIRTH | PLACE | | | |
| BAPTISM | CHURCH | | | |
| CONFIRMATION | WHERE | | | |
| COMMUNICANT | HOW OR WHENCE | | | |
| REMOVED | WHITHER OR WHY | | | |
| MARRIED | WHOM | | | |
| | | | | |
| BURIED | PLACE | | | |
| CHILDREN | | | | |
| | | | | |
| BROTHERS: SISTERS: | | SOCIAL CONTACTS: SPECIAL TALENTS: | | |
| ATTENDING CHURCH | CONTRIBUTOR | CHURCH SCHOOL | ORGANIZATIONS | CHURCH PAPERS |
| REMARKS | | | | |
| | | | | |

OVER FOR FURTHER REMARKS AND DATES OF CALLS

# SAMPLE CALLING CARD

## ST. STEPHEN'S EPISCOPAL CHURCH

Pittsfield, Massachusetts

Parish Office Telephone 2-5243

| | |
|---|---|
| The Rev. Malcolm W. Eckel<br>Rector | The Rev. Alvin P. Lafon<br>Assistant |

### SERVICES

Sundays

| | |
|---|---|
| 8:00 A.M. | Holy Communion |
| 9:00 A.M. | Family Worship and Church School |
| 9:45 A.M. | Choral Eucharist |
| 11:00 A.M. | Morning Prayer and Sermon<br>Choral Eucharist and Sermon<br>first Sunday each month |

Thursdays and Holy Days

7:00 and 10:00 A.M. Holy Communion

(*Reverse*)

"Church Going People are Happier People"

We welcome all to St. Stephen's, the Parish established to meet peoples' needs. Sunday services are arranged to provide full opportunity for all to worship and study. Families especially are invited to worship and study together.

A full week-day program of fellowship, study and recreation is also provided. Youth, women's and men's groups meet regularly. An open invitation is extended to anyone to attend these groups.

The clergy are always available for consultation and home visits. Arrangements can be made by calling the Parish Office.

## FORM OF NEWS RELEASE

From _____ For immediate release
Official capacity _____ (or)
Address _____ For release on _____
Telephone No. _____ (date)

(leave 1½ to 2 inches at the beginning so that the news editor can write in his caption)

First paragraph: give facts: what, where, when, who, why.

Second paragraph: mention special features, giving names of persons in charge. If there are many, break up into several paragraphs.

Comments: If it is to be a lecture, perhaps with pictures, give background information about the speaker, special trips made, etc.

If possible, send pictures along with the copy to the City News Editor. (It helps if you make yourself known personally to him.)

Be sure news releases are sent early enough to be *news*. Newspapers are not much interested in telling about events *after* they have taken place.

Releases should be typed with lines double-spaced.

If copy goes over to another page, write at bottom of sheet ("more on next page").

At end of copy, write the symbol of "finished": "thirty"—or "30"—or "XXX".

## PROVEN IDEAS IN EVERY MEMBER CANVASS

(*adapted*)

DISTRIBUTED AT THE THIRTY-FIRST ANNUAL LAYMEN'S CONFERENCE, Diocese of Massachusetts, 1960.

### *Introduction*

Some people are of the opinion that the work of a church is on some kind of a mystical or spiritual plane, while the raising of funds for the work of the Church is worldly, but probably a necessary evil. They would rather have nothing to do with the financial affairs of their church.

Attitudes like this do not seem to harmonize with the example of Jesus. If you will refer to the Bible you will find from Genesis to Revelation references to silver and gold as a vital part of religious dedication. This is because they are beautiful, precious, and typify sacrifice. Aside from personal service, they are without a doubt the best gifts that are offered, for they represent the accumulation of industry, the reward of privation, and an attitude of devotion to the Church.

The work of every educational institution falls into two parts —academic and business. Without the one, we could not have the other. So it is with the Church. All of the activities of the Church require material resources, and these become the channel through which religion imparts its blessings; thus, we can say that church finance has spiritual significance.

We are stewards of our personal talents and our material possessions, and we should both use and distribute them for the benefit of all, according to our ability. The Every Member Canvass is the motivation toward the fulfillment of our ideals. To live, to grow, is our challenge.

## *Objectives of Canvass*

A successful church must have two practical objectives in addition to securing greater attendance.

(1) To secure the necessary money to pay bills or run the church.

(2) The operation of a plan whereby each member makes a proportionate contribution.

You can plainly see that if we fail in the first objective, we will, of necessity, have to curtail the work of the church.

If we fail in the second obligation, our membership deprives itself of spiritual growth.

The canvass is not primarily a drive for money, but rather an intensive effort to carry the whole message of the whole Church to the last man.

No parish has a right to ask for money only. That is not its commission. Our Lord says, "My Son, give me thy heart" . . . not thy pocketbook. The pocketbook should follow, for where the heart is, there the treasure is also. But we cannot expect the heart to follow if we go only after the treasure. We must put first things first, and a proper canvass does that.

## *Five Important Phases of a Canvass*

A canvass has five important phases—Organization, Selection and Education of Canvassers, Establishment of an accurate list of prospects, Publicity, and Follow-Up.

### Organization

A poor start is worse than none at all. The most important part of a canvass is the organization and the setting up of the machinery to run the canvass. A skillful organization and an efficient administration are a necessity. This cannot be emphasized too strongly, as it is the keystone of the canvass.

Before the summer sets in, the chairman for the Every Member Canvass should be selected and appointed by the vestry. This enables him to select his committee and formulate the plans so that, by the end of September, the ground work is completely laid.

Duties and responsibilities must be allocated to capable committeemen. Experience has proved that a general committee of five works very well. Extreme care should be used in selecting the members of the committee to be sure that they have the *willingness to serve, the ability to get things done,* and that they are dependable, so as to be sure that each member will ultimately carry out his duties and responsibilities to a successful conclusion. If the members of the committee do not have the proper qualifications, you will find yourself with a one-man committee, and the chairman will do all the work.

Select those that are best qualified. If you have a sales manager or a teacher, assign this person, for example, to select, educate, and train the canvassers. A person in the advertising or promotional field is the one for handling the publicity. The Treasurer of the church is the one best qualified to acquaint the canvassers with all the vital financial statistics. The fourth member of the committee can be assigned to other miscellaneous duties. For instance, if your plan calls for a kick-off dinner, and you have a caterer available, give him this job. The chairman, of course, has the responsibility of setting up the entire organization and supervising the entire project, and he sees to it that all of his plans are carried out.

Of course, we must not forget that the Rector is the guiding hand in all activities, and he should be invited to attend all the meetings of the canvass committee. All vestrymen, without any exception, should participate in the canvass activities.

Prepare an organization chart showing the committee, the parish split up into districts, the district chairmen, and all the canvassers by districts. Make a schedule showing things to do and important dates. A suggested form of Time-Table follows:

| SUGGESTED DATES | |
|---|---|
| June 1 | Chairman appointed. |
| June 15 | Committee appointed. |
| Sept. 3 | Get budget from Finance Committee. |
| Sept. 11-12 | Laymen's Conference. |
| Oct. 1 | First committee meeting—formulate all plans and assign duties to members of committee. |

| | |
|---|---|
| Oct. 2 | Select canvassers. |
| Oct. 4 | Send letters to canvassers, asking them to participate. Enclose return postcard for their reply. |
| Oct. 15 | Supper meeting—first in series of educational meetings for canvassers.<br>Topics to be discussed:<br>1. What Church Stands For<br>2. Budget Analyzed<br>3. The Approach |
| Oct. 16 | Parish paper to be mailed. |
| Oct. 24 | Special missionary service. |
| Nov. 4 | Special canvass meeting—second in series of educational meetings for canvassers—prominent speaker. |
| Nov. 10 | Mail letters of appeal and pledge cards. (For direct mail canvass only.) |
| Nov. 12 | Men's Club meeting—prominent speaker. |
| Nov. 13 | Mail parish paper. |
| Nov. 14 | Pledge Sunday—special sermon. |
| Nov. 18 | Supper meeting—final instructions and distribution of canvass cards. |
| Nov. 21 | Canvass Sunday—canvassers report in P.M. to district chairman—special sermon. |
| Nov. 28 | Commence follow-up. |
| Dec. 5 | Write first follow-up letter. |
| Dec. 12 | Send out final follow-up letter. |
| Dec. 17 | Make final canvass report to vestry. |

### Selection and Education of Canvassers

The selection of workers who will make the canvass is most important. They are selected or rejected with one thought in mind; namely, the fitness of the individual for the task to be done. In making your selections, use your Men's Club membership list, and, in addition, men who have previously canvassed together with new members or even boys who are now reaching the age where they can be of assistance in this work—particularly Galahad boys.

You may have your Rector write a letter to these men and boys asking for their help, or your committee may want to do this.

Inasmuch as women do most of the church work, try to use men only for the canvass. Women, however, make good canvassers.

Hold at least two instruction meetings. Tell your canvassers what you want them to do and how they are to do it. Equip them with all the information they need to do a good job. Good canvassers are very scarce, and they are the result of education.

Very few can present the problem in a way that will convince the individuals that not only will they receive fine sermons and good music, but also, by attending Church and giving, they will receive inspiration, peace of mind, confidence, consolation, added strength, purpose in life, satisfaction, self-development, and encouragement. Every individual is seeking happiness and peace, but many are seeking these in the wrong places.

We should talk to the people in terms of benefits to them instead of their duty to support the Church. Later will come the sense of duty and obligation to themselves. Later they will become missionary minded. It is difficult, it is agreed, to get a layman to talk this way. It sounds too much like preaching—yet it must be used if the canvass is to be successful.

In a commercial field, sales managers know the power of visual selling. They equip their men with sales portfolios for the prospects to see, and it is said that one picture equals one thousand words. The eye absorbs the message much more readily than the ear. This is not a new thought, but rather a new application of a proven rule. This rule can apply with Church and Every Member Canvass. The canvasser should be equipped with the portfolio which tells the exact story briefly and graphically, and this, combined with the moving power, makes his visit a success.

**A Good Canvasser**

1. Is informed on:

   The activities of the parish. He knows the program and the service offered by his church. He is able to talk convincingly of its ministry.

   The budget (if you use one) required to support the program. He will figure the per capita cost as well as the total, and estimate the resources of the congregation.

The cause of which the local church is an integral part. The cause is God's Kingdom—nothing less. The field is the world.

2. Is prepared by:

Prayer that he may worthily represent Christ's cause. The canvass is a spiritual undertaking, and requires the strength and guidance of the Holy Spirit.

Participation in the church program, proving his interest and conviction.

Pledging, because it is easier to convince a prospective contributor if the canvasser has signed his own pledge.

3. Is persistent in:

Confidence in himself and his prospect. Patient and friendly discussion will often clear up criticism and misunderstanding.

Courtesy toward the prospect. Be a good listener. Do not argue or contradict.

Cultivation of the basic principles of Christian giving.

### Establishment of an Accurate List of Prospects

Every church should have its membership roll, so called, divided into two categories. First, a list of those who are the active members or the backbone, and can be called upon at any time to respond generously with their time and financial assistance. Secondly, a list of those who want the benefits our Church can bring, but who are on the list because they come to church occasionally or because of a funeral, wedding, or sickness. They demand more of the Rector's time than some of the "pillars of the church."

Because the Rector makes a courtesy call, upon request, is no more the reason why the person on whom he is calling should be on the church rolls, than the name of a family who listens to a radio program should be considered a company's prospect for a particular product. Until these individuals show a greater interest in the church, they should be treated as a business would treat a partially interested customer.

We should, however, keep a list of them, and work and develop this list to try to make them more interested. It seems practical and ethical that everyone who accepts what a church has to offer should be willing to return the courtesy with some sort of contributory support and association and attendance at church. Some people are holiday church visitors, taxing the facilities at Christmas and Easter, and they grudgingly drop a single dollar bill in the plate as a fulfillment of their obligation. This is the group that has been referred to as "Neither antireligious nor incurably unreligious, but they have not been convinced that the Church has the answer for human hope or right."

Above all, don't discourage your canvassers by asking them to call on this group, as their percentage of accomplishments will be very low. It is quite possible that they may later be brought into line and convinced that they have an obligation. Their names should then be transferred to the active list. Many times a canvasser might have ten calls to make, and eight or nine of them would be persons such as those mentioned above. If canvassers consistently meet with badly selected names on their list, the results of the canvass are naturally doubtful. Give the canvassers an accurate list of those who are considered to be at least favorable to the cause.

**Suggestions for Cultivating the "Inactive Group"**

(1) Divide your parish into districts, if you have not already done so.

(2) Organize district committees composed mostly of women with a few selected men, probably the wardens and members of the vestry.

(3) Appoint a leader carefully selected, as district chairman for each district, preferably a woman.

(4) Have members of the committee make quarterly calls on each prospect to "talk church" and church activities. Topic of conversation should be arranged beforehand.

(5) By this process, eliminate those who are positively not interested, and encourage those who are interested.

(6) Encourage church organizations, both men's and women's, to carry on membership drives.

(7) As the project progresses, you will be able to transfer many individuals from the inactive list to the active list.
(8) Supplement this plan by carefully prepared letters and probably other information to be selected as appropriate for such a program.
(9) Have the clergy make a call on these individuals.
(10) More and better general publicity.

**Publicity**

Publicity is the life blood of all promotion. No canvass can be a complete success without it. Our problem is to advance the interest of Every Member Canvass. Get a slogan. It should be talked about throughout the entire parish and also in the city. Use the following media:

(1) Local newspapers
(2) Radio and TV
(3) Sunday Service Bulletin
(4) Material supplied by General Church
  (a) Posters
  (b) Episcopalian Magazine
  (c) Mailing Pieces
  (d) Sound motion pictures
(5) Sermon materials
(6) Co-ordinate the canvass with the various meetings of the men's and women's organizations throughout the Church.
(7) Prepare to have visiting speakers from the missionary field.
(8) Make the canvass the focal point and the chief topic of conversation throughout the parish.

The publicity program should be carefully planned by one of experience, in order to get the most effective results.

All mailing pieces and letters should have appeal. We should strive for an agreeable "point of contact" with the reader's probable thoughts, and travel with those thoughts. Every reader has passed through the experience of reading something that so accords with his own views, that he almost says aloud, "That's so."

The most enjoyable sermons are those which to some degree, at least, accord with our own reflections. The minister or the writer may lead us on to new convictions, but he at least accomplishes his mission by dropping into our channel of thought and guiding it, rather than repelling it or irritating it. A single unfortunate statement may be sufficient to interfere with the delicate task of guiding minds to the desired conclusion. Don't forget that human thoughts prefer to be led rather than pushed.

**Follow-up**

The follow-up is usually the weakest part of the canvass. The members of the committee are inclined to feel fairly satisfied with their results, and no concentrated effort is expended to clean up the delinquents and procrastinators. Probably this is due to the fact that no definite plan for the follow-up is laid down before the canvass commences.

Know beforehand what your follow-up is to be. Keep the organization intact. Review returns. Know where you stand. Usually it takes about two weeks to clean up all the work.

When the personal contacts cease, then the follow-up should be made. Know in advance just exactly what kind of a letter or letters you are going to send out to round up the tardy non-participants. Personal calls are better than letters. Concentrate very thoroughly on this particular phase of the canvass. The follow-up is almost as important as the business of securing pledges. It may be the difference between success and failure. The results will surprise you.

## *Canvassing by Direct Mail*

Many churches canvass by direct mail. This is not recommended unless there is a shortage of man-power.

It is generally agreed that the only way to canvass is by personal contact. If you are now canvassing by direct mail, it is suggested that an effort be made to canvass by personal contact as soon as practicable.

Generally, parishioners like to be visited. This affords an opportunity to acquaint them more thoroughly with the many activities of the church and to interest them in these activities. The results of canvassing by personal contact prove that larger pledges can be obtained.

If you are compelled to canvass by direct mail you may find

that one mailing may be adequate, but more often several are needed. Remember there are more and more people who seem to put off until tomorrow the job that should be done today. A mailed reminder often proves a judicious prod.

The mailing pieces should be designed with the greatest of care by one experienced in this sort of endeavor.

## *Evaluate Your Canvass*

Evaluate your canvass at the close. Analyze it for strong and weak points, and keep accurate records of criticisms and appraisals. All these records and this information will be most helpful in future Canvasses. Remember, someone else may be the canvass chairman next year.

## *Hints to Canvassers*

### Walking Points

As you start out, do not go as a beggar. You go into the presence of your prospect with a commission to get the prospect properly inducted into the *Fellowship of Giving.*

You are, though your unit of it may be small, representing a tremendous enterprise.

You are asking support for a program that seeks to get at the root of crime, sin, depression and despair; that helps people to lasting good and triumph over ill.

Head up! Do not beg; do not cajole. What you have to offer—a share in a preaching, ministering, enlightening and helping enterprise—is worth any person's consideration.

### Talking Points

Be sure to give careful thought, preferably with the whole group of canvassers, or visitors, to the talking points of your church for the year.

Talk the need of the giver to give. Talk participation in a real program. What has the Church done that is worth commending to its regular members, its adherents and its neighbors? What is the Church planning to do that is worth advertising and sharing with others?

Bear witness yourself to the value of the program. Encourage church attendance. Pick out the talking point on which you can sincerely and enthusiastically express yourself.

### Stalking Points

Get your man! Please remember that Christ—and of course His Church—is interested in the individual. You are asked to "stalk" a person, not a pocketbook. The gift without the giver is bare.

This requires genuine friendliness. There should be no arguing, no criticism, expressed or implied, no condescension, no humility or timidity. But complete and always welcome friendliness.

There should also be understanding, sympathy and interest in the individual. And above everything, prayer, "unuttered or expressed," that a canvass call will cement the ties of fellowship in the brotherhood of the Church.

## *Ten Commandments for the Canvasser*

1. Go out representing God's cause—not the needs of the financial officers of the church.
2. Never ask people to help pay the bills of the corporation. Insist on getting the idea over to yourself and them that the canvassers are offering a Christian program that is worth supporting.
3. Do not debate. Having your talking points clearly in mind. State them with conviction and sincerity. Answer questions intelligently.
4. Ask for your assignments early enough to get acquainted with your prospects, if that is needed, to give thought to how to win them to a fuller sharing in the work of the Church, and to demonstrate your friendliness through some kindly service before your canvass contact.
5. Radiate confidence in your prospects' good will. Believe in it yourself, however hard it may be for you. Your contact will be much more compelling if you obviously expect the best from them.

6. Avoid criticism yourself; receive it without protest; show respect for it; try honestly to get the objector's point of view.
7. Be simple and direct—not devious, apologetic or timid.
8. Endeavor to shape your presentation to offer clearly what your listener actually needs or wants from the service of your church.
9. If you can bear witness, simply and definitely, to what the cause you are advocating means and has done for you, you have perhaps the most effective contact you can make.
10. Make your own pledge before you ask others. Be able to say, "I myself have invested," before suggesting it to others.

When one evaluates the benefits of a church to the community, to the family, to individuals—particularly growing children—it is easy to appreciate why one should take on the duties of a canvasser with interest and sincere energy. It is a task of consecration.

A good canvasser is human and realizes that he is not the judge of what his brother should give for his family. He understands that demands are many, and the joy of giving must be spontaneous and self-inspired.

## *What to Do About Unpaid Pledges*

Inasmuch as the activities of a church are planned according to anticipated receipts, it is important that the money come in as planned. If there are delinquents and there is a shrinkage in receipts of 10% to 15% or possibly more, the current year will close with a deficit. Following are two suggestions which may help to avoid such a deficit.

1. Mail to each person making a pledge a quarterly statement or letter showing the amount pledged for the period to date, amount paid, and amount in arrears. Care should be used in the preparation of this statement so as not to cause any offense. It should be a statement of fact, not a dun.
2. Set up a committee of carefully selected men to make personal calls on delinquents. Pick a chairman competent to handle such an activity. The size of the committee will obviously depend on the number of delinquents. If practicable use all of the members of the vestry. Members of this committee should

be trained by the chairman to approach the delinquents in a manner so as not to cause any offense. This committee should have monthly meetings for the purpose of discussing their problems and making reports.

We all know that no one likes to be told that he owes money. Some are of the opinion that this is a delicate subject and there is a natural reaction against this type of procedure. However a call may reveal that a person is unable to pay due to illness or some unfortunate circumstance in the family—or a person may have a gripe. This is the information the church needs. The clergy may be of some help in case of illness, or, if a person has a gripe, here is an opportunity for reconciliation. The outcome may be that the parishioner may resume paying his pledge.

A parishioner likes to be told he has been missed at the church services, and keep in mind that although the family has a pledge to the church, the church has a pledge to the family. This pledge is to care for that family just as much after the canvass as during the canvass.

## *Conclusion*

Do not forget the successful Every Member Canvass depends upon *member participation.* It succeeds only to the extent that each member is reached and given an opportunity to subscribe.

The success of the financial program of the Church depends to a great extent upon the success of your canvass. Lay your plans early and follow them through carefully in every detail with perseverance and determination, and the results may exceed your expectations.

# A PLAN FOR NEW BUILDING OR RADICAL REMODELING

(Committee to be appointed by the vestry, but be representative of the whole parish.)

(1) Committee to study needs of the parish—not only fabric but manpower. Every person should have a chance to "put in his nickel's worth" even if some suggestions seem absurd and quite beyond the resources of the parish.
(2) Get the parish to the point where it realizes that something must be done.

If physical needs seem important, vestry to appoint committee to choose an architect, consult bishop and others; but do not try to get an architect on a competitive basis, or be misled into taking a man who offers his services because he is a member of the parish.

Ask the architect to make preliminary sketches only, at a fair price, and on the understanding that, if they are not satisfactory and it is decided to do nothing, payment of this price will discharge all obligations.

Take time to convince the vestry that to meet demands some professional fund-raising concern must be called in. All sorts of economically-minded persons will object. You will have to pay, but you will probably get far more than what you pay for, as compared with a purely local effort. Have vestry decide which money-raising concern to employ, after consulting with the bishop or the archdeacon, or other churches and organizations who have employed such agencies.

General discussion of needs, plans and resources, by congregational meeting, in the parish leaflet, in organizations of the parish, etc.

Vestry then asked to commit themselves to the general enterprise, but not to particular plans.

Get cubic-foot estimate for plan most approved as drawn by architect.

Get potential figure of parish resources from money-raising concern.

Parish meeting to commit parish to general undertaking.

Sign contract with money-raising concern, which vestry chooses, and go ahead with campaign, saying that what will be built will depend upon the amount raised. No promises to be made as to what this will eventually be.

Enter into contract with architect to draw plan, first without specifications, and study plans over and over, getting all advice possible from other sources—the bishop, archdeacon, friends who have lately engaged in building operations.

When pledges have been received over three or five year period, and the amount available has been fairly accurately determined in consultation with the bishop as to how much can be reasonably borrowed, have the architect revise plan down to this ceiling. Get cubic-foot estimate of revised plans.

> **Beware:** almost every architect is an optimist and thinks he can build for far less than actual final cost; so you should allow 20% overage on estimate. Ask architect to draw up specifications after you are sure that every detail has been examined over and over again.

Any changes, after specifications are drawn, will cost much more than if you had a correction in the original, even in such matters as the placing of floor plugs, where switches are to be placed, or which way the doors are to swing, etc.

Have architect choose contractors who will bid on it. Do not automatically take the lowest bid, but take lowest bid of reputable contractor.

If much of the work is in renovation, contractors will all bid high to cover themselves. It may, therefore, be advisable not to ask for bids in such a case, but to choose a contractor and ask him to give you a maximum top price. He will, of course, call for bids from sub-contractors.

The following two pages reproduce a four-page leaflet for Godparents. Page 290 shows the front and back pages of the leaflet, and the two inside pages will be found on page 291. (Godparents Ctf. No. 1, published Morehouse-Barlow Co.)

### Prayer for a Birthday

Watch over my Godchild, ...................... ...................., O Lord, as *his* days increase; bless and guide *him* wherever *he* may be, keeping *him* unspotted from the world. Strengthen *him* when *he* stands; comfort *him* when discouraged or sorrowful; raise *him* up if *he* fall; and in *his* heart may Thy peace which passeth understanding abide all the days of *his* life; through Jesus Christ our Lord. *Amen.*

### For Anniversary of Baptism

Grant, O Lord, that as my Godchild, ............. ........................, has been received into the congregation of Christ's flock and signed with the sign of the Cross, in token that hereafter *he* should not be ashamed to confess the faith of Christ crucified, so he may manfully fight under His banner against sin, the world, and the devil, and may continue Christ's faithful soldier and servant unto *his* life's end; through the same Jesus Christ our Lord and Saviour. *Amen.*

### For One About to Be Confirmed

O God, who through the teaching of Thy Son Jesus Christ didst prepare the disciples for the coming of the Comforter; Make ready, I beseech Thee, the heart and mind of Thy servant, my Godchild, .......... ............................, who at this time is seeking to be strengthened by the gift of the Holy Spirit through the laying on of hands, that drawing near with penitent and faithful heart, *he* may evermore be filled with the power of His divine indwelling; through the same Jesus Christ our Lord. *Amen.*

*This is to Certify that*

______________________________

*is a* GODPARENT *to*

______________________________

*who was Born*______________________19___

*and who became*

A MEMBER OF CHRIST,
THE CHILD OF GOD, AND
AN INHERITOR OF THE
KINGDOM OF HEAVEN

*through*

**HOLY BAPTISM**

*in*______________________________

(church)

______________________________

(city)

*on*______________________________19___

Other Sponsors______________________

______________________________

(*Signed*)___________________________

# SUGGESTIONS FOR GODPARENTS

You are a Sponsor for your godchild, and therefore responsible for *him* through the solemn promises you have made to God for *him*. Yours is a sacred relationship from which there should come much happiness and spiritual gain, both to you and to your godchild.

In carrying out your trust the following suggestions will prove helpful.

1. Form the habit of praying regularly for your godchild by name, and also when you make your Communion.

2. Cultivate your godchild's friendship. Multiply helpful contacts. Remember *his* birthdays and baptismal anniversaries with an appropriate letter or gift.

3. When your godchild is old enough see that *he* is enrolled in the Church school and that *he* is faithful in attendance.

4. Encourage *him* to attend the Church services. Go with *him* when possible.

5. See that *he* has a Bible and Prayer Book and that *he* uses them.

6. Remember your promises as a Sponsor to take heed "that this Child learn the Creed, the Lord's Prayer, and the Ten Commandments, and all other things which a Christian ought to know and believe to his soul's health" and "that this Child, so soon as sufficiently instructed, be brought to the Bishop to be confirmed by him."

7. Teach *him* to look forward eagerly to Confirmation, and by all means, be present with *him* at that service.

8. Go with your godchild to *his* First Communion and encourage *him* to receive *his* Communion regularly thereafter.

✠

## *A Godparent's Prayer*

O LORD Jesus Christ, who dost embrace children with the arms of Thy mercy, and dost make them living members of Thy Church; Give grace, I pray Thee, to my Godchild,

. . . . . . . . . . . . . . . . . . . . . . . . . . . . . . . . . . . . . . . . . . ,

to stand fast in Thy faith, to obey Thy word, and to abide in Thy love; that, being made strong by Thy Holy Spirit, *he* may resist temptation, and may rejoice in the life that now is, and dwell with Thee in the life to come; through Thy merits, O merciful Saviour, who with the Father and the Holy Ghost livest and reignest one God, world without end. *Amen.*

On pages 294 and 295 is a reproduction of a leaflet concerning requirements for Confirmation. The first page shows the front and back pages, the following page reproduces the inside section.

## PRAYERS

Defend Me, O Lord, with thy heavenly grace; that I may continue thine forever; and daily increase in thy Holy Spirit more and more, until I come unto thy everlasting kingdom; through Jesus Christ our Lord. *Amen.*

O Almighty Lord, and everlasting God, I pray thee to direct, sanctify, and govern, my heart and my body, in the ways of thy laws, and in the works of thy commandments; that, through thy most mighty protection, both here and ever, I may be preserved in body and soul; through our Lord and Saviour Jesus Christ. *Amen.*

### *On Entering Church*

O Lord, I am in thy holy House. Help me to keep my thoughts on thee, that I may hear thee speaking in my heart, through Jesus Christ. *Amen.*

### *On Leaving Church*

O God, grant that what we have said with our lips we may believe in our hearts, and practise and show forth in our lives, to the glory of thy great Name; through Jesus Christ our Lord. *Amen.*

# REQUIREMENTS *for* CONFIRMATION

IN THE DIOCESE OF WESTERN MASSACHUSETTS

PUBLICATIONS OF

*Christ Church Cathedral*

SPRINGFIELD, MASSACHUSETTS

# DIOCESAN REQUIREMENTS FOR CONFIRMATION

QUESTION: What is your bounden duty as a member of the Church?

ANSWER: My bounden duty is

I. *to follow Christ,*

which includes,

(1) some knowledge of the contents of the Bible, and some plan of Bible reading;
(2) some knowledge of the life and teaching of Christ;
(3) some knowledge of the history and organization of our Church.

II. *to worship God every Sunday in His Church,*

which includes,

(4) an established practice of Church attendance;
(5) knowledge and use of the Prayer Book.

III. *to work,*

which includes,

(6) activity and responsibility in Church School, Parish or Community.

IV. *and pray,*

which includes,

(7) the practice of daily prayer;

and

(8) the ability to repeat from memory some of the prayers of the Church.

V. *and give for the spread of His kingdom.*

which includes,

(9) a pledge to the Parish;
(10) a pledge to the general work of the Church.

# A PRAYER FOR A MARRIED COUPLE

*by Bishop Slattery*

O God, our heavenly Father, protect and bless us. Deepen and strengthen our love for each other day by day. Grant that by thy mercy, neither of us ever say one unkind word to the other. Forgive and correct our faults, and make us instantly to forgive each other, should one of us unconsciously hurt the other. Make us and keep us sound and well in body, alert in mind, tender in heart, devout in spirit. O Lord, grant us each to rise to The Other's Best. Then, we pray thee, add to our common life such virtue as only thou canst give; and so, O Father, consecrate our life and our love completely to thy worship and to the service of all about us, especially those whom thou hast appointed us to serve, that we may always stand before thee in happiness and peace; through Jesus Christ our Lord.

*Amen.*

# A LIST OF QUESTIONS FOR THOSE CONTEMPLATING MARRIAGE

Consider these questions. Talk them over together. If the Minister can help to answer them, ask him to do so.

## *The Marriage Service*

1. Have you read the service, so that you know what it says about Christian marriage and what you are to promise?
2. Are you planning your wedding as you yourselves wish it, so that you will always cherish the memory of it?
3. Have you considered others, particularly your parents and relatives, in deciding who will be present at it?

## *Your Religion*

4. Are you members of the same Church?
5. Have you ever talked together of your ideas of God, or of what it means to be a Christian?
6. Does the Church to which you belong meet your spiritual need?
7. What part will the Holy Communion and the worship of the Church play in your lives?
8. If you are not members of the same Church, have you seriously studied each other's religion to find out if you might unite on one Church?
9. If not, have you counted the cost of a divided loyalty and faced it intelligently?
10. Do you find reality in prayer?
11. Will you start your marriage with an adventure in prayer, beginning with prayers together the night that you are married and learning more of it continually together?

### *Interests*

12. What interests have you in common? Have you considered how you will develop them?
13. What separate interests, hobbies, or obligations have you which might take time (evenings and holidays) or money from what you might otherwise spend together? Have you considered together the continuation of these activities?

### *Security*

14. Have you talked over together the matter of your salary or income?
15. Do you expect it to continue as it is, increase, or diminish?
16. How much of this income will be spent in starting housekeeping, your wedding, or paying off debts?
17. Have you budgeted your income so that you know how much you will need for rent, food, fuel, clothing, doctors, recreation, "good will" (that is, donations, gifts, organization dues, etc.) and savings?
18. How much can you afford to put aside for sickness, for increasing overhead expenses, for children, for education?
19. Have you any relatives who are, or might become, wholly or temporarily dependent on you? Does the other realize this?

### *Parents and In-Laws*

20. Is either of you over-dependent on your parents, or inconsiderate of them or of your in-laws?
21. Is there any feeling of tension with parents or in-laws which could be cleared up at this time.
22. Does either of you feel restrained by the other in carrying out what you believe to be your rightful and loving obligations to your own family?
23. Are there any particular circumstances of sickness, loneliness, or isolation that will necessitate either of you being with your parents a great deal? If so, does the other realize this?

24. Are conditions such that at any time you might have to live with relatives or they with you? If so, do you both understand this?

## *Personal Questions*

25. Is there anything in marriage which you fear? Do you fear yourself? Each other? The finality of marriage? Do you fear having children, or any of the physical aspects of marriage?
26. Have you, to your own knowledge, any disease, or likelihood of disease, which might affect your future? Have you seen a reliable doctor in regard to this?
27. Is there anything in the life of either of you which you have concealed, or intend to conceal from the other?
28. Is there any information which you do not possess, and feel you should have before you are married?

# BIBLIOGRAPHY

GENERAL BACKGROUND READING AND REFERENCE WORKS

The Church's Teaching Series, Seabury Press.

*Chapters in Church History,* P. M. Dawley.

*The Faith of The Church,* J. A. Pike and W. N. Pittenger.

*The Worship of The Church,* M. H. Shepherd, Jr.

*The Holy Scriptures,* R. C. Dentan.

*The Episcopal Church and Its Work,* P. M. Dawley.

*Christian Living,* S. F. Bayne, Jr.

*History of the American Episcopal Church,* W. W. Manross. Morehouse-Barlow Co.

*The Episcopal Church in The United States,* James T. Addison. Charles Scribner's Sons.

*A History of the Church of England,* J. R. H. Moorman. Morehouse-Barlow Co.

*The Oxford Dictionary of the Christian Church,* F. L. Cross (Ed.). Oxford University Press, New York.

*The Critical Years,* Clara O. Loveland. Seabury Press.

*This Church of Ours,* Howard Johnson (Ed.). Seabury Press.

*Annotated Constitution and Canons,* White and Dykman. Seabury Press.

*The Constitution and Canons of the Protestant Episcopal Church.* Available from The National Council of the Protestant Episcopal Church.

THE HOLY SCRIPTURES

*Is The Bible Inspired?* J. Burnaby. S.P.C.K.-Seabury Press.

*How to Read The Bible,* W. K. L. Clarke. S.P.C.K.-Seabury Press.

*Translating The Bible,* F. C. Grant. Seabury Press.

*A Layman's Guide to The Old Testament,* P. S. Robinson. S.P.C.K.-Seabury Press.

*God and History in The Old Testament,* Harvey Guthrie. Seabury Press.

*One Body and One Spirit:* A Study of the Church in The New Testament, O. J. F. Seitz. Seabury Press.

*Inherit the Promise:* Six Keys to New Testament Thought, Pierson Parker. Seabury Press.

THE PRAYER BOOK

*Oxford American Prayer Book Commentary,* Massey Shepherd. Oxford University Press, New York.

*A History of The Book of Common Prayer,* Procter and Frère. St. Martin's Press.

*Dynamic Redemption:* Reflections on The Book of Common Prayer, Bayard Jones, Seabury Press.

PARISH ADMINISTRATION

*I am a Vestryman,* T. R. Ludlow. Morehouse-Barlow Co.

*What Every Vestryman Should Know,* H. Anstice. Morehouse-Barlow Co.

*Handbook for Parishes,* G. R. Madison, Seabury Press.

Joint Commission Publications, Seabury Press.

*Service Music and Anthems*
*Ideals in Church Music*
*Music for Church Weddings*
*Music for Church Funerals*
*Architecture and the Church*
*Church Buildings and Furnishings*

*A Glossary of Architectural and Liturgical Terms,* E. N. West. Seabury Press

*The Changing Church,* K. M. McClinton. Morehouse-Barlow Co.

ECUMENICAL MOVEMENT

Various studies and pamphlets are issued by the National Council of Churches (Office of Publication and Distribution) 475 Riverside Drive, New York 27, N. Y.; and the World Council of Churches, 475 Riverside Drive, New York 27, N. Y.

*The Yearbook of American Churches,* an annual publication of the National Council of Churches (see above) is a useful reference work and contains information on all religious bodies in the U.S.A., as well as lists of agencies having ecumenical and international affiliations.

*The Church is There,* Leslie Cooke. Seabury Press.